THE NEW TESTAMENT AND
THE SCRIPTURES OF ISRAEL

Edited by
Maarten J.J. Menken and Steve Moyise

Published under
LIBRARY OF NEW TESTAMENT STUDIES
377
formerly the Journal for the Study of the New Testament Supplement Series

Editor
Mark Goodacre

THE MINOR PROPHETS
IN THE NEW TESTAMENT

Edited by
MAARTEN J. J. MENKEN
and
STEVE MOYISE

t&t clark

Published by T&T Clark
A Continuum imprint
The Tower Building, 11 York Road, London SE1 7NX
80 Maiden Lane, Suite 704, New York, NY 10038

www.continuumbooks.com

British Library Cataloguing-in-Publication Data
A catalogue record for this book is available from the British Library

ISBN: HB: 978-0-567-03305-5

Typeset by Free Range Book Design & Production Limited
Printed and bound in Great Britain by the MPG Books Group,
Bodmin and King's Lynn

CONTENTS

ABBREVIATIONS

AB	Anchor Bible
ABRL	Anchor Bible Reference Library
AGJU	Arbeiten zur Geschichte des antiken Judentums und des Urchristentums
AnBib	Analecta biblica
ASNU	Acta seminarii neotestamentici upsaliensis
ASOR	American Schools of Oriental Research
ATD	Das Alte Testament Deutsch
BDAG	W. Bauer, F. W. Danker, W. F. Arndt and F. W. Gingrich, *Greek–English Lexicon of the New Testament and Other Early Christian Literature* (Chicago: University of Chicago Press, 3rd edn, 1999)
BDF	F. Blass, A. Debrunner and R.W. Funk, *A Greek Grammar of the New Testament and Other Early Christian Literature* (Cambridge: Cambridge University Press, 1961)
BECNT	Baker Exegetical Commentary on the New Testament
BETL	Bibliotheca ephemeridum theologicarum lovaniensium
Bib	*Biblica*
BibInt	*Biblical Interpretation: A Journal of Contemporary Approaches*
BIS	Biblical Interpretation Series
BKAT	Biblischer Kommentar: Altes Testament
BNTC	Black's New Testament Commentaries
BWANT	Beiträge zur Wissenschaft vom Alten und Neuen Testament
BZAW	Beihefte zur ZAW
BZNW	Beihefte zur ZNW
CBC	Cambridge Bible Commentary
CBET	Contributions to Biblical Exegesis and Theology
CBQ	*Catholic Biblical Quarterly*
CBR	*Currents in Biblical Research*
ConBNT	Coniectanea biblica, New Testament Series
DJD	Discoveries in the Judaean Desert
EHS	Europäische Hochschulschriften
ET	English Text
ETL	*Ephemerides theologicae lovanienses*
GTA	Göttinger theologische Arbeiten

HALOT	L. Koehler, W. Baumgartner, and J. J. Stamm, *The Hebrew and Aramaic Lexicon of the Old Testament* (Trans. M. E. J. Richardson, 4 vols, Leiden: Brill, 1994–1999)
HBS	Herders Biblische Studien
HKNT	Handkommentar zum Neuen Testament
HNT	Handbuch zum Neuen Testament
ICC	International Critical Commentary
JAOS	*Journal of the American Oriental Society*
JBL	*Journal of Biblical Literature*
JSNT	*Journal for the Study of the New Testament*
JSNTSup	*Journal for the Study of the New Testament, Supplement Series*
JSOTSup	*Journal for the Study of the Old Testament, Supplement Series*
JTS	*Journal of Theological Studies*
KAT	Kommentar zum Alten Testament
KEK	Kritisch-exegetischer Kommentar über das Neue Testament
KJV	King James Version
LD	Lectio divina
LNTS	Library of New Testament Studies
NA[27]	Nestle and Aland, *Novum Testamentum Graece* (Stuttgart: Deutsche Bibelgesellschaft, 27th edn, 1993)
NBC	New Biblical Commentary
Neot	*Neotestamentica*
NETS	*A New English Translation of the Septuagint* (eds A. Pietersma and B. Wright; Oxford and New York: Oxford University Press, 2007)
NGS	New Gospel Studies
NICNT	New International Commentary on the New Testament
NIGTC	New International Greek Testament Commentary
NJPS	New Jewish Publication Society
NKJV	New King James Version
NovT	*Novum Testamentum*
NovTSup	*Novum Testamentum*, Supplements
NRSV	New Revised Standard Version
NTD	Das Neue Testament Deutsch
NTS	*New Testament Studies*
OPTAT	Occasional Papers and Technical Articles for Translators
OTL	Old Testament Library
POut	De Prediking van het Oude Testament
RevQ	*Revue de Qumran*
RSV	Revised Standard Version
SAC	Studies in Antiquity and Christianity
SB	Sources bibliques
SBL	Society of Biblical Literature

SBLDS	SBL Dissertation Series
SBLMS	SBL Monograph Series
SBLSCS	SBL Septuagint and Cognate Studies
SBLSymS	SBL Symposium Series
SBS	Stuttgarter Bibelstudien
SNTA	Studiorum Novi Testamenti Auxilia
SNTSMS	Society for New Testament Studies Monograph Series
ST	*Studia theologica*
STDJ	Studies on the Texts of the Desert of Judah
SubBi	Subsidia biblica
TCS	Texts from Cuneiform Sources
TDNT	*Theological Dictionary of the New Testament* (eds G. Kittel and G. Friedrich; trans. G. W. Bromiley; 10 vols; Grand Rapids: Eerdmans, 1964–76)
TU	Texte und Untersuchungen
TynBul	*Tyndale Bulletin*
UBS⁴	United Bible Societies' *Greek New Testament*, 4th edn
VT	*Vetus Testamentum*
VTSup	*Vetus Testamentum*, Supplements
WBC	Word Biblical Commentary
WMANT	Wissenschaftliche Monographien zum Alten und Neuen Testament
WUNT	Wissenschaftliche Untersuchungen zum Neuen Testament
ZAW	*Zeitschrift für die alttestamentliche Wissenschaft*
ZNW	*Zeitschrift für die neutestamentliche Wissenschaft und die Kunde der älteren Kirche*

LIST OF CONTRIBUTORS

Jutta Leonhardt-Balzer is Lecturer at the University of Aberdeen (UK) and author of *Jewish Worship in Philo of Alexandria* (Mohr-Siebeck, 2001).

Cilliers Breytenbach is Professor for the Literature, Religion and History of Early Christianity at the Humboldt-Universität (Berlin, Germany) and author of *Nachfolge und Zukunftserwartung nach Markus* (TVZ, 1984).

Radu Gheorghita is Associate Professor of Biblical Studies at Midwestern Baptist Theological Seminary (Kansas City, USA) and author of *The Role of the Septuagint in Hebrews: An Investigation of its Influence with Special Consideration to the Use of Hab 2:3-4 in Heb 10:37-38* (Mohr-Siebeck, 2003).

Clay Alan Ham is Professor of New Testament at Lincoln Christian College (Illinois, USA) and author of *The Coming King and the Rejected Shepherd: Matthew's Reading of Zechariah's Messianic Hope* (Sheffield Phoenix Press, 2005).

Marko Jauhiainen is Systems Analyst at TAMK University of Applied Sciences (Finland) and author of *The Use of Zechariah in Revelation* (Mohr-Siebeck, 2005).

Karen H. Jobes is the Gerald F. Hawthorne Professor of New Testament Greek and Exegesis at Wheaton College and Graduate School (Illinois, USA) and co-author of *Invitation to the Septuagint* (Baker Academic, 2000).

Maarten J. J. Menken is Professor of New Testament Exegesis at the Faculty of Catholic Theology of the University of Tilburg (The Netherlands) and author of *Matthew's Bible* (Leuven University Press – Peeters, 2004).

Steve Moyise is Professor of New Testament at the University of Chichester (UK) and author of *Evoking Scripture: Seeing the Old Testament in the New* (T&T Clark, 2008).

Huub van de Sandt is Lecturer at the University of Tilburg (The Netherlands) and co-editor of *Matthew, James and Didache: Three Related Documents in their Jewish and Christian Settings* (SBL, 2008).

Introduction

In his encomium on the great figures of Israel's past ('Praise of the Fathers'), Ben Sira says of the Minor Prophets: 'May the bones of the twelve prophets also sprout afresh from their graves, for they encouraged Jacob, and they rescued the people by their confident hope' (Sir. 49.10). To him, the importance of the Minor Prophets is that they kept Israel's hopes alive. And indeed, the Book of the Twelve, as we know it, contains many prophecies that concern God's near intervention in human history, or at least can be read that way by those seeking solace and guidance from the book. This intervention involves both salvation and judgement.

It is probably for this reason that the New Testament authors quote from or allude to the Book of the Twelve relatively often and make it worthwhile to devote a volume to it in this series, following the volumes on Psalms, Isaiah and Deuteronomy. According to the lists in *The Greek New Testament* (4th edn), there are 30 explicit quotations from the Minor Prophets in the New Testament, taken from 22 different texts: Hosea (6); Zechariah (5); Habakkuk (3); Joel (2); Amos (2); Micah (2); Jonah (1); Haggai (1). These will be discussed in chapters on Mark, Matthew, Luke–Acts, John, Paul and Hebrews. In addition, there is a chapter on James, 1 and 2 Peter and Jude, and a chapter on the book of Revelation, both of which contain only allusions.

The collection starts with a contribution by Jutta Leonhardt-Balzer on the Minor Prophets in Second Temple Judaism. Apart from the Qumran scrolls, the evidence for their use is not overwhelming, but there are quotations in Philo, and allusions in several of the Old Testament Pseudepigrapha. In Qumran, *pesharim* (running commentaries, giving both the biblical text and its interpretation) have been found on Hosea, Micah, Nahum, Habakkuk, Zephaniah and Malachi. There are also quotations in other documents, such as the Damascus Rule (CD), the Florilegium (4Q174) and the Catena (4Q177). It would appear that the Minor Prophets appealed to the Qumran community, who read these texts (along with other Jews) as prophetic texts directed to themselves and as revealing – on condition that one had the proper hermeneutical key – God's plan behind human history.

The materials from the Minor Prophets in Mark's Gospel are discussed by Cilliers Breytenbach. There are two quotations and a number of allusions, generally based on the LXX (with the exception of the quotation from Mal. 3.1 in Mk 1.2). Zechariah and – to a much lesser degree – Joel are used in Mark to depict the final judgement and the eschatological events preceding it, such as the scattering of the disciples (Zech. 13.7 in Mk 14.27). Passages from Zechariah are prominent in Mark's story of Jesus' last week in Jerusalem. Mal. 3.1 and 3.22-23 (ET 4.4-5)[1] serve to characterize John the Baptist as the one who prepares the way for Jesus, and Jonah 1 has significantly influenced the story of the calming of the storm in Mk 4.35-41.

Matthew's Gospel contains ten quotations from the Minor Prophets, more than any other prophetic book (Isaiah is next with eight). They are taken from Hosea, Jonah, Micah, Zechariah and Malachi. These are discussed by Clay Alan Ham, who does not find any evidence that Matthew necessarily read them as one 'book'. The evangelist interprets some quotations in a (directly or indirectly) messianic sense (Mic. 5.1 [ET 5.2] in Mt. 2.6; Mal. 3.1 in Mt. 11.10; Zech. 9.9 in Mt. 21.5; Zech. 13.7 in Mt. 26.31; Zech. 11.12-13 in Mt. 27.9-10). In other instances, the fulfilment is typological (Hos. 11.1 in Mt. 2.15; Jonah 2.1 [ET 1.17] in Mt. 12.40). Quotations from the Minor Prophets are also used to support Jesus' teaching on a righteousness surpassing that of the Pharisees (Hos. 6.6 in Mt. 9.13 and 12.7), or to depict the distress of the time of the end (Mic. 7.6 in Mt. 10.35-36).

There are three relatively brief quotations from the Minor Prophets in Luke's Gospel, and four fairly extensive quotations in Acts. Huub van de Sandt argues that the quotations from Mal. 3.1 in Lk. 7.27 and from Mic. 7.6 in Lk. 12.53 come from Q and were adapted by Luke. The other quotations (Hos. 10.8 in Lk. 23.30; Joel 3.1-5 [ET 2.28-32] in Acts 2.17-21; Amos 5.25-27 in Acts 7.42-43; Hab. 1.5 in Acts 13.41; Amos 9.11-12 in Acts 15.16-17) were directly derived by Luke from a LXX text closely related to the Alexandrian manuscript group. The original context of these quotations in the LXX has demonstrably influenced Luke's use of them. The three long quotations in Acts 7, 13 and 15 serve to legitimize the Gentile mission. The two Amos quotations display several links; the first one depicts God's punishment of an idolatrous Israel, the second one the renewal of Israel which Luke perceives in the Christian community made up of Jews and Gentiles.

Maarten Menken deals with the Minor Prophets in John's Gospel. There are two quotations, two instances of secondary influence of a Minor Prophets passage on a quotation, and a series of allusions. The quotation from Zech. 9.9 in Jn 12.15 probably comes from the LXX;

---

1.   At a number of places in the Minor Prophets, the Masoretic text (MT), the Septuagint (LXX) and the English Text (ET) employ different numbering systems. Unless otherwise stated, references will be given first to the Masoretic text, with the alternatives in parenthesis.

the evangelist has heavily edited it, in the interest of his Christology. The textual form of the quotation from Zech. 12.10 in Jn 19.37 is that of an early Christian testimony, in Greek, to the second coming of Christ; John has applied the clause to looking in faith on the crucified Jesus as the risen Lord. John largely depends on early Christian tradition for his use of the Minor Prophets and he interprets them mainly on the principle that the Scriptures testify to Jesus (Jn 5.39).

All quotations from the Minor Prophets, as well as a few allusions to them in the *Corpus Paulinum*, are discussed by Steve Moyise. Paul shows great interest in Hab. 2.4b ('the righteous will live by faith'); he cites it in Rom. 1.17 and Gal. 3.11. Quotations from Malachi, Hosea and Joel function in Paul's argument in Romans 9–11, and in 1 Cor. 15.55 he appends Hos. 13.14b to Isa. 25.8, presenting both prophetic words in a striking textual form and with a striking meaning. Paul appears to be a serious interpreter, using methods of interpretation that were also accepted by his fellow Jews, but drawing conclusions that are clearly influenced, if not determined, by his Christian faith. He applies, for instance, Hosea's words on God's commitment to Israel (2.1, 25 [ET 1.10, 2.23]) to the inclusion of the Gentiles in the Christian community (Rom. 9.24-26).

The Minor Prophets materials in Hebrews consist of two quotations and some allusions. In his contribution, Radu Gheorghita observes that all these materials (one allusion excepted) occur in the latter part of Hebrews, with its interest in eschatology. In the case of the two quotations (Hab. 2.3-4 in Heb. 10.37-38 and Hag. 2.6 in Heb. 12.26), Gheorghita discusses their textual form and their intertextual links with the other Old Testament passages used in the same context in Hebrews, compares the historical situations of the addressees of source text and target text, and describes the theological meaning of the quotation in Hebrews, taking into consideration the modifications made by the author. It appears that both quotations receive a legitimate eschatological interpretation; the former one serving as an exhortation to persevere in faith, the latter one announcing that God's final intervention will concern both earth and heaven.

Although the letters ascribed to James, Peter and Jude do not contain any marked quotations from the Minor Prophets, they do contain several interesting allusions to which Karen Jobes gives attention. As far as the provenance of the allusions can be determined, James and 1 Peter depend on the LXX, while Jude probably draws on the Hebrew (2 Peter does not offer much more than language and themes shared with the Twelve). James makes use of Hosea, Amos and Malachi, 1 Peter of Hosea and Malachi (and possibly of Zechariah), and Jude of Zechariah. James, 2 Peter and Jude use the Minor Prophets to exhort their audience to live under the new covenant; 1 Peter does so to strengthen Christian identity in a hostile society. Especially interesting is the way in which James and

1 Peter connect the 'bookends' of the Book of the Twelve, Hosea and Malachi.

The Book of Revelation contains several allusions to the Minor Prophets; formal quotations from Scripture are, as is well known, completely absent from it. Marko Jauhiainen discusses the Minor Prophets materials in Revelation. He starts with some considerations (inspired by Z. Ben-Porat) on how a reader detects and assesses a 'literary allusion', that is, an allusion to a specific Old Testament text. Most of Revelation's literary allusions to the Minor Prophets are to Zechariah or Joel; there is one such allusion to Hosea. They concern the imminent reversal of fortunes (judgement of the sinners and salvation of the faithful), John's high Christology, and the vocation of Christians. Almost all of them would function whether John has a Hebrew or Greek text of the Old Testament in mind (the exception being the allusion to Zech. 12.10 in Rev. 1.7, which, according to Jauhiainen, presupposes a Hebrew text).

Not all New Testament documents are dealt with in this volume: several Pauline or Deutero-Pauline letters are missing (2 Corinthians, Philippians, Colossians, 1 and 2 Thessalonians, 1 and 2 Timothy, Titus, Philemon), as well as 1, 2 and 3 John. These writings do not contain quotations from the Minor Prophets, nor allusions that would be regarded as certain by most scholars. Neither is there a separate chapter on Q (as there was in the volumes on Psalms and Isaiah); instead, these materials are discussed within the chapters on Matthew and Luke–Acts.

Anyone familiar with this field of study will know that there is no consensus on how terms like quotation, allusion and echo should be used, or indeed on what methods or approaches should be applied. For example, some take what might be called a 'maximalist' view regarding the New Testament author's interest in the Old Testament context. They assume that the New Testament author interpreted a quotation or allusion within its immediate or wider Old Testament context. Others take a 'minimalist' view of such matters: they think that the New Testament author read the text he quoted or alluded to in an 'atomistic' way, detached from its Old Testament context. Mediating positions are also possible, which presuppose that both the contextual and the atomistic reading occur in fact, and that the New Testament exegete should try to determine which of the two applies in an individual case. For this reason, it was decided to allow each contributor to use whatever methods and approaches that they find most illuminating for the particular text being discussed.

Nevertheless, some general trends can be perceived. New Testament authors usually employ the LXX version of the Minor Prophets, but in some cases there are indications for the use of the Hebrew text or of another Greek translation. There is some evidence that at the beginning of the era the collection of twelve prophetic booklets was considered to constitute one book, but in actual practice New Testament authors hardly give evidence of seeing the collection as a unit. Judging from the quantity of quotations and allusions, and relating this quantity to the size of the twelve booklets, we can observe a clear interest among New Testament authors in Hosea, Joel and Zechariah (especially Zechariah 9–14); neglected (to different degrees) are Obadiah, Nahum, Zephaniah and Haggai. In the case of Amos, Micah, Habakkuk and Malachi, the interest is limited to a few selected passages, and in the case of Jonah, it concerns the biography of the prophet, who is considered to be a 'type' of Christ. Finally, to return by way of *inclusio* to the beginning of this introduction, we can conclude that Ben Sira was not the only one to view the Twelve as prophets who 'encouraged Jacob' and who 'rescued the people by their confident hope'. If we consider the Qumran scrolls and the New Testament, we can observe that many passages from the Twelve Prophets are interpreted in an eschatological sense, often even more specifically in a messianic sense. In Luke–Acts and Paul, the eschatological interpretation includes passages from the Minor Prophets which are read as predicting the creation of one new people of God, consisting of Jews and Gentiles. All this is not to say that the eschatological way of reading is the *only* way the Minor Prophets were read in early Judaism or early Christianity, but it certainly was the *predominant* way. It is also a way of reading that makes the Minor Prophets relevant to a contemporary theology of hope.

CHAPTER 1

THE MINOR PROPHETS IN THE JUDAISM OF THE SECOND TEMPLE PERIOD

Jutta Leonhardt-Balzer

Introduction

Compared to the references to the Torah, the Psalms or Isaiah, the Minor Prophets (Hosea, Joel, Amos, Obadiah, Jonah, Micah, Nahum, Habakkuk, Zephaniah, Haggai, Zechariah, Malachi)[1] are not referred to very frequently in Second Temple Judaism. However, there is significant evidence that they were read and used. The Septuagint even places them before the Major Prophets (in a different order from the Masoretic text).

Hebrew editions of the Minor Prophets were found in Qumran and Wadi Murabbaʿat, in Greek in Naḥal Ḥever. In addition to the ancestor of the Masoretic text these versions attest to many textual variations and range from about 150 BCE to approximately 100 CE.[2] There is no evidence that there was one Hebrew version which was favoured over the others,[3] but the Greek manuscript (end of the first century BCE) is a recension of the Septuagint, which aims to align the translation with the proto-Masoretic text,[4] indicating a tendency to favour the Hebrew.

All the twelve books are represented in the Qumran fragments (4QMinor Prophets[a-g] = 4Q76–82),[5] and most of the editions have the

---

1. Biblical passages are quoted from the NRSV.
2. Cf. R. Fuller, 'Minor Prophets', in L. H. Schiffman and J. C. VanderKam (eds), *Encyclopedia of the Dead Sea Scrolls* (Oxford: Oxford University Press, 2000), I, pp. 554–7 esp. 555.
3. Although parallels to the Targum have been found especially in the *pesharim* on Nahum and Habakkuk, cf. R. P. Gordon, 'The Targum to the Minor Prophets and the Dead Sea Texts: Textual and Exegetical Notes', *RevQ* 31 (1974), 425–9.
4. Cf. Fuller, 'Minor Prophets', p. 555.
5. Cf. R. E. Fuller, 'The Twelve', in E. Ulrich, F. Moore Cross, R. E. Fuller, J. E. Sanderson, P. W. Skehan and E. Tov (eds), *Qumran Cave 4: X. The Prophets* (DJD, 15; Oxford: Clarendon, 1997), 221–318, PL XL–LXIV; B. Ego, A. Lange, H. Lichtenberger and K. De Troyer (eds), *Biblia Qumranica: 3B. Minor Prophets* (Tübingen: Mohr Siebeck, 2004).

Masoretic order. However, in 4Q76 (4QXII^a) Malachi comes before Jonah. It is not an older version, but a secondary adaptation of the first half of the second century BCE. The change moves the eschatological perspective from Mal. 1.11, 14 towards Jonah 1.5, 10, 14–16 and 3.5-10 and broadens the hope of salvation for Israel of Mal. 3.22-24 into the expectation of salvation for the Gentiles.[6] The variation shows that the Septuagint is not the only tradition that interpreted the Twelve by changing their order.[7] That the Twelve were seen as a unit can be seen from Sir. 49.10, where the Twelve Prophets are mentioned together as comforters of Israel.[8]

In addition to the Hebrew and Greek texts of the Minor Prophets, literal quotations of them occur in the Qumran *pesharim*, in the Damascus Document, in 4QFlorilegium and in 4QCatena A. Outside of Qumran, quotations of the Minor Prophets can only be found in the allegorical commentaries of the Alexandrian exegete Philo (Zech. 6.12 [LXX] in *Conf.* 62f and Hos. 14.9 [LXX] in *Mut.* 139 and *Plant.* 138). Beyond these literal quotations one study identifies approximately 70 allusions to the Minor Prophets in Early Jewish writings,[9] some of which are based on misunderstandings,[10] some are very vague. In this chapter, only clear quotations and allusions from Second Temple Jewish sources are discussed.[11]

Quotations

Qumran Writings[12]

Although there are a few quotations of the Minor Prophets in the sectarian rules (CD), most of the quotations occur in exegetical texts, such as 4QFlorilegium, 4QCatena A and especially the *pesharim*. All the Qumran *pesharim* on the Minor Prophets interpret the texts in the

---

6.   Cf. O. H. Steck, 'Zur Abfolge Maleachi – Jona in 4Q76 (4QXII^a)', *ZAW* 108 (1996), 249–53.

7.   Cf. J. Barton, *Oracles of God: Perceptions of Ancient Prophecy in Israel after the Exile* (London: Darton, Longman and Todd, 1986), pp. 82, 85.

8.   Cf. Barton, *Oracles*, p. 135.

9.   Detailed list of quotations and allusions can be found in H. B. McLean, *Citations and Allusions to Jewish Scripture in Early Christian and Jewish Writings through 180 CE* (Lewiston, NY: Edwin Mellen Press, 1992), pp. 113–20. Because of his focus on the New Testament, he missed some quotations in the Qumran writings, which have been included here.

10.   Thus McLean identifies a reference to Zech. 1.1 in Josephus, *War* 4.335, although the passage does not refer to the prophet but a different Zechariah during the Jewish War.

11.   Therefore post-70 CE writings such as 4 Ezra are not considered here.

12.   For a convenient edition in Hebrew and English, see F. García Martínez and E. J. C. Tigchelaar, *The Dead Sea Scrolls Study Edition* (2 vols; Leiden: Brill, 1997–1998).

order of the biblical book, first quoting a verse or passage of the biblical text (the *lemma*) and then adding an interpretation, usually with an introductory formula ('its *pesher* / interpretation is ...'), which applies the text to a situation outside the original context.[13] All of the texts seem to be 'continuous' *pesharim* which follow the biblical order but can omit certain passages not regarded as relevant for the purposes of the sect.[14] The link between the passage and the *pesher* can be made by focusing on individual words or broader literary connections.[15] The interpretation sometimes just paraphrases or expands the biblical text, sometimes it changes a form or the subject of a clause, sometimes a vague reference in the text is made clear,[16] but in any case the *lemma* and the *pesher* are usually closely related.[17]

Among the Qumran writings *pesharim* have been found on Isaiah, Hosea, Micah, Nahum, Habakkuk, Zephaniah, Malachi and the Psalms.[18] Thus there are *pesharim* on half of the 'Minor' Prophets versus only one on the 'Major' Prophets and one on the Psalms. Together with the biblical manuscripts this is evidence of the great importance of the Minor Prophets for the community. It has been suggested that the *pesharim* were revised over time to adapt the interpretation to the historical developments, so that only one copy of each *pesher* has been found.[19] The remaining copies can be dated to the first century BCE.[20]

Pesher Habakkuk

The *pesher* on Habakkuk (1QpHab), on Habakkuk 1–2, is the most complete *pesher* preserved from Qumran.[21] In many places the biblical

---

13. Cf. S. L. Berrin, 'Pesharim', in L. H. Schiffman and J. C. VanderKam (eds), *Encyclopedia of the Dead Sea Scrolls*, vol. 2 (Oxford: Oxford University Press, 2000), pp. 644–7, esp. 644.

14. Cf. Pesher Psalms (4Q171) which moves from Psalm 37 to Psalm 45 and Pesher Isaiah (4Q162) which omits Isa. 5.15-24; see Berrin, 'Pesharim', pp. 644–5.

15. Cf. Berrin, 'Pesharim', p. 645.

16. M. J. Bernstein, 'Pesher Habakkuk', in Schiffman and VanderKam, *Encyclopedia*, vol. 2, pp. 647–51, esp. 648–9.

17. Cf. S. L. Berrin, 'Lemma / Pesher Correspondence in Pesher Nahum', in L. H. Schiffman, E. Tov and J. C. VanderKam (eds), *The Dead Sea Scrolls Fifty Years after Their Discovery: Proceedings of the Jerusalem Congress, July 20–25, 1997* (Jerusalem: Israel Exploration Society, 2000), pp. 341–50, esp. 344–9. On the definition of a *pesher*, see also J. H. Charlesworth, *The Pesharim and Qumran History: Chaos or Consensus* (Grand Rapids, MI: Eerdmans, 2002), pp. 68–70.

18. J. E. Bowley, 'Prophets and Prophecy in Qumran', in P. W. Flint and J. C. VanderKam (eds), *The Dead Sea Scrolls after Fifty Years: A Comprehensive Assessment*, vol. 2 (Leiden: Brill, 1999), pp. 354–78, esp. 355.

19. Cf. Berrin, 'Pesharim', p. 645.

20. Cf. Charlesworth, *Pesharim*, pp. 77–80.

21. Cf. Bernstein, 'Pesher Habakkuk', p. 647.

text is different from the Masoretic (frequently corrupt) tradition.[22] The two fundamental topics of the interpretation are the politics in Jerusalem, especially among the Temple priests on the one hand and the devastating consequences of the activities of the Kittim on the other.[23]

The Habakkuk text is seen as referring to 'the beginning of the generation' (1QpHab I,2 on Hab. 1.1-2). The main issue with the people is that 'they have rejected the Law of God' (I,11 on Hab. 1.4a). The 'wicked' in Hab. 1.4bc is related to the 'Wicked Priest', while the 'righteous' is the 'Teacher of Righteousness' (I,13). Hab. 1.5 is read as referring to 'the traitors with the Man of the Lie' who do not believe the words of God through the 'Teacher of Righteousness' and have no interest in God's covenant (II,1–4). The people mentioned in the text are called the 'traitors in the last days' and 'violators of the covenant', who do not believe the 'priest whom God has placed within the Community' (II,5–10). The 'Man of the Lie' thus is the opponent of the 'Teacher of Righteousness' and led those who rejected the Teacher's teachings. The name is probably based on Mic. 2.11, the preacher of lies who is believed by the people.[24] Thus the *pesher* on Habakkuk also uses other prophetic texts in its reading of the text and the sect's history.

Following Hab. 1.6-12 the perspective moves to foreign foes: the Chaldeans in the text are identified with the 'Kittim', who spread fear, are treacherous, conquer the land and whose military power is overwhelming (II,10–IV,14). The Kittim are the sect's name for the Romans, but as there are no references to specific events in the Roman conquest of Palestine the *pesher* dates from before this time. The *terminus post quem* is based on the references to internal events, which indicate Hasmonean times.[25]

After the long passage on the power and cunning of the 'Kittim' the interpretation returns to the conflict of the followers of the 'Teacher of Righteousness' and their opponents: Hab. 1.12-13a is seen as a promise of God not to let the nations destroy his chosen ones, but to hand over the judgement of the world to them, especially that over those of his people who, unlike them, have not been faithful in adversity (IV,16–V,6). Hab. 1.13a is quoted again, and read, together with 1.13b, in terms of the contrast between those who did not give in to desire on the one hand and the 'House of Absalom' and the council, who did not support the 'Teacher of Righteousness' against the 'Man of the Lie', on the other (V,6–12).

Following Hab. 1.14-16 and 'the fish of the sea', the interpretation returns to the Kittim and their wealth (V,12–VI,2). The sacrifices of

22. Cf. R. Fuller, 'Minor Prophets', p. 557; Bernstein, 'Pesher Habakkuk', pp. 647–8.
23. Bernstein, 'Pesher Habakkuk', pp. 648–9; Charlesworth, *Pesharim*, pp. 2, 74, 109–12, 117.
24. Charlesworth, *Pesharim*, pp. 94–7.
25. Bernstein, 'Pesher Habakkuk', p. 649.

the fisherman to his net of Hab. 1.16a are linked to the practice of the 'Kittim' to sacrifice to their standards, another reference to the Romans (VI,2–5). Hab. 1.16b-17 is seen in terms of the Kittim's demand for tributes and the killing done by their armies without heed for age or gender (VI,5–12).

In Hab. 2.1-2 the biblical text turns to the prophet himself, leading the *pesher* to a hermeneutically important remark: God told Habakkuk about the future until the 'last generation' and the prophet wrote it all down, but he was not informed about the 'end' of the era. Thus the prophetic texts are seen as oracles about the future, but they are incomplete as their authors did not know about the final end (VI,12–VII,2). The 'runner' who reads these sayings in Hab. 2.2 is interpreted as the 'Teacher of Righteousness', who is given full insight into the divine 'mysteries' of the prophets (VII,3–5). The appointed time of the vision in Hab. 2.3 is read as the 'Teacher of Righteousness', who has the key for the full understanding of God's plan and to the full interpretation of the writings of the prophets (VII,5–8).[26] Thus the prophets are given the mystery and the Teacher receives the interpretation.[27] The Teacher is never called a prophet himself, because his task is not to produce oracles; he provides the exegesis, and yet he has the authority of divine inspiration.[28]

As the eschaton did not come with the Teacher and history went on, Hab. 2.3 about the delay of the appointed time is seen as referring to 'the men of truth', who remain faithful to God and their place in God's plan (VII,9–14). After a fragmentary reference to 'proud' in Hab. 2.4a (VII,14–16) they are identified with the 'righteous', who will 'live by their faith', in Hab. 2.4b. They are 'all who observe the Torah in the house of Judah' and will be saved because they are faithful to the 'Teacher of Righteousness' (VII,17–VIII,3).

The warning about the corrupting influence of wealth in Hab. 2.5-6 serves as a point of reference for the 'Wicked Priest', who at the beginning of his office was seen as trustworthy and is regarded as having later betrayed God and the Torah for his own prosperity (VIII,3–13). This 'Wicked Priest' must be distinguished from the previously mentioned 'Man of the Lie':[29] The interpretation of Hab. 2.7-8 mentions a priest who rebelled (VIII,13–IX,2) and who is related to the later priesthood, for the fate of the plunderer in Hab. 2.8a refers to the 'last priests of Jerusalem' and their accumulation of riches from the nations. The author expects the 'Kittim' to conquer them (IX,2–7). This expectation results from the interpretation of the shedding of blood in Hab. 2.8b, which is

---

26.   Cf. Bowley, 'Prophets', p. 361.
27.   Cf. Barton, *Oracles*, pp. 196–7.
28.   Cf. Bowley, 'Prophets', p. 371.
29.   Cf. Bernstein, 'Pesher Habakkuk', p. 650.

related back to the 'Wicked Priest' who was given by God into the hands of his enemies together with his council because of their 'wickedness' against the 'Teacher of Righteousness' and God's elect (IX,7–12). Thus the text is read on different levels: in relation to the time of the Teacher, in relation to the present of the author and in relation to the time of the end, of the 'last priests' – probably expected to be very close. It is possible that the 'Wicked Priest' originally referred to a specific person, but that in the course of the history of the sect the term was reapplied to the present.[30]

Of the interpretation of the quotation of Hab. 2.9-11 only a reference to a priest remains (IX,10–X,1), and the *pesher* then expands on God's judgement in Hab. 2.10 (X,2–5). The town built by bloodshed of Hab. 2.12-13 is related to the 'Spreader of Lie' and his false teachings which led many astray (X,5–13), and Hab. 2.14 is read against this as announcing the revelation of true knowledge (X,13–XI,2). As the 'Spreader of Lie' and the 'Man of the Lie' act similarly and introduce the contrast between those with the true insight and those who reject this, they can probably be identified as the same person.

The warning against making people drunk at festivals in Hab. 2.15 is then taken to refer to the 'Wicked Priest' and his persecution of the 'Teacher of Righteousness' on the Day of Atonement (XI,2–8), implying that the sect used the solar calendar, not the lunar calendar of the Jerusalem priesthood, so that their festivals fell on different days.[31] Consequently, Hab. 2.16 is read as judgement over the priest who 'did not circumcise the foreskin of his heart' (XI,8–16), Hab. 2.17 as judgement over the 'Wicked Priest' for his behaviour towards 'the poor' and 'the simple folk of Judah' as well as for the desecration of God's Temple (XI,17–XII,10). And Hab. 2.18-20 is quoted as warning against idolatry (XII,10–XIII,3).

Thus the prophetic book was read as a code for which the 'Teacher of Righteousness' had received the key. Those who followed him were the only ones able to truly observe the Torah and understand the prophets, unlike the 'Man of the Lie' and his people, who rejected their interpretation. Their interpretation, however, uses cryptic ciphers for every reference to a specific person or event.[32] Therefore to someone outside the community it is not clear which persons and events are referred to: until now there is no convincing theory for the identification of the 'Teacher of Righteousness', and almost every Hasmonean high priest has been suggested as 'Wicked Priest'.[33] Probably the key to the code was given to the members of the community in oral instruction,

---

30.   Cf. Charlesworth, *Pesharim*, pp. 36–7, 91–3.
31.   Cf. Bernstein, 'Pesher Habakkuk', p. 650; Charlesworth, *Pesharim*, pp. 89–90.
32.   Cf. Berrin, 'Pesharim', p. 644.
33.   Bernstein, 'Pesher Habakkuk', p. 649.

which would also enable the sect to update its interpretation to the present – requiring, however, another step of inspired exegesis.

Pesher Nahum

The Nahum *pesher* (4QpNah = 4Q169), like the one on Habakkuk, contains references to the sect's history by means of an eschatological reading of the text.[34] The quotations of the Nahum *pesher* disagree with the Masoretic text in many places, originally due to orthographic differences.[35]

The first remaining section (frags 1+2) refers to Nah. 1.3-6 with its emphasis on God's power over nature, storms, the sea and land. The author associates the forces of nature described in Nah. 1.3 (1–5) with the Kittim, again to be identified with the Romans. The perishing of Bashan and Carmel in Nah. 1.4 is seen as announcing God's destruction of the Kittim (5–9). Nah. 1.5-6 on the power of God is quoted (9–11), but the interpretation is missing.

The second part (frags 3+4) interprets Nah. 2.13-14. Nah. 2.13 (ET 2.12) is quoted with its reference to the unrestricted movements of the lion and his cubs and applied to 'Demetrius, king of Yavan', and his attempt to enter Jerusalem at the suggestion of 'the seekers of smooth things'.[36] The commentary states that this attempt failed because God did not allow the kings of Yavan to conquer Jerusalem, unlike the chiefs of the Kittim (4QpNah frags 3–4 I 1–3). The quotation of Nah. 2.14 (ET 2.13) and the prey of the lion is interpreted as the 'Lion of Wrath', who took revenge on the 'seekers of smooth things' and hanged them alive – probably a reference to crucifixion and regarded as an atrocity by the author of the *pesher* (frags 3–4 I 4–8). The 'seekers of smooth things' can be identified as the Pharisees,[37] the 'Lion of Wrath' as Alexander Jannaeus, and the whole passage refers to the events mentioned in Josephus, *Ant.* 13.372–384 (95–88 BCE), Alexander's conflict with Demetrius III Eucaerus, the Seleucid king, and his crucifixion of 800 Pharisees accused of siding with Demetrius.[38] The Kittim reference alludes to the later event of Pompey's entering the Temple. Once more the *pesher* technique combines references to events on several temporal levels, although, on the

---

34. Cf. S. L. Berrin, 'Pesher Nahum', in Schiffman and VanderKam, *Encyclopedia*, vol. 2, pp. 653–5, esp. 653.

35. Cf. Fuller, 'Minor Prophets', p. 557.

36. Cf. Berrin, 'Pesher Nahum', p. 653; Charlesworth, *Pesharim*, pp. 97–8.

37. Cf. Berrin, 'Pesher Nahum', p. 653; Charlesworth, *Pesharim*, pp. 97–8.

38. E. Schürer, *The History of the Jewish People in the Age of Jesus Christ (175 B.C.– A.D. 135)* III.1 (rev. and ed. G. Vermes, F. Millar, M. Goodman; Edinburgh: T&T Clark, 1986), pp. 431–2; Berrin, 'Pesher Nahum', pp. 653–4; Charlesworth, *Pesharim*, pp. 99–106, 112–16.

whole, col. I is concerned with Alexander Jannaeus's persecution of the Pharisees in the eighties BCE, col. II with the Pharisaic influence during Salome Alexandra's reign (76–67 BCE, cf. Josephus, *Ant.* 13.405-432) and cols III–IV with the civil conflict during the struggle of their two sons Hyrcanus II and Aristobulus II for the throne, which was ended by Pompey's conquest of Judea.[39]

Nah. 2.14 (ET 2.13) on God's judgement is read as referring to the destruction of Alexander Jannaeus, his council, the priests and their accumulated wealth (frags 3–4 I 8–II 1). Nah. 3.1 and the 'city of bloodshed' with its plunder is interpreted as the city of Ephraim, associated with the 'seekers of smooth things' (frags 3–4 II 1–2). The violent fate of this city in Nah. 3.1-3 is seen in terms of the violence which is to end the reign of the 'seekers of smooth things' (3–4 II 3–6), the influence of the Pharisees under Salome Alexandra. The *pesher* on Nah. 3.4 and the prostitute describes the teaching of the 'seekers of smooth things' as leading nations and rulers, Jews and proselytes astray (3–4 II 7–10). Nah. 3.5 on God's judgement (3–4 II 10–12) is read in terms of the nations and their despicable customs (3–4 III 1). But the interpretation of the announcement of judgement in Nah. 3.6-7 returns to the 'seekers of smooth things' and the final judgement which will show the wicked deeds of Ephraim and the 'glory of Judah' (3–4 III 1–5). The destruction of Nineveh in Nah. 3.7 in particular is read as proclaiming the end of the 'seekers of smooth things' and their misdirection of the people (3–4 III 5–8).

Moving on in history to the reign of another group No-Amon, i.e. Thebes, in the quotation from Nah. 3.8 is not read as the city but as the nation of Amon and interpreted as Manasseh (3–4 III 8–9). The interpretation of the water surrounding Thebes in Nah. 3.8 sees the waters as armies (3–4 III 10–12). The allies of Thebes in Nah. 3.9 are identified as 'the wicked ones of Judah', who associated with Manasseh (3–4 III 11– IV 1). The description of Manasseh in the interpretation of Nah. 3.10 implies that Manasseh is the currently ruling power in Jerusalem, whose exile and destruction is foreseen, based on the text's reference to exile, captivity and death (3–4 IV 1–4). The 'you also will get drunk' in Nah. 3.11 is read as referring back to 'the wicked in Ephraim', who will share the fate of Manasseh (3–4 IV 4–8).[40] This parallel between Ephraim – the Pharisees – and Manasseh together with the text's explanation that they rule in Jerusalem has led to the identification of Manasseh as the Sadducees, the only known aristocratic group in Jerusalem.[41] It is only fitting that the sect used the two northern tribes

---

39. Cf. Berrin, 'Pesher Nahum', p. 654.
40. Of the passages on Nah. 3.12 (3–4 IV 8), Nah. 3.13 and 3.14 (3–4 V1–3) not much has been preserved beyond the quotations of the text.
41. See Charlesworth, *Pesharim*, pp. 106–9, but with a note of caution.

who defected from the Jerusalem Temple as names for their opponents[42] to express their fundamental criticism of the Jerusalem cult which is seen as aberrant and corrupt.

Thus the Nahum *pesher* regards the details of the prophetic text as a cipher referring to people and events of its recent past, present and the future it expects. The overall aim is the application to the present, not the reading of the text in its historical setting.

Pesher Hosea

There remain only few fragments of the *pesher*, the quotations of which, as far as can be determined, seem to be close to the Septuagint readings.[43] The prophet's comparison of Israel's relationship with God to that of an unfaithful wife and her husband is easily interpreted in terms of those who, in the sect's view, reject God's commandments in the present.[44] 4QpHos[a] (4Q166) cols I and II interprets Hos. 2.8-14 (ET 2.6-12). The thorns which block the unfaithful wife's path in Hos. 2.8-9 are seen as the people's 'blindness and confusion' during the 'era of their disloyalty' (I,6–9), and her wish to return to her husband is related to the 'return of the captives' (I,16). The judgement of God over the unfaithful wife is applied to the people (II,1–6 on Hos. 2.11-12) as foretelling hunger and the desertion of their foreign allies (II,8–14 on Hos. 2.12-13) and as announcing the end of all festivities which have been aligned with foreign festivals (II,14–17 on Hos. 2.15).[45] The last part is another reference to the argument about the calendar, phrased almost as a quotation of *Jub.* 6.35,[46] which is a warning to strictly observe the solar calendar.

There is also a fragment of the *pesher* Hosea in 4QpHos[b] (4Q167). Frag. 2 quotes Hos. 5.13-15, frags 5–6 Hos. 6.4, frags 7–8 Hos. 6.7, frags 10+26 Hos. 6.9-10, frags 10a+4+18+24 Hos. 6.11–7.1, frags 11–13 Hos. 8.6-8, and frags 15+16+33 col. II Hos. 8.14, but only the interpretation on Hos. 5.13-15 remains sufficiently preserved for comment. What is left of the interpretation of Hos. 5.13 mentions a 'lion' (frag 2.2), and based on the lion attacking the house of Judah in Hos. 5.14 there is the announcement of 'the last priest who will stretch out his hand to strike Ephraim' (frag. 2.3). As in the Nahum *pesher* Ephraim and the lion are mentioned in the same context, thus the 'lion' can be identified as Alexander Jannaeus, and Ephraim as the Pharisees.[47] The similarity

42. Cf. Berrin, 'Pesher Nahum', p. 653.
43. Cf. Fuller, 'Minor Prophets', p. 556.
44. Cf. M. J. Bernstein, 'Pesher Hosea', in Schiffman and VanderKam, *Encyclopedia*, vol. 2, pp. 650–1.
45. The interpretation of the quotation of Hos. 2.14 in II,17–19 is missing.
46. Cf. Bernstein, 'Pesher Hosea', p. 651; Charlesworth, *Pesharim*, pp. 101, 106.
47. Cf. Bernstein, 'Pesher Hosea', p. 651; Charlesworth, *Pesharim*, p. 101.

of the context shows that the ciphers were handled consistently in the different *pesharim*, another indication of ongoing additional – probably oral – instruction about the interpretation of the Minor Prophets.

Pesher Micah

The Micah *pesher* 1QpMic (1Q14) has a biblical text that differs from the Masoretic and the Septuagint text (which agree in this case).[48] There are passages with interpretation in 1QpMic frags 8–10 3–11 on Mic. 1.5-6, in frag. 11 1–4 on Mic. 1.8-9 and in frags 17–18 1–5 on Mic. 6.15-16. Mic. 1.5-6 refers to God's judgement over Jerusalem as 'the high place of Judah' and to the destruction of Samaria. In the *pesher* Samaria is interpreted as the 'Spreader of the Lie', who has led the 'simple' astray (4–5), and Jerusalem as the 'Teacher of Righteousness', who instructs all those who are willing to observe the law of God in the proper interpretation (6–9). In the biblical text Judah and Samaria are parallel, both doomed under God's judgement, while the *pesher* sees Jerusalem as positive, identified with the Teacher of Righteousness and his followers, who escape judgement (8). Quoting Mic. 1.8-9 (frag. 11 1–4) the wailing mentioned in Mic. 1.8 is read in terms of the 'priests of Jerusalem' and their misdirection of the people (1–2), while the Jerusalem of Mic. 1.9 is again interpreted with regard to the 'Teacher of Righteousness' and his judgement over his enemies (4).

Mic. 6.14-15 on the punishment of the people for observing 'the statutes of Omri' and 'the works of the house of Ahab' in the form of the futility of their agricultural labour is quoted in 1QpMic frag. 17–18 1–5, but of the interpretation only the eschatological application to the 'last generation' is preserved (5).

The remaining fragment in 4QpMic 1 (4Q168) consists only of a quotation of Mic. 4.8-12,[49] but Jerusalem without its king, going into exile to be saved by God from there, could easily be interpreted in terms of the community's history, and its stay in 'Damascus' (e.g. CD–B XX,10–14).

Thus even the fragmentary condition of this *pesher* allows the conclusion that the same mixture of historical and eschatological reading occurred as in the more complete *pesharim*.

48.   Cf. Fuller, 'Minor Prophets', pp. 556–7.
49.   Cf. L. A. Sinclair, 'Hebrew Text of the Qumran Micah Pesher and Textual Tradition of the Minor Prophets', *RevQ* 11 (1983), 253–63, esp. 256.

Pesher Zephaniah

The fragments are too short to allow conclusions as to the affiliation of the Hebrew text.[50] 1QpZeph (1Q15) contains fragments of Zeph. 1.18 and Zeph. 2.1-2 about God's judgement. Of the interpretation of the former nothing is left and of the latter only a reference which identifies the 'shameless nation' with the 'inhabitants of the land of Judah'. 4QpZeph (4Q170) contains only the quotation of Zeph. 1.12-13 on God's punishment of Jerusalem (frags 1+2, 4).

Thus the *pesher* mainly proves that the book was read and commented on in Qumran, which is also shown by the quotation of Zeph. 3.9a–b on God's making the nations pure of speech in a very fragmentary passage on Abraham in 4QExposition on the Patriarchs (4Q464 frag. 3 I,8).

Pesher Malachi and Commentary

Similarly of Malachi references there is only a fragment of the quotations and interpretations of Mal. 1.14 in 5QpMal (5Q10) and Mal. 3.16-18 in 4QcommMal (4Q253a).

The Damascus Document

The Damascus Document (CD) is one of the two main sectarian rules; it places the rules of the community in the context of its history and the Minor Prophets are used in the historical as well as the rule parts. Mal. 1.10 is quoted immediately after the introduction of 'one who teaches righteousness' at the end of times in the outline of the history of the sect to describe those who follow the Teacher (CD–A VI,11–14): as requested in the prophetic text they close the door to the Temple and do not participate in its defiled worship. This is the introduction of the long list of duties of the righteous in CD. Thus the sect regards its observance of the rules and separation from the Temple as fulfilling the call of the prophet.

Amos 5.26-27 is used in CD–A VII,14–16 in a historical section based on Isa. 7.17 on the separation of 'Ephraim' from 'Judah'. This is seen as the parting of the sect from 'Ephraim'. Amos 5.26-27 with the exile of 'Sikkut, their king' and 'Kiyyun, your images' beyond Damascus – negative judgement of God in Amos – is read as referring to the exile of the 'books of Torah' and that of the prophetic writings in Damascus. This then, by virtue of the identical consonants in the Hebrew, is combined with a quotation of Amos 9.11 about the eschatological raising up of

50. Cf. Fuller, 'Minor Prophets', p. 557.

the *sukkot*, the 'booths', of David (VII,16–17). Thus Amos 5.26-27 receives a messianic reading as referring to the assembly and their true interpretation of the prophets inspired by the 'star' out of Jacob (Num. 24.17), who is identified with the 'interpreter of the Torah' (VII,17–20).[51] Instead of taking up the negative connotation of the Amos text the community regarded the exile in 'Damascus' as positive reference to their own exile, as the place where God rebuilt the house of David by sending a teacher to instruct the people in the correct interpretation of the Torah and the prophets. The Messianic connotations do not relate here to a political government but to the leader of this sect.

Quotations from the Minor Prophets also serve as the basis of certain sectarian rules. In CD–A XVI,14–15, in the context of the prohibition to offer as a freewill offering anything that has been obtained by unjust means (XVI,13–20), Mic. 7.2 is quoted to support the prohibition against offering the food of one's mouth. In the same way Nah. 1.2 is used in CD–A IX,5 on the prohibition to avenge oneself (IX,2–5) to emphasize that it is God who takes revenge.

In CD–B there are clusters of quotations from the Minor Prophets. Thus Zech. 13.7 on God's striking the shepherd and scattering of the sheep is used in CD–B XIX,7–9 at the beginning of the description of the community's life to warn against the judgement of God over those who do not keep the ordinances of the sect. Immediately afterwards Zech. 11.11 is quoted in CD–B XIX,9 in order to identify those who revere him as 'the poor ones of the flock'. To them it is promised that they will escape the 'first visitation' – with reference to Ezek. 9.4 – and the future punishment, which is described quoting Hos. 5.10 on God's wrath over the princes of Judah who change boundaries (CD–B XIX,15–16). The changing of the boundaries is interpreted as licentiousness and deviation from the laws (CD–B XIX,16–21).

The quotation of Hos. 3.4 in CD–B XX,16–17 is presented in contrast to Mal. 3.16-18 in CD–B XX,17–21 in another eschatological reading of the history of the community. The Hosea quotation on the loss of king and judge serves to illustrate the wrath of God against Israel during the 40 years between the coming of the Teacher and the end of those who follow the 'Man of the Lie' (XX,14–16), and the Malachi text on the people who revere God and who are listed in the 'book of remembrance' describes the obedience of the sect and their salvation.

Thus, as in the *pesharim*, in the Damascus Document the Minor Prophets are linked with the history and the life of the sect, interpreting past events, present practices and providing a basis for future expectations.

---

51.   Cf. Bowley, 'Prophets', pp. 361–2.

4QFlorilegium

As in CD–A VII,16 Amos 9.11 God's raising up the 'booth of David' is quoted in 4QFlor (4Q174) frag. 1 col. I, 21,2, 12–13.[52] Here it is used conservatively in the context of the messianic promise to the house of David in 2 Sam. 7.12-14 (frag. 1 col. I, 21,2, 10–12).

4QCatena A

Mic. 2.10-11 is quoted in 4QCatena A (4Q177) I,10 to interpret the persecutions in Ps. 11.1, but the whole passage is fragmentary, as well as the quotation of Nah. 2.10 in 4QCatena A III,3 and of Hos. 5.8 in III,13–16.

The quotation of Zech. 3.9 in 4QCatena A (4Q177) II,1–2 only uses the idea of engraving God's words to interpret the pure and refined words of God in Ps. 12.7 (II,1). A single thought of the text is taken and used to make an exegetical point which resulted from the previous biblical text.

Conclusion Qumran

In Qumran the historical context of the Minor Prophets is irrelevant; they serve to interpret events in the sect's history and in its present in terms of an immediate eschatological expectation. Quotations can be combined with other quotations from the Minor Prophets or from other biblical books. In the *pesharim* the Minor Prophets provide the main text, which the exegesis relates to the sect's history; in the Florilegium and the Catena the Minor Prophets serve the interpretation of other texts; and in CD the history and practice of the sect provide the 'main text', interpreted through the quotations. The hermeneutics of the sect is based on their instruction in the tradition of the founder, the Teacher of Righteousness. Thus the members of the sect are the only ones who have the key to interpreting the Minor Prophets.[53] The prophets become the ignorant tradents of the divine speech to Israel; they themselves do not understand the full meaning of their words.[54] As the exegetes of the sect can point to certain events as the fulfilment of their interpretation of the prophets' words, they can expect to be believed about their reading of their future. This use of the prophets is truly apocalyptic. But the whole

---

52. As in CD the text used differs from the Masoretic text; cf. Fuller, 'Minor Prophets', p. 556.

53. Cf. Charlesworth, *Pesharim*, pp. 1–16.

54. Cf. Bowley, 'Prophets', pp. 362–5.

interpretation is not given in clear terms but in cipher, necessitating another key to translate the code, apparently never given in writing, but in the oral traditions of the sect.

Philo

Philo of Alexandria's commentaries date from the first half of the first century CE. His main aim is to interpret the Torah. Non-pentateuchal texts are only rarely quoted. Of the Minor Prophets there are only three quotations in all his writings, all three of which are in his allegorical commentaries, which aim to provide an individual, philosophical interpretation of the Torah.

In the context of the interpretation of Gen. 11.2 Philo identifies the 'east' mentioned in the passage with 'rising' (of the sun) and compares this to the rising of virtues he associates with the garden of Eden in Gen. 2.8 (*Conf.* 60–61). Interpreting the 'rising', in 62–3 Philo quotes the Septuagint version of the prophecy about the man who rebuilds the Temple and has royal status in Zech. 6.12 ('here is a man whose name is rising').[55] Philo identifies this man with the Logos, whom God raised.[56] This is a philosophical interpretation of the prophetic text, based on a specific term in the text, as in the Catena from Qumran. Philo reads the prophetic text as a hermeneutical key for understanding the Genesis passage and at the same time he uses the philosophical Logos traditions as key to the interpretation of the Zechariah passage.

The same double approach of exegetical tool and key for philosophical interpretation can be found in Philo's quotation of Hos. 14.9 LXX in *Mut.* 139 and in *Plant.* 138. Both times the Hosea quotation serves the interpretation of a verse from the Pentateuch: In *Plant.* 138 the overall context is the exegesis of Lev. 19.23-25, the laws which leave the fruits of trees in the fourth year for God (*Plant.* 95). The immediate context is the interpretation of the fifth son of Leah in Gen. 30.35, Issachar, whose name he reads with reference to Gen. 30.18 as 'reward' (*Plant.* 134–135). This 'reward' is linked with the greater context of the fruits of the fourth year as God's and the fact that the owner of the trees receives the fruits in the fifth year; then they are identified as virtue, as the fruit of human actions (136–137). Philo quotes the 'fruits' promised in Hos. 14.8 LXX and reads Hos. 14.9 ('Those who are wise, understand these things …') not as a statement but as a question: 'Who is wise …, who is understanding?' (138; Philo makes use of the LXX). This proves to him that only the wise man knows to whom the 'fruits of intelligence' belong.

---

55.   In Hebrew the name is 'branch'.
56.   Cf. Barton, *Oracles*, pp. 248–9.

Thus the prophetic text serves to argue for a philosophical interpretation of the Torah.

In the same way Philo reads Hos. 14.8-9 in *Mut.* 139. Here the context is a discussion of the laughter of Sarah after the announcement of Isaac's birth, particularly the phrase 'God has brought laughter for me' in Gen. 21.6 (*Mut.* 137–138). Philo identifies Isaac with 'laughter' and observes that there are only few who understand the true meaning that God alone gives what is excellent (138). As proof of this the quotation of Hos. 14.8-9 is introduced as 'this oracle, inspired words of fire through the mouth of some prophet' (139). Again he quotes the reference to the fruits and reads the following verse as questions and again the quotation supports the idea that only few people have access to God's fruit which is understanding and wisdom. This conclusion is accompanied by a very personal expression of admiration ('I understood the echo and the unseen one striking invisibly the instrument of the voice, and I marvelled ... also at what was said', 139). The understanding of the prophetic verse places Philo himself in a state of inspired awe.

Thus Philo's hermeneutical use of the Minor Prophet is consistent: they serve the allegorical interpretation of the Torah. Even in different interpretative contexts the same verse is used in the same interpretation. But in *Mut.*, along with the interpretation of the text, Philo also offers a kind of personal ecstatic testimony of his insight into the truth of the prophetic words. Thus, as in Qumran, the text not only serves the exegesis of a biblical text but it also addresses Philo's life directly.

Allusions

Apocalypses, Testaments and Oracles

The apocalyptic Enochic material occasionally uses the Minor Prophets. Already in the introduction of *1 Enoch* (first century CE)[57] there is an allusion to God's coming from the heavens (in *1 Enoch* it is 'heavens', in Micah 'his place') to judge (*1 En.* 1.4), a theme known from Mic. 1.3 or Isa. 1.3.[58] The older parts of the Enoch traditions also use the Minor Prophets. A certain similarity to Joel 2.10 and the darkening of the sun, moon and stars on the day of God's judgement can be found in the

---

57. On the dating of the different parts of *1 Enoch*, see E. Isaac, '1 (Ethiopic Apocalypse of) Enoch', in J. H. Charlesworth (ed.), *The Old Testament Pseudepigrapha. Vol 1: Apocalyptic Literature and Testaments* (New York: Doubleday, 1983), pp. 5–89, esp. 7.

58. The same thought of God's coming forth from his habitation can also be found in *T. Mos.* 10.3 (probably also first century CE; see J. Priest, 'Testament of Moses', in Charlesworth, *Pseudepigrapha. Vol 1*, pp. 919–34, esp. 920–1).

Book of the Heavenly Luminaries (late second century BCE) in the stars changing their course and the time of their appearance (*1 En.* 80.6–7). In the Dream Visions (middle second century BCE) there is a vague reference to Mal. 1.7, which refers to the priests offering polluted food at the altar. In the same way the behaviour of the returning exiles is described as placing polluted food on the table of the high tower they build (*1 En.* 89.73), thus applying the prophetic criticism to the second, not the first Temple. The general thought of the fighting between the generations of Mic. 7.6 is taken up in the Similitudes (first century CE, *1 En.* 56.7) and in the Epistle of Enoch (around 100 BCE, *1 En.* 99.5 and 100.2) in various combinations. Thus the prophetic criticism of the present is applied to the authors' time and their references to judgement are taken as information about the future.

The eschatological interest in the Minor Prophets can also be found in the *Testaments of the Twelve Patriarchs* (second century BCE).[59] Thus God's promise in Joel 3.1-5 (ET 2.28-32) to pour out his spirit over everyone to make them prophesy is given a messianic interpretation in *T. Jud.* 24.2-3: first the spirit is poured out over the 'Star of Jacob' (24.1-2), and then the 'spirit of grace' over the people (24.3). In the same way the reference to the 'sun of righteousness' rising over those who fear God in Mal. 3.20 (ET 4.2) is taken up in *T. Zeb.* 9.8 to describe the eschatological rising of the 'light of righteousness' over the people.

The same approach to the prophets as sources of information about the future is taken in the *Sibylline Oracles*. In *Sib. Or.* 3.544 (3.489-839, middle of the second century BCE)[60] the thought that only a third of humankind will survive parallels Zech. 13.8. In *Sib. Or.* 3.718-719 the nations are foreseen to send envoys to the Temple and study the Torah, which echoes the journey of the nations to the Temple and their instruction in the Torah in Mic. 4.2. The call of God to 'daughter Zion' in Zech. 2.10 to rejoice because He will come and dwell there is taken up in *Sib. Or.* 3.785, addressed to the 'maiden' in the eschatological kingdom. And the darkening of the sun from Joel 2.10 is taken up in *Sib. Or.* 3.801 as a sign of the end. Thus the Minor Prophets were read by the seer as maps for the events before, during and after the final judgement.

59.   H. C. Kee, 'Testament of Twelve Patriarchs', in Charlesworth, *Pseudepigrapha.* Vol 1, pp. 776–828, esp. 777–8.

60.   J. J. Collins, 'Sibylline Oracles', in Charlesworth, *Pseudepigrapha. Vol 1*, pp. 317–472, esp. 354–5.

Rewritten Bible

Jubilees (second century BCE)[61] is largely a retelling of the Genesis narrative. At the beginning, references to the Minor Prophets provide a basis for Israel's continuing relationship with God. Thus *Jubilees* uses a reference to Zech. 8.13 and the people's change from a curse to a blessing along with various passages from Jeremiah to refer to the restoration of Israel (*Jub.* 1.16). In a similar context the thought of the people as 'children of the living God' (Hos. 2.1 [ET 1.10]) is used to emphasize the close relationship between God and his people after their return from the exile (*Jub.* 1.24-25). In *Jub.* 7.34 the idea that God plants Israel on the land forever (Amos 5.26) is taken up and transferred to the descendants of Noah. But also the prophetic criticism of idols as work of human hands (Amos 5.26; cf. Jer. 10.3, 9) appears in the mouth of Abraham in *Jub.* 12.5 when he criticizes the idols of his father. Prophetic statements on judgement are likewise used; for example the thought that the animals will also suffer in the future judgement as suggested by Hos. 4.3 and Zeph. 1.3 appears in the account of the evil of future generations in *Jub.* 23.18-19. In *Jub.* 24.31-32 Amos 9.2-4 is taken up to say that there is no place in heaven, on earth or in Sheol to hide from God's judgement. Thus *Jubilees* takes the prophetic texts as not tied to a specific time; they are applied to either the account of the history of Israel before the life of the prophets or to the depiction of future judgement and salvation.

Ps-Philo's *Liber Antiquitatum Biblicarum* (first century CE)[62] narrates the history from Adam to David. When God speaks to Joshua the promise in Mal. 4.6 LXX that Elijah will unite the parents and their children is used to express that at the end God will raise the dead (*LAB* 23.13). Similarly, the concept of election and rejection as reward or punishment for one's actions is introduced into the narrative about the birth of Jacob and Esau using Mal. 1.2-3, in which God says that He loved Jacob but hated Esau. While the prophet does not give any reason, Ps-Philo adds 'God loved Jacob but he hated Esau because of his deeds' (*LAB* 32.6). Thus, in Ps-Philo the Minor Prophets are used in the interpretation of certain texts/traditions by adding certain philosophical concepts with a view to the application to the individual.

---

61.   Cf. O. S. Wintermute, 'Jubilees', in J. H. Charlesworth (ed.), *The Old Testament Pseudepigrapha. Vol 2: Expansions of the 'Old Testament' and Legends, Wisdom and Philosophical Literature, Prayers, Psalms and Odes, Fragments of Lost Judeo-Hellenistic Works* (New York: Doubleday, 1985), pp. 35–142, esp. 43–4.

62.   D. J. Harrington, 'Pseudo-Philo', in Charlesworth, *Pseudepigrapha. Vol 2*, pp. 297–377, esp. 299.

Psalms

The application of the prophets to individuals and their present can also be found in the *Psalms of Solomon* (first century CE).[63] In *Ps. Sol.* 15.3 the psalm is seen as 'the fruit of the lips', a direct reference to Hos. 14.2 and the prophet's request to the people to ask God for forgiveness so that they can 'offer the fruits of our lips'. Thus the psalm becomes the fulfilment of the prophetic call at the time when the Temple is threatened and the country is in turmoil.

Qumran

Similarly the Hodayot, the hymns from Qumran (first century BCE),[64] apply references to the Minor Prophets to their present. Thus the image of Jerusalem as a woman in labour and the inhabitants' leaving the city for Babylon to be rescued by God in Mic. 4.10 is taken up in 1QH III,7–12 (Sukenik), but here the woman in labour is the individual soul before the conversion to God. This does not exclude the eschatological use, for later the same hymn takes up the anger and wrath of God in Nah. 1.6 (1QH III,27–28 [Sukenik]): asking who can withstand God's anger the psalm addresses everyone. The hymn by contrast refers to God's future anger against the hypocrites and Belial, thus using the reference to define the sect's opponents.

That the Qumran sect itself is shaped to conform with the prophetic ideas can be seen from the beginning of the Community Rule, where the purpose of the group is defined as doing what God regards as good as He commanded through Moses and the prophets (1QS I,1–3; VIII,14–16).[65] This is demonstrated by repeated allusions to the Minor Prophets in different parts of the rule. Thus at the end of the passage on the covenant liturgy in 1QS II,24–25 the people are advised to show meekness, love and uprightness in their behaviour towards each other, which reflects Mic. 6.8 and the exhortation 'to do justice, and to love kindness, and to walk humbly with your God'. Similarly in the Instruction on the Two Spirits in IV,5 the 'sons of truth' have 'enthusiasm for the decrees of justice'; they practise compassion and reject idols. The Micah echo returns at the beginning of the main rules: in V,3–4 the community is described as striving to achieve 'truth and humility, justice and uprightness, compassionate love' etc. In VIII,1–2 the council of the community seeks to implement 'truth, justice, judgement, compassionate love and unassuming behaviour of one to another', and in the final hymn in X,26

---

63. R. B. Wright, 'Psalms of Solomon', in Charlesworth, *Pseudepigrapha. Vol 2*, pp. 639–70, esp. 640–1.
64. Schürer, *History* III.1, p. 455.
65. Cf. Bowley, 'Prophets', pp. 355, 364.

the speaker promises to act on 'justice (and) compassionate love with the oppressed'.[66] Thus without direct literal references the community aims to fulfil the Micah ideal at every level of the communal structure, in the individual, the council and in the liturgical practice.

Micah, however, is not the only prophet to be used as the basis of the community's self-identification as the eschatological people of God. In 1QS IV,21–22 there is a reference to the pouring out of the 'spirit of truth' over the 'sons of light' to cleanse them from their wickedness and to instruct them about God himself and about proper behaviour. This takes up the promise of Joel 3.1-2 (ET 2.28-29) that God will pour out his spirit so that the people will prophesy. At the end of the covenant liturgy there is a reference to the purification of the individual through God's spirit and through the observance of the community's rules (III,6–12). Thus the eschatological expectation of the spirit implied in IV,21–22, in Joel 2.21–29 and in other receptions, such as *T. Jud.* 24.2-3, was seen as fulfilled in the community. The identification of the sect defined by the rules in 1QS with the generation mentioned in Joel turns the Qumran group into a community of eschatological prophets, which fits the hermeneutics of their own inspired exegesis of the prophetic texts in the *pesharim*.

Conclusion

Thus the picture painted by quotations and allusions alike is a consistent one. In spite of the double cipher of the Qumran hermeneutical approach, its method is not very different from Philo's. For both, there is a hermeneutical key needed to understand the writings of the Minor Prophets, but while in Qumran the key is the inspired exegesis of the Teacher and his followers, Philo's key is the philosophy of his time. Furthermore, for both, the Minor Prophets not only serve an exegetical purpose, they are also relevant for the individual's life.

The same approach can be found in the allusions throughout many areas of Second Temple Jewish literature: the Minor Prophets are alluded to in exegetical, narrative, poetic and apocalyptic writings (less so in historical or wisdom texts), and everywhere their sayings are taken out of the temporal, the historical order of things and applied to situations before and after their time. Thus their sayings become disembodied words of God that can be taken out of context and applied to any new situation, as the word of God remains true in past, present and future. Consequently the Minor Prophets were treated as apocalyptic seers,[67] people who received insights into God's plan behind history, and who in their writings spoke to each new generation.

66. Translation Martinez and Tigchelaar, *The DSS Study Edition*.
67. Barton, *Oracles*, pp. 198–201.

Chapter 2

THE MINOR PROPHETS IN MARK'S GOSPEL*

Cilliers Breytenbach

Introduction

Mark's[1] indebtedness to the Book of Isaiah is well known but his use of the Minor Prophets has received comparatively little attention.[2] Mark never quotes from nor alludes to Hosea, Amos, Obadiah, Micah, Nahum, Habakkuk, Haggai and Zephaniah.[3] Of greatest significance is the Book of Zechariah, with an explicit quotation in Mk 14.27 (Zech. 13.7), as well as allusions in Mk 11.2 (Zech. 9.9-10), Mk 13.27 (Zech. 2.10 [ET 2.6]) and Mk 14.24 (Zech. 9.11). A phrase from Mal. 3.1 appears in the composite quotation (Exod. 23.20/Isa. 40.3) at the beginning of the Gospel (Mk 1.2), though it is ascribed to Isaiah. Malachi is also present in the discourse about the return of Elijah in Mk 9.11-13 (Mal. 3.22-23 [ET 4.4-5]).[4] The metaphor of the 'sickle' in the context of eschatological harvest (Mk 4.29) could be an allusion to Joel 4.13 (ET 3.13), while the severity of the judgement described in Mk 13.19 has similarities with Joel 2.2. Finally, there are a number of parallels between the stilling of the storm in Mk 4.35-41 and the story of Jonah. There is no conclusive evidence that Mark alludes to any of the other Minor Prophets.[5] With the exception of the opening citation of Mal. 3.1, which Mark probably

---

* Matthaeo Koeckerto: anno sexagesimo quinto feliciter peracto collegae carissimo in donum natalitium oblatum.

1. 'Mark' refers to the author without identifying him with any historical person.

2. The major monographs on Mark's use of the Scriptures give little attention to the Minor Prophets. A. Suhl, *Die Funktion der alttestamentlichen Zitate und Anspielungen im Markusevangelium* (Gütersloh: Gütersloher Verlagshaus, 1965) and J. Marcus, *The Way of the Lord: Christological Exegesis of the Old Testament in the Gospel of Mark* (Louisville, KY: Westminster, 1992) focus on Zechariah and Malachi.

3. On Hosea and Amos, see below. In Mk 15.32 the crucified is merely addressed with ὁ βασιλεὺς Ἰσραήλ, explaining ὁ Χριστός. There is no reason to infer that the evangelist alludes to Zeph. 3.15.

4. In Mk 9.11 a phrase from Mal. 3.23 (ET 4.5) is attributed to the scribes.

5. NA²⁷ lists Hos. 6.6 (Mk 12.33); Amos 2.16 (Mk 14.52); 8.9 (Mk 15.3); Zeph. 3.15 (Mk 15.32) but none of these are convincing.

took from tradition, it would appear that Mark made use of the LXX. We begin our study with the explicit quotation of Zech. 13.7 in Mk 14.27.[6]

Quotations

Zech. 13.7 in Mk 14.27

After the meal, Jesus and the disciples have gone back to the Mount of Olives (Mk 14.26). Jesus predicts that all the disciples will fall away, will be caused to stumble. Though this will happen because of him (cf. *v.l.* and Mk 6.3), there is a deeper reason. Mark's Jesus grounds his prediction by citing from the Scripture: 'for it is written'. This introductory formula signals to the recipients of the text that words of God, who determines the course of events, will follow. The evangelist altered the second person plural imperative of the text he cited from Zech. 13.7 πατάξατε,[7] into the first person indicative πατάξω in Mk 14.27b in order to let the cited words appear not as God's command but as his intention: 'I will strike the shepherd, and the sheep will be scattered'. Zech. 13.7 is also cited in the Damascus Codex (XIX,8), in connection with the day of judgement, when God visits the earth. The entire Jerusalem prophecy of Zechariah seems to have been applied to the last days. The *Lives of the Prophets*, preserving traditions that reach back into pre-Christian times, explicitly characterized Zechariah's prophecy in Jerusalem as based 'on his visions about the end of the Gentiles, Israel, the temple ...' He announced a twofold judgement, on the nations and on Israel.[8] Mark places the quotation in an eschatological context.

Mk 14.28 interprets the quotation.[9] The close link between the quotation in Mk 14.27b and Mk 14.28a is signalled not only by the contrastive ἀλλά, but also from v. 28, where it becomes clear that the images of the struck shepherd and the scattered flock from Zech. 13.7 are mapped onto Jesus and his disciples in v. 27. This seems to be the reason why the evangelist had to rewrite the text from Zechariah. In order to make the reference to Jesus possible, he altered the plural τοὺς ποιμένας

6.   Intertextuality is to be approached from the perspective of the reader; cf. C. Breytenbach, 'Das Markusevangelium, Psalm 110,1 und 118,22f. Folgetext und Prätext', in C. Tuckett (ed.), *The Old Testament in the Gospels* (BETL, 131; Leuven: Leuven University Press – Peeters, 1997), pp. 197–220, esp. 197–201.

7.   Late minuscules have the Markan reading.

8.   Cf. *Liv. Pro.* 15.5.

9.   Cf. also S. L. Cook, The Metamorphosis of a Shepherd: The Tradition History of Zechariah 11:17 + 13:7-9', *CBQ* 55 (1993), pp. 453–66, esp. 463–6.

in Zech. 13.7 LXX into the singular τὸν ποιμένα. But what does the first line of the metaphor mean? The verb πατάσσω in the quotation means 'to physically strike a blow, to strike or to hit' but it can also express a 'deadly blow'. From v. 28 it is evident that Jesus is the shepherd who will be struck, since he will be raised up. Τὸ ἐγερθῆναί με indisputably refers to his resurrection, thus πατάξω τὸν ποιμένα in v. 27 must refer to the death of Jesus. The shepherd will be given a deadly blow. What is the meaning of the second line of the metaphor, τὰ πρόβατα διασκορπισθή σονται? One has to note the alteration in the quotation. Unlike codices Vaticanus and Sinaiticus which read ἐκσπάσατε[10] in Zech. 13.7, Mk 14.27 has διασκορπισθήσονται. The verb means, like the Hebrew פוץ, 'to scatter, to disperse'. Adapting to the time of πατάξω, the evangelist changed from an aorist imperative second person to a future passive third person.[11] The scattering of the flock will happen in the future. Verse 28 determines that the disciples are depicted in terms of the flock. After the death of Jesus, they will be scattered like sheep without a shepherd. This will be part of the eschatological events leading up to great suffering of the disciples and the destruction of the temple (Mark 13). But there is a positive announcement. The Greek verb προάγω means 'to lead forward, on, onward, to escort on the way'. So after his resurrection, Jesus will resume his role as shepherd and lead his flock to Galilee. The text implies that the dispersion which starts with his death will then end.[12]

Combined Quotations

Exod. 23.20 and Mal. 3.1 in Mk 1.2b

The quotation in Mk 1.2b-3 is introduced 'as it is written in the prophet Isaiah' with no reference to Malachi. The quotation itself has three peculiarities. Firstly, Mk 1.2b-c is a conflation between Exod. 23.20 and Mal. 3.1. The two texts are combined by the relative pronoun ὅς. Secondly, typically for Mark,[13] a second citation (from Isa. 40.3 LXX) is

10. ἐκσπάω 'to draw out, to draw forth'.
11. The reading διασκορπισθήσονται in codex Alexandrinus and in the sixth century codex Marchalianus is clearly influenced by the Synoptics; διασκορπισθήτω/σαν in codex Sinaiticus is due to late correction.
12. Through careful analysis of the context, D. S. du Toit, *Der abwesende Herr. Strategien im Markusevangelium zur Bewältigung der Abwesenheit des Auferstandenen* (WMANT, 111; Neukirchener Verlag: Neukirchen–Vluyn, 2006), p. 139, has illustrated convincingly that διασκορπισθήσονται cannot refer to the flight of the disciples.
13. The combination of quotations is a technique by which Mark composed his text; cf. C. Breytenbach, 'Die Vorschriften des Mose im Markusevangelium. Erwägungen zur Komposition von Mk 7,9-13; 10,2-9 und 12,18-27', *ZNW* 97 (2006), 23–43.

added in Mk 1.3.[14] Thirdly, the conflation in Mk 1.2b-c is a traditional quotation, since the very same conflation between Exod. 23.20 and Mal. 3.1 forms the basis of the independent tradition from Q.[15] Both traditions, Mk 1.2b and Lk.^{Q} 7.27b-c/Mt.^{Q} 11.10b-c have, instead of the bi-composite verb ἐξαποστέλλω in Mal. 3.1, the composite ἀποστέλλω and an additional phrase, πρὸ προσώπου σου. Although the latter comes from Exod. 23.20a ('I am going to send a messenger in front of you'), both Mk and Q do not follow the Greek translations of Exod. 23.20b in the second line, but unanimously read ὃς κατασκευάσει τὴν ὁδόν σου.[16] Their common text thus rather recalls 'to prepare a way before me' of Mal. 3.1 than 'to guard you on the way' from Exod. 23.20. The addition of the article before ὁδόν signifies that the synoptic tradition focuses on the specific path of Jesus. The second person σου, following τὴν ὁδόν, might still reflect the influence of Exod. 23.20 preceding the lines taken from Malachi in the Mk/Q tradition. It uses κατασκευάσει ('to make ready for some purpose, prepare') instead of ἐπιβλέψεται ('to look attentively at, look upon') as Mal. 3.1 LXX does. This might indicate that the Mk/Q tradition reflects the פנה (pi. with דרך 'to clear a path') of the Hebrew original.[17]

The early synoptic tradition, which must have been taken over by Mark, thus expressed the role of John the Baptist through a conflated citation (Exod. 23.20 and Mal. 3.1). It is precisely the notion from the Hebrew text of Malachi entailed in the traditional quotation that the messenger 'prepares' the way, which led Mark to add (Mk 1.3) the quotation from Isa. 40.3 LXX to the tradition (Mk 1.2b-c) and to introduce the whole complex quotation with καθὼς γέγραπται ἐν τῷ Ἠσαΐᾳ τῷ προφήτῃ (Mk 1.2a).[18] Exodus and Malachi are not even mentioned. The traditional quotation is taken to be part of Isaiah. For Mark, the beginning of the Gospel (= good news) about Jesus Christ [the Son of God] is in accordance with what has been written in the prophet Isaiah.[19]

---

14. Cf. the synopsis of the texts in S. Pellegrini, _Elija – Wegbereiter des Gottessohnes_ (HBS, 26; Freiburg: Herder, 2000), 226–7.

15. With the exception that Matthew adds ἐγώ after ἰδού both texts are identical. Even this prevented a unanimous reconstruction of a Q-text, as can be seen from the differing proposals of the _International Q-Project_ and the _Critical Edition of Q_. Cf. F. Neirynck, _Q-Parallels_ (Leuven: Peeters, 2001), pp. 78–9.

16. Cf. Mk 1.2c//Lk.^{Q} 7.27c/Mt.^{Q} 11.10c.

17. Similarly Theodotion with ἑτοιμάσει.

18. Mk 1.1-2a should read: Ἀρχὴ τοῦ εὐαγγελίου Ἰησοῦ Χριστοῦ [υἱοῦ θεοῦ] καθὼς γέγραπται ἐν τῷ Ἠσαΐᾳ τῷ προφήτῃ ...

19. On the importance of Isaiah for Mark, cf. M. Hooker, 'Isaiah in Mark's Gospel', in S. Moyise and M. J. J. Menken (eds), _Isaiah in the New Testament_ (London and New York: T&T Clark, 2005), pp. 35–49.

Allusions

Allusions to Hosea[20] and Amos[21] are improbable, whilst Mark's readers might be led to recognize phrases and motives from Jonah, Malachi, Joel and Zechariah.

Jonah 1.4, 10 in Mk 4.35-41

It can rightly be asked whether the episode on the calming of the storm (Mk 4.35-41) is narrated against the backdrop of Jonah. The similarities between Jonah 1.4 and Mk 4.37 are striking indeed. The corresponding detail of Jonah fast asleep, snoring in the bowels of the ship (Jonah 1.5) and Jesus sleeping in the stern on a cushion (Mk 4.38) beg for a more detailed comparison.[22] In both narratives the wind causes a rough sea endangering the ship. In both stories the main character must be woken up and is reprimanded by the others on the ship. The verbal reoccurrences from Jonah in Mark's episode are not limited to τὸ πλοῖον and θάλασσα (the latter refers to the lake, cf. Mk 4.41). In Mk 4.41 the motive of fear of those accompanying Jesus is expressed in the same words (including *figura etymologica*) that the crew in Jonah

---

20. The phrase 'and after six days' (Mk 9.2) marks the shift in time between the transfiguration narrative and the preceding context. Some have suggested an allusion to Hos. 6.2, but that phrase rather recalls Exod. 24.16, urging the reader to understand the transfiguration against the backdrop of Moses' encounter with the Lord on Sinai (cf. Exod. 24.9-18). When Jesus comments in Mk 12.33c that to love God wholeheartedly, with all the understanding and strength, and to love one's neighbour as oneself, 'is much more important than all whole burnt-offerings and sacrifices', Mark alludes to a well-known motive, reaching back to the times of Hosea. A direct allusion to Hos. 6.6, however, is not recognizable. Cf. Hos. 6.6: διότι ἔλεος θέλω καὶ οὐ θυσίαν καὶ ἐπίγνωσιν θεοῦ ἢ ὁλοκαυτώματα ('For I will have compassion rather than sacrifice, and the knowledge of God rather than whole burnt-offerings'). H. B. Swete, *The Gospel according to Mark* (London: Macmillan, 1902), p. 286 opted for 1 Kingdoms 15.22: καὶ εἶπεν Σαμουηλ εἰ θελητὸν τῷ κυρίῳ ὁλοκαυτώματα καὶ θυσίαι ὡς τὸ ἀκοῦσαι φωνῆς κυρίου ('and Samuel asked if whole burnt-offerings and sacrifices are such a delight to the Lord, as to obey the voice of the Lord?').

21. According to Mark's passion narrative, from the sixth (= noon) to the ninth hour, the three hours before Jesus died, 'darkness came over the whole land until three in the afternoon' (Mk 15.33). The corresponding time and the motive of global darkness might – so Irenaeus, *Haer.* IV 33.12 – recall Amos 8.9, but the absence of the sun setting at midday and the evangelist's choice of words do not allow the conclusion that he alludes to the prophet's words: 'That the sun shall go down at midday, and the light shall be darkened on the earth by day'. It is unlikely that the young man fleeing naked (Mk 14.52) alludes to Amos 2.16 ('the naked shall flee away in that day, said the Lord'). For Swete, *Gospel*, p. 354, the incident recalls Gen. 39.12-19.

22. Cf. E. Lohmeyer, *Das Evangelium des Markus* (KEK, I/2; Göttingen: Vandenhoeck & Ruprecht, 1963), p. 92.

1.10²³ uses (καὶ ἐφοβήθησαν οἱ ἄνδρες φόβον μέγαν): καὶ ἐφοβήθησαν φόβον μέγαν καὶ ἔλεγον. Additionally, the outcome of both stories is identical, in that the sea is calmed (Jonah 1.15; Mk 4.39). Albeit that the dangerous situation, caused by wind and raising waves, the fear of the crew pleading for help, and a passenger who assists in rescuing, are common motives of this type of narrative,²⁴ the similar terminology, the contrast between the fear of the crew and the sleeping passenger make it likely that Mark drew on the Greek version of the episode from Jonah in telling his story,²⁵ thus focusing on Jesus' power as Son of God (1.11). His word silences the natural forces.²⁶

Mal. 3.22-23 LXX in Mk 9.11-13

Mk 9.11-13 is the second part of a larger episode (Mk 9.9-13), which can be classified as an argument on the basis of Scripture.²⁷ After the transfiguration Jesus orders Peter, John and James to tell nobody what they have seen until after the Son of Man has risen from the dead (Mk 9.9). The disciples seem to include the resurrection of the Son of Man in the general eschatological resurrection of the dead.²⁸ Trying to understand this, they ask what this rising from the dead could mean (Mk 9.10b). The reason for their lack of understanding becomes evident from their question. It is put in words which allude to Mal. 3.22 LXX²⁹: 'Why do the scribes say that Elijah must come first?' How can the Son of Man rise from the dead if, according to the scribes, Elijah must first return before there can be a resurrection of the dead? Although Mark does not

---

23.   Mark points to Jonah 1.10 rather than 1.16 (καὶ ἐφοβήθησαν οἱ ἄνδρες φόβῳ μεγάλῳ τὸν κύριον). 8HevXIIgr has the Tetragrammaton.

24.   Cf. the analysis of the motives by G. Theißen, *Urchristliche Wundergeschichten* (Gütersloh: Gütersloher Verlagshaus, 1974), pp. 107–11. For parallel narratives from Greek and Jewish tradition see W. Cotter, *Miracles in Greco-Roman Antiquity* (New York: Routledge, 1999), pp. 132–42.

25.   Cf. R. Kratz, *Rettungswunder* (EHS, XXIII/123; Frankfurt: Lang, 1979), 207–16. See also A. Y. Collins, *Mark: A Commentary* (Hermeneia; Philadelphia: Fortress, 2007), pp. 259–60.

26.   The words of the Markan Jesus 'my soul is very sorrowful' (Mk 14.34) might rather cite Psalm 42 or 43 than allude to the words of Jonah that he is 'grieved unto death' (Jonah 4.9).

27.   Cf. Marcus, *Way*, pp. 100–10.

28.   I have analysed the argument and its presuppositions in some detail elsewhere. Cf. C. Breytenbach, 'Das Markusevangelium als traditionsgebundene Erzählung? Anfragen an die Markusforschung der achtziger Jahre', in C. Focant (ed.), *The Synoptic Gospels: Source Criticism and the New Literary Criticism* (BETL, 110; Leuven: Leuven University Press – Peeters, 1993), pp. 77–110, cf. pp. 102–5.

29.   The verbal agreement is confined to Ἠλίαν and ἐλθεῖν. Both words function differently in both texts.

quote Mal. 3.22, there are more indicators in his narrative that he alludes to the tradition in Mal. 3.22-23 LXX, that Elijah will be sent before the great and terrible day of the Lord. John the Baptist has been sent (cf. Mk 1.2b). According to Mark he proclaimed baptism after conversion (Mk 1.4). According to Malachi, the returning Elijah will restore the relationships between father and son and neighbours (Mal. 4.6/Mal. 3.23 LXX; cf. Sir. 48.10). Mk 9.11 thus presupposes the tradition about Elijah redivivus from Malachi. In Mk 9.12 Jesus agrees that Elijah comes to restore 'everything' (Mk 9.12a), which will include the restitution of the above mentioned relationships. The verbal similarities are confined to ἀποκαταστήσει in Mal. 3.23 LXX and ἀποκαθιστάνει in Mk 9.12a, but it is clear that the evangelist alluded to the Malachi tradition. Jesus' answer draws on the common synoptic tradition that Elijah returned as John the Baptist (cf. Lk.Q 7.27/Mt.Q 11.10) and resolves the problem of the disciples: Since Elijah has already come as John the Baptist, the precondition of the scribes is already fulfilled. Consequently the eschatological resurrection can be inaugurated by the Son of Man.

Zech. 9.9-10 in Mk 11.1-11

According to Zechariah the return of the Lord to Jerusalem will start from the Mount of Olives (Zech. 14.4-6). Jesus sets out from Bethany on the eastern slope of the Mount of Olives (Mk 11.1). Is this an allusion to the prophet's words?[30] There is harder evidence for an allusion to Zech. 9.9 in the next verse (Mk 11.2).[31] The Hebrew text of Zech. 9.9 wants to stress the purity of the חמור ('pack animal'). The king rides on a עיר ('male ass' or 'colt ass'); it is the offspring of a אתון ('filly ass'). The Greek translation renders חמור adequately with ὑποζύγιον 'under the yoke', a term for a pack animal. It then, however, translates עיר with πῶλον, which designates a foal, a young horse.[32] The words בן־אתנות ('a filly of a donkey') are rendered by the adjective νέον 'young'. With πῶλον Mk 11.2, 4, 7 thus repeatedly takes up a term from Zech. 9.9. Mark, however, does not specify that the πῶλος is a donkey. In both

---

30. The saying of the Markan Jesus 'For mortals it is impossible, but not for God; for God all things are possible' (Mk 10.27b) presupposes a widely attested Jewish belief in God's omnipotence (cf. Gen. 18.14; Job 42.2; Jdt. 9.14; 13.4; 3 Macc. 5.51; Philo, *Spec.* 4.127; *Abr.* 175; Mk 14.36, 62) and is not confined to Zech. 8.6. That family ties will be severed during the last days is a common apocalyptic motive (cf. *1 En.* 100.1-2; *Jub.* 23.19) shared by Mk 3.21; 13.12 and Zech. 13.3.

31. Suhl, *Funktion*, pp. 57–8, denies any influence from Zech. 9.9. Notwithstanding his treatment of the Johannine parallel, one can agree with Lührmann that the story has roots in Zech. 9.9. Cf. D. Lührmann, *Das Markusevangelium* (HNT, 3; Tübingen: J.C.B. Mohr, 1987), p. 188.

32. Cf. BDAG, *s.v.*

the Hebrew source and its Greek translation this is evident. In fact, it is merely because Mark expands on the νέον from Zech. 9.9 by telling his reader in Mk 11.2 that the πῶλος has never been ridden (ἐφ᾽ ὃν οὐδεὶς οὔπω ἀνθρώπων ἐκάθισεν) that one can infer that he alludes to the Greek translation of Zech. 9.9.[33] The royal motive of the coming kingdom of David which Mark adds in 11.10 to the quotation of Ps. 117.26 LXX in Mk 11.9 is clearly taken from Zech. 9.9 (ἰδοὺ ὁ βασιλεύς σου ἔρχεταί σοι).[34] Matthew was certainly correct in highlighting the allusion by quoting Zech. 9.9 in Mt. 21.5.[35] Against the backdrop of Zech. 9.9 Mark depicts Jesus as entering Jerusalem, as the one who comes in the name of the Lord, and whose advent fuels the hope of his entourage that the return of the Davidic reign is imminent. What this hope entails can be inferred from Zech. 9.10 LXX: 'And he shall root the chariots out of Ephraim, and the horse out of Jerusalem. The bow of war shall be destroyed and abundance and peace from the nations. And he shall govern over the waters as far as the sea, and over the rivers on earth's end'. In 12.35-37 the Markan Jesus dashes this hope by arguing on the basis of David's 'own words' that the Christ is not a Son of David.[36] Since the narrator has introduced Jesus as the Christ (cf. Mk 1.1), the reader is left with the question: 'Why does he enter Jerusalem as a king?' According to Mark, Jesus is the harbinger of the kingdom of God, not that of David.[37] All his enemies will be subdued under him (12.36); he will gather the elect from everywhere (13.27).

Joel 4.13 (ET 3.13) in Mk 4.29; Joel 2.2 in Mk 13.19

The allusions to Joel are confined to the depiction of the final judgement.[38] Mark 4.29 depicts the moment when the final judgement commences metaphorically with the phrase 'to send in the sickle' designating the action with which the final judgement commences, as is the case in Joel 4.13 (ET 3.13). Since this is not common eschatological imagery,

33.   Cf. Lohmeyer, *Evangelium*, p. 229.

34.   The Greek can be rendered as 'Rejoice greatly, O daughter of Zion. Announce aloud, O daughter of Jerusalem; behold, your King is coming to you, he is just and liberates, he is unassuming and riding on a pack animal, a young foal'.

35.   Cf. the contribution of Clay Alan Ham in this volume.

36.   Cf. Breytenbach, 'Markusevangelium', pp. 201–14.

37.   Cf. the similar exposition of L. Schenke, *Das Markusevangelium* (Stuttgart: Kohlhammer, 2005), p. 264.

38.   The phrase that 'the sun will be darkened, and the moon will not give its light, and the stars will be falling from heaven, and the powers in the heavens will be shaken' in Mk 13.24-5 is quoted from Isa. 13.10; 34.4. This imagery, which is also used by Joel 2.10 and (in the Hebrew text) in 3.4 and 4.15, is widely attested in Jewish apocalyptic literature (cf. *Sib. Or.* 3.800-1; 4.346-9, 476-80; *As. Mos.* 10.5; *4 Ezra* 5.4-5; 7.39; *T. Levi* 4.13).

it could be an allusion.[39] That the day of the Lord will be the darkest and gloomiest day ever (Joel 2.2) is comparable to the great tribulation announced in Mk 13.19.

Zech. 2.10 in Mk 13.27

At the hour of judgement, Mark's Jesus will return as Son of Man at the right hand of Power (14.62).[40] This combination of Dan. 7.13 and Ps. 110.1[41] implies that the Son of Man comes as Lord to whom all enemies will then have been subjected (cf. Mk 12.35-37).[42] In Mk 13.27 the Son of Man of Dan. 7.13 is again the one who 'will gather his elect from the four winds, from the ends of the earth to the ends of heaven'. Taking into account (1) that in Mark's Gospel the 'Son of Man' and 'Lord' both refer to Jesus' coming seated at the right hand of God, and (2) that Mk 13.27 and Zech. 2.10 LXX both have the motive of the four winds (ἐκ τῶν τεσσάρων ἀνέμων)[43] in combination with the gathering (ἐπισυνάξει/ συνάξω)[44] of the addressees, one might argue that Mk 13.27 recalls the *Greek* translation of Zech. 2.10 ('from the four winds of heaven I will gather you, says the Lord': ἐκ τῶν τεσσάρων ἀνέμων τοῦ οὐρανοῦ συνά ξω ὑμᾶς λέγει κύριος), rather than Deut. 30.4.

Zech. 9.11 in Mk 14.24

It is exactly the link between the kingdom of God and Jesus which requires that Mk 14.23-24 should be interpreted coherently with Mk 14.25. After giving the cup to the Twelve, the Markan Jesus declares: 'Truly I tell you, I will never again drink of the fruit of the vine until that day when I drink it new in the kingdom of God' (14.25). In which way is the cup associated with the dawn of God's kingdom? In Mark, Jesus elucidates the drinking of the wine in the cup as his 'blood of the covenant, which is poured out for many'. The sharing of the cup clearly refers to Jesus' death, but what meaning does it attribute to it? One should not utilize Mt. 26.28 to introduce the notion of forgiveness of sin into Mk 14.24. For Mark, Jesus' authority to forgive sin is not connected

---

39.   Suhl, *Funktion*, p. 154; du Toit, *Herr*, p. 125.
40.   See Breytenbach, 'Markusevangelium'.
41.   Cf. R. Watts, 'The Psalms in Mark's Gospel', in S. Moyise and M. J. J. Menken (eds), *The Psalms in the New Testament* (London and New York: T&T Clark, 2004), pp. 25–45, esp. 41.
42.   Cf. Breytenbach, 'Markusevangelium', pp. 207–8, 213–4.
43.   For this motive cf. *1 En.* 18.1-2; *4 Ezra* 13.5 and Rev. 7.1.
44.   For this motive cf. *4 Ezra* 4.12-3; 13.5. The Greek συνάξω deviates from the Hebrew פרשׂ 'to expand' (cf. *T. Ash.* 7.2-7).

to his death (cf. Mk 2.5, 10). Since man can give nothing in return for his life (Mk 8.37), it is the Son of Man who gives his life as a ransom for many (Mk 10.45). When one places the blood of the covenant in Mk 14.24 in its narrative context, it is best understood as an exchange for the doomed life of many. Mark might be recalling the covenant of Exod. 24.8 via its reception in Zech. 9.11-12[45]: 'You also, by the blood of the covenant, have sent forth your prisoners from the pit that has no water'.[46] A בּוֹר, a well or cistern, with no water in it, often served as a prison (Gen. 37.20; 40.15; Isa. 24.22), which is clearly the meaning in Zech. 9.11. Indeed, its translation λάκκος can metaphorically refer to sheol (cf. Ps. 27.1 LXX). Both Mk 14.24 and Zech. 9.11 are followed by a positive statement. In Mk 14.25 it is the advent of the royal reign of God, and in Zech. 9.12 the restitution of the people, who now live on Zion: 'You shall reside in fortresses, o prisoners of the assembly, and for one day as expatriate, I will recompense you double'.[47] If Mk 14.24 is read in the light of Zech. 9.11, the turn in Mark's Christology becomes clear. The drinking of the wine in the cup symbolizes the death of Jesus in terms of the covenant. His death sets the prisoners free, having a ransoming effect (Mk 14.24 with Zech. 9.11). Since Peter's confession (8.29), Mark has prepared a line of interpretation, which he now follows through. Jesus is the Christ, but has to suffer as Son of Man (8.29, 31). Man is not able to give any exchange for his own life (8.37). The Christ, the Son of Man, came to serve and to give his life in exchange for all humans (10.45). He enters Jerusalem on a foal, just, as one who saves and is humble. As Christ he is not the Son of David (12.36), neither does he come to reinstitute David's kingdom as the crowd expects him to do (11.10). As the narrative develops, he recaps on the announcement that he came to give his life as ransom (10.45) by explaining that the sharing of the cup symbolizes his death as having, in terms of the covenant, a ransoming effect for many (14.24). When he returns, he will gather the elect (13.27).

Conclusion

With the exception of the traditional conflated quotation from Exod. 23.20/Mal. 3.1 in Mk 1.2b-c, Mark follows the Greek translations

---

45.   This line of interpretation has been recognized by Lohmeyer, *Evangelium*, p. 307; Marcus, *Way*, p. 157, and J. R. Donahue and D. J. Harrington, *The Gospel of Mark* (Sacra Pagina Series, 2; Collegeville, MI: Liturgical Press, 2002), p. 399. None of the interpretations understand the allusion in the context of Mk 8.37; 10.45 (see below).

46.   Zech. 9.11: Καὶ σὺ ἐν αἵματι διαθήκης ἐξαπέστειλας δεσμίους σου ἐκ λάκκου οὐκ ἔχοντος ὕδωρ.

47.   Καθήσεσθε ἐν ὀχυρώματι δέσμιοι τῆς συναγωγῆς καὶ ἀντὶ μιᾶς ἡμέρας παροικεσίας σου διπλᾶ ἀνταποδώσω σοι.

of the Minor Prophets. Quotations or allusions from Jonah, Joel, Zechariah and Malachi can be accepted with some confidence and are used in a variety of ways. Thus for a single narrative (Mk 4.37-41), an episode from Jonah forms the backdrop, while imagery from Joel serves to express the final judgement (Mk 4.29; 13.19). Citations from and allusions to Malachi are integrated into broader conceptions that draw on Isaiah to depict John the Baptist as the one preparing Jesus' path (Mk 1.2-3; 9.1-13). Finally, quotations from and allusions to Zechariah play an important role in portraying the Messianic expectations that the crowd were associating with Jesus (11.1-11), the prediction of the dispersion and gathering of the Twelve (14.27), the ransoming effect of the Son of Man's death (10.45; 14.24), and the announcement of his eschatological advent (13.27). Thus, although Mark's use of the Minor Prophets is not as extensive as the Book of Isaiah, it nevertheless plays an important role in his narrative.

CHAPTER 3

THE MINOR PROPHETS IN MATTHEW'S GOSPEL

Clay Alan Ham

Introduction

A recent trend in the study of the Minor Prophets[1] considers the twelve
books as a literary whole.[2] This inclination, however, is not new but
ancient, for both Jewish and Christian traditions regard the Twelve
Prophets as one 'book'. Early textual evidence (4QXII[a–g]=4Q76–82,
8ḤevXIIgr, and MurXII) suggests that the twelve Minor Prophets were
indeed copied together on one scroll.[3] The Wisdom of Ben Sira (Sir.
49.10) refers to them collectively in the earliest mention of the 'Twelve
Prophets'. Both Josephus (*Ag. Ap.* 1.38) and 4 *Ezra* 14.46 count the
Twelve as one 'book' among the prophets, as does the later rabbinic
tradition (*b. B. Bat.* 13b, 14b). Cyprian (*Ep.* 54) attributes a citation
from Hos. 8.4 to the 'twelve prophets' (cf. Justin, *Dial.* 87). More
unambiguous are the comments by Melito of Sardis, 'the twelve in one
book', cited in Eusebius (*Hist. eccl.* 4.26) and the statement in Jerome's

---

1.   Apparently, Augustine (*City of God* 18.29) is the first to label the last twelve of
the prophetic books in the Hebrew Bible as the 'Minor' Prophets.
2.   E.g., K. Budde, 'Eine folgenschwere Redaction des Zwölfprophetenbuchs', *ZAW*
39 (1922), pp. 218–29; P. R. House, *The Unity of the Twelve* (Bible and Literature Series,
27; JSOTSup, 97; Sheffield: Almond Press, 1990); J. D. Nogalski, *Literary Precursors
to the Book of the Twelve* (BZAW, 217; Berlin: de Gruyter, 1993); idem, *Redactional
Processes in the Book of the Twelve* (BZAW, 218; Berlin: de Gruyter, 1993); R. J. Coggins,
'The Minor Prophets: One Book or Twelve?' in S. E. Porter, P. Joyce and D. E. Orton
(eds), *Crossing the Boundaries: Essays in Biblical Interpretation* (FS M. D. Goulder; BIS,
8; Leiden: Brill, 1994), pp. 57–68; J. W. Watts and P. R. House (eds), *Forming Prophetic
Literature: Essays on Isaiah and the Twelve* (FS J. D. W. Watts; JSOTSup, 235; Sheffield:
Sheffield Academic Press, 1996); and C. D. Bowman, 'Reading the Twelve as One: Hosea
1–3 as an Introduction to the Book of the Twelve (the Minor Prophets)', *Stone–Campbell
Journal* 9 (2006), 41–59.
3.   R. E. Fuller, 'The Form and Formation of the Book of the Twelve', in J. W. Watts
and P. R. House (eds), *Forming Prophetic Literature: Essays on Isaiah and the Twelve* (FS
J. D. W. Watts; JSOTSup, 235; Sheffield: Sheffield Academic Press, 1996), pp. 86–101.

prologue to the Twelve Prophets in the Vulgate that 'the Twelve Prophets are one book'.

In spite of this general perception, evidently the earliest interpreters of the Twelve do not read them as one book.[4] This is clearly the case with Matthew's Gospel, which, while making frequent use of the Twelve to demonstrate that Jesus is the Messiah who fulfils the Hebrew Scriptures, does not display a coherent reading of the Twelve as 'one book'. It cannot even be said that Matthew knows every one of the Twelve Prophets, for Matthew cites only five of them: Hosea, Jonah, Micah, Zechariah, and Malachi.[5] Nonetheless, when taken together, these citations suggest that Matthew grants a prominence to the collection of the Twelve Prophets among the Old Testament sources cited within the Gospel. NA[27] and UBS[4] list thirteen citations from Deuteronomy, eight from Isaiah, eight from Psalms, six from Exodus, five from Leviticus, and two from Genesis. Of the prophets, then, Matthew's Gospel cites texts from the 'book' of the Twelve Prophets more times (10) than it does from any other prophetic book, including Isaiah (8). This phenomenon is similar to the way in which the sect of the Dead Sea Scrolls regards the collection of the Twelve,[6] particularly as evidenced in their *Damascus Document* which quotes and discusses three texts from Isaiah, two from Ezekiel, but eleven from the Twelve.[7] Francis Watson suggests further that the Jewish sectarians and Christian evangelists use these texts 'to show that the history of the sect's origins is at the same time the predetermined history of God's saving action in the last days, and of positive and negative human responses to it'.[8] This assertion gives credence to the significant function of the material

---

4.   E. Ben Zvi, 'Twelve Prophetic Books or "The Twelve": A Few Preliminary Considerations', in Watts and House, *Forming Prophetic Literature*, pp. 125–56, esp. 130–9; P. L. Redditt, 'The Production and Reading of the Book of the Twelve', in J. D. Nogalski and M. A. Sweeney (eds), *Reading and Hearing the Book of the Twelve* (SBLSymS, 15; Atlanta: Society of Biblical Literature, 2000), pp. 11–33, esp. 25–30; H. Utzschneider, 'Flourishing Bones: The Minor Prophets in the New Testament', in R. G. Wooden and W. Kraus (eds), *Septuagint Research: Issues and Challenges in the Study of the Greek Jewish Scriptures* (SBLSCS, 53; Atlanta: Society of Biblical Literature, 2006), pp. 273–92, esp. 274–82.

5.   Even if the presence and intention of allusions listed in NA[27] and UBS[4] were established, this would demonstrate that Matthew knows only three more of the Twelve (Joel, Amos, and Haggai). It would appear that no material in Matthew is drawn from Obadiah, Nahum, and Zephaniah. Cf. n. 12 below.

6.   J. Trebolle Barrera, 'Qumran Evidence for a Biblical Standard Text and for Non-standard and Parabiblical Texts', in T. H. Lim *et al.* (eds), *The Dead Sea Scrolls in Their Historical Context* (Edinburgh: T&T Clark, 2000), pp. 89–106, esp. 89–98.

7.   F. Watson, *Paul and the Hermeneutics of Faith* (London and New York: T&T Clark, 2004), pp. 80–101; citations in *CD* are taken from seven of the Twelve: Hosea (3x), Joel (1x), Amos (2x), Micah (2x), Nahum (1x), Zechariah (1x), and Malachi (1x).

8.   Watson, *Paul and the Hermeneutics of Faith*, p. 101.

from the Minor Prophets in the New Testament[9] and particularly in Matthew.

The extensive use of the Old Testament in Matthew presents ample opportunity for study,[10] and such is the case with the Gospel's application of materials from the Minor Prophets. Matthew cites from Hosea three times (Hos. 11.1 in Mt. 2.15 and Hos. 6.6 in Mt. 9.13 and 12.7), Jonah one time (Jonah 1.17 [ET 2.1] in Mt. 12.40), Micah two times (Mic. 5.1 [ET 5.2] in Mt. 2.6 and Mic. 7.6 in Mt. 10.35-36), Zechariah three times (Zech. 9.9 in Mt. 21.5, Zech. 13.7 in Mt. 26.31, and Zech. 11.12-13 in Mt. 27.9-10), and Malachi one time (Mal. 3.1 in Mt. 11.10). Of these ten citations, eight are explicit, that is, introduced by formulas (Mt. 2.6, 15; 9.13; 11.10; 12.7; 21.5; 26.31; 27.9-10); of these, three are among the so-called formula quotations (Mt. 2.15; 21.5; 27.9-10).[11] The other two citations (Mt. 10.35-36; 12.40) are implicit, that is, lacking an introductory formula but of such length to make for an obvious and intentional quotation.[12] Since several studies have carefully discussed the form of the citations found in Matthew's

---

9.   C. A. Evans, 'The Messiah in the Old and New Testaments: A Response', in S. E. Porter (ed.), *The Messiah in the Old and New Testaments* (McMaster New Testament Series; Grand Rapids: Eerdmans, 2007), pp. 230–48, esp. 235–6.

10.   W. D. Davies and D. C. Allison, *The Gospel according to Saint Matthew* (ICC; 3 vols; Edinburgh: T&T Clark, 1988–97), I, pp. 34–56, list 41 quotations in Matthew. W. Dittmar, *Vetus Testamentum in Novo: Die alttestamentlichen Parallelen des Neuen Testaments im Wortlaut der Urtexte und der Septuaginta* (Göttingen: Vandenhoeck & Ruprecht, 1903), pp. 1–72, E. Hühn, *Die alttestamentlichen Citate und Reminiscenzen im Neuen Testamente* (Tübingen: Mohr Siebeck, 1900), pp. 1–49, NA[27], pp. 770–806, and UBS[4], pp. 887–90, add another 23 texts to the list of potential citations in Matthew. Arriving at a definite number of citations is complicated by several factors, including the distinction of 'implicit citation' and 'allusion', the existence of combined citations, and the identification of a citation's source.

11.   For a summary of the research on the formula quotations in Matthew, see C. A. Ham, *The Coming King and the Rejected Shepherd: Matthew's Reading of Zechariah's Messianic Hope* (New Testament Monographs, 4; Sheffield: Sheffield Phoenix Press, 2005), pp. 3–5. More detailed studies of the introductory formula include W. Rothfuchs, *Die Erfüllungszitate des Matthäus-Evangeliums: Eine biblisch-theologische Untersuchung* (BWANT, 88; Stuttgart: Kohlhammer, 1969), pp. 27–44, and G. M. Soares Prabhu, *The Formula Quotations in the Infancy Narratives of Matthew: An Enquiry into the Tradition History of Mt 1–2* (AnBib, 63; Rome: Pontifical Biblical Institute, 1976), pp. 45–62.

12.   Any comprehensive examination of the 25 potential allusions to the Minor Prophets in Matthew listed in NA[27] and UBS[4] cannot occur within the constraints of this study. It would be expected that no more than 15 of the 25 could be confirmed as intentional allusions. This estimate is based on the use of stereotypical language for judgement in all texts that purportedly allude to Joel or Amos (Joel 3.4-8 and Amos 1.9-10 in Mt. 11.21-22, Joel 2.2 in Mt. 24.21, Joel 2.10, 31; 3.15 in Mt. 24.29, and Amos 8.9 in Mt. 27.45) and on a detailed study of Matthew's allusions to Zechariah in Ham, *The Coming King and the Rejected Shepherd*, pp. 84–106, which argues that only eight of 18 possible allusions to Zechariah in Matthew can be ascertained with some certainty.

Gospel,[13] this essay examines the function of the final form of these ten citations from the Minor Prophets in their Matthean contexts and, where appropriate, compares the use of these same texts in Jewish and Christian literature.

Mic. 5.1 (ET 5.2) in Mt. 2.6

'And you, Bethlehem, in the land of Judah,
are by no means least among the rulers of Judah;
for from you shall come a ruler who is to shepherd my people Israel'.[14]

Of the four gospels, only Matthew explicitly[15] substantiates Bethlehem as the birthplace of Jesus with a prophetic text. Mt. 2.6 is the first of four citations in the chapter (Mt. 2.15 quotes Hos. 11.1, Mt. 2.18 cites Jer. 31.15, and Mt. 2.23 refers to an unattested text). Mt. 2.1-12 focuses on events relating to Bethlehem. The Magi visit Herod in Jerusalem, asking him about the child born king of the Jews (2.1-3); Herod inquires about the location of the birthplace of the Messiah (2.4-6) and directs the Magi to Bethlehem, where they pay homage to the child (2.7-12). Rhetorically, a citation of Mic. 5.1 (ET 5.2) is placed on the lips of the chief priests and scribes who reply to Herod's inquiry about the Messiah. Their answer, 'in Bethlehem of Judea', is then supported with wording from Mic. 5.1, a text which contrasts a weakened ruler of Israel (Mic. 4.9, 14) with a new ruler for Israel, born in the small town of Bethlehem, who will revive the ancient dynasty of David (5.2-3) and restore security to Israel (5.4-5a).

John 7.41-42 also gives evidence of the Jewish expectation that the Messiah, a descendant of David, comes from Bethlehem. Later Jewish literature verifies this. For example, the interpretive translation found in *Tg.* Mic. 5.1 exhibits a decisively 'messianic' reading, identifying the one who shall come forth as 'the anointed One'.[16] So too is Mic. 5.1

---

13.   Most notable is M. J. J. Menken, *Matthew's Bible: The Old Testament Text of the Evangelist* (BETL, 173; Leuven: Leuven University Press – Peeters, 2004); see also R. H. Gundry, *The Use of the Old Testament in St Matthew's Gospel with Special Reference to the Messianic Hope* (NovTSup, 18; Leiden: Brill, 1967), and K. Stendahl, *The School of St. Matthew, and Its Use of the Old Testament* (ASNU, 20; Lund: Gleerup, 1954; repr. Philadelphia: Fortress Press, 1968).

14.   All English citations from the Hebrew Bible/Old Testament and the New Testament are taken from the NRSV, unless otherwise noted.

15.   The citation is not introduced with the characteristic Matthean formula (cf. Mt. 1.22-23; 2.15, 17–18, 23; 4.14-16; 8.17; 12.17-21; 13.35; 21.5; 27.9-10) but with γέγραπται, an introductory formula found in Mt. 2.5; 4.4, 6, 7, 10; 11.10; 21.13; 26.24, 31.

16.   Another text, which does not refer to Mic. 5.1, also describes Bethlehem as 'the place from which the King Messiah will reveal himself at the end of days' (*Tg. Ps.-J.* Gen. 35.21).

common among the early Christian literature, for its specific geographic identification suits well the argument of proof from prophecy (e.g. Justin, *1 Apol.* 34.1; *Dial.* 78.1; Irenaeus, *Epid.* 63; *Haer.* 4.33.11; Tertullian, *Adv. Jud.* 13.2).[17] Likewise, Eusebius (*Dem. ev.* 7.2.2) argues that only two famous men have been born in Bethlehem, David and Jesus, and that, since David lived and died long before, the prophecy in Micah must refer to Jesus.

In Mt. 2.6, the chief priests and scribes locate the birthplace of the Messiah in Bethlehem according to the prophecy of Mic. 5.1. The wording of the citation differs from both the MT and the LXX.[18] In contrast to the LXX, Matthew replaces 'house of Ephrathah' with 'land of Judah', adds the adverb 'by no means' (οὐδαμῶς), changes the adjective 'little' to the superlative form 'least' (ἐλαχίστη), replaces 'clans' with 'rulers' (ἡγεμόσιν), and adds from 2 Sam. 5.2 'shepherd my people Israel'. These modifications serve to emphasize Matthew's Davidic Christology;[19] specifically, they underscore that Jesus' birth in Bethlehem fulfils the expectation that the future Davidic leader would arise from there, an interpretation in both Jewish and Christian literatures. The identification of Bethlehem in 'Judah' reminds the reader of the opening genealogy that traces Jesus' lineage through the patriarch Judah (Mt. 1.2-3). While Mic. 5.1 comments on the insignificance of Bethlehem as 'one of the little clans of Judah', Mt. 2.6 apparently reverses the text from Micah[20] in light of its fulfilment; Matthew claims that, since Jesus the Messiah has been born there, glory has come to Bethlehem, that is, it is now 'no longer least'.[21] Matthew's citation forms a small midrash on two texts originally about David: Mic. 5.1 and 2 Sam. 5.2. The connection between them is made possible, in part, by the description of the ruler of Israel in the context of Mic. 5.1 as one who will 'shepherd' his flock (Mic. 5.3), and the connection between Matthew and 2 Samuel is seen in the two words 'rule' (ἡγέομαι) and 'shepherd' (ποιμαίνω). 'Shepherd' overlaps semantically with 'ruler', and both are appropriate descriptions for a 'king' (2 Sam. 5.3; cf. 1 Kgs 22.17), since kings in the ancient Near East are often portrayed as shepherds.[22] Thus, Matthew's

---

17. R. E. Heine, *Reading the Old Testament with the Ancient Church: Exploring the Formation of Early Christian Thought* (Grand Rapids: Baker, 2007), pp. 120–1.

18. See Menken, *Matthew's Bible*, pp. 256–63, and Stendahl, *The School of St. Matthew*, pp. 99–100.

19. Davies and Allison, *The Gospel according to Saint Matthew*, I, p. 243.

20. G. Geiger, 'Falsche Zitate bei Matthäus und Lukas', in C. M. Tuckett (ed.), *The Scriptures in the Gospels* (BETL, 131; Leuven: Leuven University Press – Peeters, 1997), pp. 479–86, esp. 480. On the reception of the wording of Matthew's citation among certain textual witnesses, see J. L. North, 'Reactions in Early Christianity to Some References to the Hebrew Prophets in Matthew's Gospel', *NTS* 54 (2008), pp. 254–74, esp. 255–8.

21. R. T. France, *The Gospel of Matthew* (NICNT; Grand Rapids: Eerdmans, 2007), p. 73.

22. J. Jeremias, 'ποιμήν', in *TDNT*, VI, pp. 485–502, esp. 486–7.

citation of Mic. 5.1 and 2 Sam. 5.2 implies that Jesus has come as the Davidic ruler/king who shepherds God's people, one who, unlike 'all the chief priests and scribes of the people' (Mt. 2.4), saves 'his people from their sins' (Mt. 1.21).[23]

Hos. 11.1 in Mt. 2.15

'Out of Egypt I have called my son'.

Mt. 2.13-23 portrays three events: the angel of the Lord directs Joseph to take Jesus and his mother to Egypt (Mt. 2.13-15), Herod orders the murder of the children in Bethlehem (2.16-18), and the angel of the Lord instructs Joseph to return to the land of Israel (2.19-23). Each episode concludes with a reference to the Old Testament. The citation of Hos. 11.1 in Mt. 2.15 is the second of the ten so-called formula quotations, each of which shares a similar redactional formula ('to fulfil what had been spoken through the prophet'), serves as editorial commentary from the evangelist,[24] and manifests a mixed-text form less close to the LXX than is the case with references to the Old Testament elsewhere in Matthew.[25] The evangelist, then, supports the command to flee to Egypt and the resulting obedience of Joseph in so doing (Mt. 2.13-14) with a citation from Hos. 11.1, a text which depicts the relationship of Yahweh and Israel with parental language reminiscent of the exodus. Even though Israel is loved as a son and has been raised with kindness (Hos. 11.1-4), Israel risks through rebellion a 'return to the land of Egypt' (Hos. 11.5), here represented in the contemporaneous threat posed by Assyria.

Evidently no examples exist of early Jewish references to Hos. 11.1 that are explicitly messianic.[26] The text is applied, in a sense akin to the context in Hosea 11, to the immaturity of Israel as a nation, prone to the ways of idolatry like their ancestors in the wilderness (*Exod. Rab.* 43.9 [on Hos. 11.1]; *Num. Rab.* 12.4 [on Hos. 11.1]; *Song Rab.* 3.9 § 1). Other references to Hos. 11.1 in Jewish literature reflect variation

---

23.   J. P. Heil, 'Ezekiel 34 and the Narrative Strategy of the Shepherd and Sheep Metaphor in Matthew', *CBQ* 55 (1993), 698–708, esp. 700.

24.   On that account German scholarship has used the term *Reflexionszitate*, appearing as early as H. J. Holtzmann, *Die Synoptiker – Die Apostelgeschichte* (HKNT, 1; Freiburg: Mohr Siebeck, 1889), p. 41, to distinguish the formula quotations from other citations in Matthew.

25.   E. Massebieau, *Examen des citations de l'ancien testament dans l'évangile selon Saint Matthieu* (Paris: Fischbacher, 1885), pp. 93–4, calls the collection of quotations 'citations apologétiques' and notes that they both are introduced with a common formula and show an awareness of the Hebrew text.

26.   C. L. Blomberg, 'Matthew', in G. K. Beale and D. A. Carson (eds), *Commentary on the New Testament Use of the Old Testament* (Grand Rapids: Baker, 2007), pp. 1–109, esp. 7.

regarding two issues: the sense of the preposition מִן (either 'out of' or 'ever since' Egypt)[27] and the rendering of בֵּן (either 'son' or 'sons'). Both alternative renditions are found in *Tg*. Hos. 11.1: 'When Israel was a child, I loved him *and brought him near to my worship* and ever since Egypt I called *them sons*'.

In Mt. 2.15, the evangelist supports Jesus' sojourn in Egypt by citing Hos. 11.1. The wording of citation differs from the LXX, since Matthew contains the singular 'son' found in the MT and the Greek translations of Aquila, Symmachus, and Theodotion (cf. *Gos. Naz.* frg. 1).[28] This singular form is significant in Matthew, since the evangelist has shifted the referent of 'son' from Israel in Hos. 11.1 to Jesus in Mt. 2.15. Thus, the 'fulfilment' of the text is better regarded as typological than messianic. As a result, the evangelist makes a striking portrayal of Jesus as the true Israel, whose sojourn in and departure from Egypt intimates a 'new exodus',[29] during which Jesus proves faithful where Israel has not been (e.g. Mt. 4.1-11). Even so, the text also has clear Christological significance, since 'son' is the only title used for Jesus in Matthew 2.[30] 'Son' reoccurs in Mt. 4.3-6, where Jesus as God's son personifies the obedient Israel.

Hos. 6.6 in Mt. 9.13 and 12.7

'I desire mercy, not sacrifice'.

Twice Matthew explicitly refers to Hos. 6.6, in a controversy over eating with those considered sinful and in a controversy over Sabbath regulations. In Mt. 9.9-13, Jesus calls Matthew to follow him (9.9), eats with tax collectors and sinners (9.10), and answers the Pharisees' question about his actions (9.11) with a proverb, a quotation, and a statement of mission (9.12-13). In Mt. 12.1-8, Jesus answers the Pharisees' accusation about his disciples' actions (12.1-2) with two comparisons, a quotation,

27. Cf. the NRSV, 'Out of Egypt I have called my son', with the NJPS, 'I have called him My son ever since Egypt'.

28. For this reason, some suggest that the evangelist has independently translated the MT. So E. E. Ellis, *The Old Testament in Early Christianity: Canon and Interpretation in the Light of Modern Research* (Grand Rapids: Baker, 1991), p. 78; Gundry, *The Use of the Old Testament in St. Matthew's Gospel*, p. 149; Stendahl, *The School of St. Matthew*, p. 101; *contra* Menken, *Matthew's Bible*, pp. 133–42.

29. In the words of F. D. Bruner, *Matthew: A Commentary* (2 vols; Grand Rapids: Eerdmans, rev. edn, 2004), I, pp. 75–6, 'As Matt 1 taught the *New Genesis* by the birth of the promised Son of David, so Matt 2 teaches the *New Exodus* in the migration in and out of Egypt by Jesus the new Moses'.

30. U. Luz, *Matthew 1–7: A Commentary* (trans. W. C. Linss; Minneapolis: Augsburg Press, 1989), p. 146.

and a pronouncement (12.3-8). Both pericopes are triple tradition texts (Mt. 9.9-13 // Mk 2.13-17 // Lk. 5.27-32 and Mt. 12.1-8 // Mk 2.23-28 // Lk. 6.1-5); however, neither account in Mark and Luke includes the citation from Hos. 6.6. In both Mt. 9.13 and 12.7, the citation is introduced by the brief formula 'what this means' (τί ἐστιν) preceded, in one instance, by the command 'go and learn' (πορευθέντες μάθετε) and, in the other, by the condition 'if you had known' (εἰ ἐγνώκειτε). The wording of the formulas, without parallel in Mark or Luke, reflects a rabbinic expression that refers to the exposition of Scripture.[31] Thus, these formulas seek to elicit from the Pharisees a correct interpretation of the words derived from Hos. 6.6 (cf. Mt. 24.32; Jn 13.12).[32] In Hos. 6.4-6, Yahweh expresses reluctance to aid Ephraim and Judah on account of their lack of fidelity (חסד) to the covenant (Hos. 6.4); as a consequence, Yahweh has sent the prophets to pronounce judgement against them (6.5), for Yahweh desires fidelity over sacrifice (6.6).

The synonymous parallelism in Hos. 6.6 clarifies the contrast made between fidelity and sacrifice as relative (i.e. the first 'over' the second) rather than absolute (i.e. the first 'but not' the second). Likewise, the interpretative rendering in *Tg.* Hos. 6.6 precludes the outright rejection of sacrifice. The *Sibylline Oracles* allude to a more absolute reading of Hos. 6.6, 'God wants not sacrifice but mercy instead of sacrifice' (*Sib. Or.* 2.82; cf. 8.334, 390), but some of the oracles betray Christian interpolation,[33] making difficult any assessment of these texts in relation to the textual allusion. Although the general principle may be evidenced elsewhere in the synoptic tradition (cf. Mk 12.33), the earliest Christian literature more commonly refers to other wording from the context of the citation in Mt. 9.13 // Mk 2.17 // Lk. 5.32 ('I have come to call not the righteous but sinners') but does not include the language from Hos. 6.6 regarding mercy and sacrifice (e.g. *Barn.* 5.9; *2 Clem.* 2.4; Justin, *1 Apol.* 15.8). Later Clement of Alexandria (*Quis div.* 39) does quote Hos. 6.6 but applies it along with Ezek. 18.23 to the topic of true repentance.

The only Old Testament quotation repeated in Matthew is Hos. 6.6. Both instances use the same wording, which is a literal rendering of the MT, agreeing with the LXX.[34] In Mt. 9.13, Hos. 6.6 is cited as part of Jesus' answer to the Pharisees' question about his actions in eating with

---

31. Ellis, *The Old Testament in Early Christianity*, pp. 86-7.

32. D. Hill, 'The Use and Meaning of Hosea 6.6 in Matthew's Gospel', *NTS* 24 (1977-78), 107-19, esp. 111.

33. H. R. Drobner, *The Fathers of the Church: A Comprehensive Introduction* (trans. S. S. Schatzmann; Peabody: Hendrickson, 2007), pp. 43-4.

34. LXX B reads ἤ ('rather than') instead of καὶ οὐ ('and not'). While LXX B does render the relative comparison intended in Hos. 6.6, the reading may have resulted from a harmonization with the second line in the synonymous parallelism of the text. R. T. McLay,

those regarded as sinful. Like the parallels in Mk 2.17 and Lk. 5.31-32, his answer is supported by a proverb and a statement of mission. Only Matthew inserts the citation from Hos. 6.6 and thereby explains Jesus' behaviour in light of this Old Testament text. In a sense, however, the citation disrupts the context, since the notion of sacrifice is absent from what has preceded, but the rabbinic formula that introduces the citation ('Go and learn what this means') indicates to the reader that what Hosea has said about the importance of covenant fidelity is now directed to the Pharisees.[35] The Hebrew term for fidelity (חסד) used in Hos. 6.6 means covenant loyalty to Yahweh shown in social relationship; the same implication is conveyed with the Greek term 'mercy' (ἔλεος), by far the most common word used to translate חסד in the LXX.[36] That Jesus has shown 'mercy' to sinners reveals part of Matthew's surpassing righteousness (Mt. 5.20) and anticipates Jesus' healing of the sick (9.27; 15.22; 17.15; 20.30-31).

In Mt. 12.7, Hos. 6.6 is cited in Jesus' response to the Pharisees' accusation about the disciples' action in plucking heads of grain on the Sabbath. Like the parallels in Mk 2.25-28 and Lk. 6.2-5, his answer is supported by a comparison with David and his companions (1 Sam. 21.1-6) and a pronouncement about the Son of Man. Only Matthew inserts a second analogy (i.e. the 'work' of the priests), a traditional argument ('something greater than the temple is here'), and a scriptural citation ('I desire mercy, not sacrifice'). In one sense, the application of this citation of Hos. 6.6 appears as similar to the previous one in Mt. 9.13, justifying the disciples' behaviour in light of an Old Testament text. Also, as with the preceding reference, the prophetic message of Hosea is directed to the Pharisees, who still do not 'know' the meaning of Hos. 6.6 and, as a result, have failed to show mercy (cf. Mt. 23.23) and condemned those who are guiltless. However, in Mt. 12.7 where the citation appears a second time, it follows the statement about the temple, which reduces the importance of the contrast between 'mercy' and 'sacrifice' and heightens the Christological function of the citation: sacrifice is less significant now, since the One greater than the temple is present in Jesus' ministry of mercy.[37]

The Use of the Septuagint in New Testament Research (Grand Rapids: Eerdmans, 2003), p. 41, cautions against the assumption that Matthew shows a dependence on the LXX, since the translations of Hos. 6.6 in the LXX and Matthew use the expected vocabulary.

35. U. Luz, *Matthew 8–20: A Commentary* (trans. J. E. Crouch; Hermeneia; Minneapolis: Fortress, 2001), p. 33.

36. *HALOT*, pp. 336–7; R. Bultmann, 'ἔλεος', in *TDNT* II, pp. 477–87, esp. 479–81; and H. Conzelmann and W. Zimmerli, 'χάρις', in *TDNT* IX, pp. 372–402, esp. 381–7.

37. L. Lybæk, 'Matthew's Use of Hosea 6,6 in the Context of the Sabbath Controversies', in C. M. Tuckett (ed.), *The Scriptures in the Gospels* (BETL, 131; Leuven: Leuven University Press – Peeters, 1997), pp. 491–9, esp. 496–9.

Mic. 7.6 in Mt. 10.35-36

'For I have come to set a man against his father,
and a daughter against her mother,
and a daughter-in-law against her mother-in-law;
and one's foes will be members of one's own household'.

Matthew 10 comprises the second of the five discourses in the Gospel. Its setting in the life of Jesus relates to the sending of the Twelve (Mt. 10.1-15), although the warnings and instructions throughout the chapter also reflect a later setting within the Matthean community (10.16-42). This 'missionary' discourse indicates that the proclamation of the gospel inevitably encounters persecution, manifest primarily in hostility of governing authorities (10.17-19, 26–31) and polarized responses among family (10.21, 34–37). This domestic strife is underscored by reference to Mic. 7.6 in Mt. 10.35-36 but without an introductory formula. Mic. 7.6 appears at the end of a prophetic lament, which begins with an introductory formula, lists reasons for the offences worthy of woe (7.1-4a), and describes divine punishment (7.4b-6) in a complete social breakdown in which no one, not even the closest family members, can be trusted.

The language of Mic. 7.6 is found among later Jewish texts to refer to the distress of the last days during which the Messiah comes (e.g. *Song Rab.* 2.13 § 4).[38] Similar is *b. Sot* 49b, which alludes to Mic. 7.6 in its explanation of the increase in evil and degradation during the war with Vespasian (cf. *Jub.* 23.16-19; *1 En.* 56.7; *Tg.* Mic. 7.6). Even though the general theme of strife among household relatives reappears in several Christian texts (e.g. *Mart. Pol.* 6.1-2; *Gos. Thom.* 16), Mic. 7.6 evidently does not occur elsewhere in extant Christian literature from the first century.[39]

The parallel to Mt. 10.35-36 in Lk. 12.53 may suggest that the saying has come from the so-called Q source; however, the wording in Luke is less close to Mic. 7.6. While Matthew replicates the same three pairs of relatives listed in Mic. 7.6 with focus on hostility from the younger to older generation (son/father, daughter/mother, daughter-in-law/mother-in-law), Luke expresses the hostility as mutual between the generations ('father against son and son against father'). In addition, Matthew contains the final phrase of Mic. 7.6 ('one's foes will be members of one's own household'), which Luke omits. In Matthew, the rendering of Mic. 7.6 has been accommodated to the preceding verb phrase (ἦλθον γὰρ διχάσαι), which has also resulted in the three-fold repetition of

---

38. S. T. Lachs, *A Rabbinic Commentary on the New Testament: The Gospels of Matthew, Mark, and Luke* (Hoboken, NJ: Ktav, 1987), p. 186.

39. É. Massaux, *The Influence of the Gospel of Saint Matthew on Christian Literature Before Saint Irenaeus* (ed. A. J. Bellinzoni; trans. N. J. Belval and S. Hecht; NGS, 5; 3 vols; Macon: Mercer University Press, 1990–93), II, pp. 48–9.

the preposition 'against' (κατά). These variations make difficult any conclusion about the use of a particular version of the Old Testament text;[40] nonetheless, the application of the text in Matthew seems similar to its Jewish parallels. If the later Jewish texts expect the division of families at the coming of the Messiah, no less can be said for Matthew's Gospel which connects Mic. 7.6 to the mission of Jesus that brings not peace but a sword.[41]

Mal. 3.1 in Mt. 11.10

'See, I am sending my messenger ahead of you,
who will prepare your way before you'.

Mt. 11.2-15 consists of Jesus' response to questions from disciples of John the Baptist (11.2-6) and Jesus' commendation of John the Baptist to the crowds (11.7-15) as one who is 'more than a prophet' (11.9). This assertion about John is explained by a citation from Mal. 3.1 with wording from Exod. 23.20, two texts combined elsewhere in Lk. 7.27. However, the presence of the same combination of texts in Mk 1.2 complicates any determination of the source of the composite citation among the various gospel traditions.[42] The citation itself is introduced by a formula (cf. Mt. 3.3) similar to one used among the Dead Sea Scrolls (cf. *CD* I, 13; 4Q174=4QFlor I, 11-12). Mal. 2.17–3.5 contains a prophetic disputation. Following a claim against the people and their rebuttal (Mal. 2.17), Yahweh answers their questions about divine morality and justice with a pronouncement of coming purification and judgement. Specifically, Mal. 3.1 contains the announcement that a messenger (מלאך) will prepare the way for the coming of Yahweh as the one who will enforce the covenant; Mal. 3.1 may itself allude to Exod. 23.20 where Yahweh promises to send an angel (מלאך) before Israel to protect them on the journey to Canaan.[43]

Later Jewish literature connects the 'messenger' named in Mal. 3.1 with Elijah in Mal. 3.23-24 (ET 4.4-5) 'as the angel who will announce the coming of the Lord and of true salvation' (*Exod. Rab.* 32.9 [on Mal. 3.1]; cf. *b. 'Ed.* 3.7). The expectation of Elijah's return, however, predates the New Testament period (Sir. 48.1, 10) and is rooted in both the Torah (Deut. 18.15) and Former Prophets (2 Kgs 2.1-11). It also

---

40. Menken, *Matthew's Bible*, p. 247; Stendahl, *The School of St. Matthew*, p. 90.

41. Luz, *Matthew 8–20*, pp. 110–11; Davies and Allison, *The Gospel according to Matthew*, II, pp. 219–20.

42. Nonetheless, Menken, *Matthew's Bible*, pp. 247–8, considers the quotation among those in Matthew derived from Q.

43. M. A. Hahlen and C. A. Ham, *Minor Prophets 2: Nahum–Malachi* (The College Press NIV Commentary; Joplin: College Press, 2006), pp. 557–8.

appears throughout the synoptic tradition (Mt. 11.14; 17.10-13; Mk 9.11-13; Lk. 1.17; cf. Jn 1.21). Among the early Christian literature, Justin (*Dial.* 49) discusses in detail the identification of John the Baptist as Elijah who comes before the Messiah.

In Mt. 11.7-10, Jesus addresses three rhetorical questions to the crowds about John the Baptist and supports the claim that John is 'more than a prophet' with a Scripture quotation. The text cited is a conflation of Mal. 3.1 and Exod. 23.20. Several interpretative alterations suggest that the citation has the character of an implicit midrash seeking to apply the citation to a current situation.[44] Notably, 'the way before me' (Mal. 3.1) is changed to 'your way before you' (Mt. 11.10). In Mal. 3.1, the announcement envisions only two characters, I/Yahweh and the 'messenger' who is later identified as Elijah in Mal. 4.5-6; however, the change in pronouns in Mt. 11.10 portrays three characters, I/Yahweh, the messenger, and the one whose way the messenger prepares.[45] This preparatory role has already been attributed to John the Baptist in Mt. 3.3, a text which intimates that the one whose way John prepares is the 'Lord', and later the identification of John the Baptist as Elijah is made overtly (Mt. 11.14; 17.12-13). Thus, if the initial function of the citation from Mal. 3.1 underscores the recognition of the messenger Elijah in John the Baptist, then the citation also has a more startling implication: the coming of Jesus is the coming of Yahweh, for Jesus stands in the place of Yahweh.[46]

Jonah 2.1 (ET 1.17) in Mt. 12.40

'For just as Jonah was three days and three nights in the belly of the sea monster'.

Following the debate over the source of Jesus' power (Mt. 12.22-37) comes the request for a miraculous sign to substantiate that power (12.38-42). The structure of the pericope begins with Jesus' Jewish opponents' petition for a sign (12.38) and with Jesus' counter that no sign will be given except the sign of Jonah (12.39). This counterclaim is then supported by an appeal to the experience of Jonah (12.40) and by two illustrations that serve as indictments against the sceptical response from 'this generation' (12.41-42). Parallel to this text is Lk. 11.29-32, suggesting that the source of the tradition may have been Q; however, Luke omits the reference to Jonah 2.1 (ET 1.17), a text which portrays

---

44.   Ellis, *The Old Testament in Early Christianity*, p. 95.

45.   J. Nolland, *The Gospel of Matthew: A Commentary on the Greek Text* (NIGTC; Grand Rapids: Eerdmans, 2005), p. 456.

46.   R. T. France, *Jesus and the Old Testament: His Application of Old Testament Passages to Himself and His Mission* (London: Tyndale, 1971), pp. 92, 155; cf. the reference to Isa. 35.4-5 ('Here is your God, He will come...') in Mt. 11.5.

Jonah 'in the belly of the fish three days and three nights'. Jonah 2.1-11 consists of Yahweh's provision of a large fish to swallow Jonah (Jonah 2.1), Jonah's response in prayer (2.2-10), and Yahweh's call for the fish to spew Jonah out on dry land (2.11 [ET 2.10]).

The story of Jonah is known broadly among the various Jewish literatures.[47] It appears in Josephus (*Ant.* 9.213) and 3 Macc. 6.8, and *T. Zeb.* 4.4 may allude to the experience of Jonah in its portrayal of Joseph's confinement 'in the cistern three days and three nights'. Later traditions emphasize the temporal description of 'three days and three nights' as an indication that divine help comes on (or no later than) the third day (e.g. *Gen. Rab.* 56.1 [on Jonah 2.1], *Deut. Rab.* 2.17 [on Jonah 2.1], and *Est. Rab.* 9.2 [on Jonah 2.1]; cf. Exod. 3.18; 5.3; 15.22). Similar are the early Christian texts that present the resurrection of Jesus 'on the third day in accordance with the scriptures' (1 Cor. 15.4; cf. Mt. 16.21; Lk. 24.21, 46; Jn 2.19). In view of its use of Hos. 6.6 in Mt. 9.13 and 12.7 (cf. Hos. 11.1 in Mt. 2.15), it seems possible that Matthew's Gospel could have on this point referred to Hos. 6.2 ('after two days he will revive us; on the third day he will raise us up, that we may live before him'). Nonetheless, the Gospel opts for Jonah 2.1, likely because of the mention of Jonah already present in the Gospel's source (Mt. 12.39, 41 // Lk. 11.29-30, 32). In so doing, the Gospel does implicitly in its comparison of the Son of Man and Jonah what later Christian writer Tertullian does explicitly in his portrayal of Jonah as a type of the suffering of Jesus (*Pud.* 10; cf. Justin, *Dial.* 107; Irenaeus, *Haer.* 3.20.1-2).

In Mt. 12.40, Jesus counters the request from his Jewish opponents to produce a sign with an appeal to the experience of Jonah. The reference to Jonah 2.1 appears with no introductory formula, but the degree of agreement in wording with the LXX and its rendering of the MT[48] accounts for its recognition as an implicit citation. The wording figures into an analogy between Jonah and the Son of Man, specifically relating to their confinement and the duration of their ordeals ('three days and three nights').[49] But, as evidenced in the two illustrations that follow

---

47. See S. Chow, *The Sign of Jonah Reconsidered: A Study of its Meaning in the Gospel Traditions* (ConBNT, 27; Stockholm: Almquist & Wiksell, 1995), pp. 25–44.

48. Gundry, *The Use of the Old Testament in St. Matthew's Gospel*, pp. 136–7. Stendahl, *The School of St. Matthew*, pp. 132–3, has argued that the quotation is a post-Matthean insertion on the basis of its omission in Justin (*Dial.* 107.1); however, this idea assumes a conclusive identification of the source used by Justin, according to Menken, *Matthew's Bible*, p. 253.

49. G. M. Landes, 'Matthew 12.40 as an Interpretation of "The Sign of Jonah" Against its Biblical Background', in C. L. Meyers and M. O'Conner (eds), *The Word of the Lord Shall Go Forth* (ASOR, 1: Winona Lake: Eisenbrauns, 1983), pp. 665–84, esp. 669. The various references to this three-day period in Matthew ('on the third day' in 16.21; 17.23; 20.19; 27.64, and 'after three days' in 27.63) are best understood in the context of the Hebrew method of counting part of a day as a whole day (cf. Gen. 40.13, 20; 1 Sam. 30.12; 2 Chron. 10.5, 12; Est. 4.16; 5.1; Hos. 6.2).

(Mt. 12.41-42), the logic of this typological comparison is from lesser to greater. Thus, the story of Jonah prefigures the gospel of Jesus the Son of Man: his death, descent, proclamation, and resurrection.[50] The sign of Jonah reappears in Mt. 16.4 before the renaming of Simon son of Jonah and his triumph over the gates of Hades (16.17-18). This 'sign' may have been remembered by Jesus' Jewish opponents (Mt. 27.62-63); even if they do not accept it, the testimony of the Ninevites and the queen of the South intimate that other Gentiles will (cf. Mt. 28.16-20).

Zech. 9.9 in Mt. 21.5

'Tell the daughter of Zion, Look, your king is coming to you,
humble, and mounted on a donkey, and on a colt, the foal of a donkey'.

After the preparatory instructions given to the disciples (Mt. 21.1-3) occurs a citation from Zech. 9.9 in Mt. 21.4-5. Introduced by Matthew's characteristic wording, it is the ninth of the so-called formula quotations. With it, the evangelist anticipates Jesus' entry into Jerusalem on a donkey (21.6-11). The imperative that begins the citation ('Tell') likely comes from Isa. 62.11;[51] the remainder of the citation takes up wording from Zech. 9.9 but with certain omissions, most notably 'triumphant and victorious'. Zechariah 9 begins with a prophecy of punishment against the nations. The judgement speech portrays the conquest of Yahweh who marches against the traditional enemies of Israel (9.1-8) followed by a prophetic call to rejoice at the victorious procession of the king (9.9-10).

Evidently, extant Jewish literature from the Second Temple period does not quote Zech. 9.9. Although *Sib. Or.* 8.324 refers to the king's entry into Jerusalem, its Christian redactor may well know the LXX text of Zech. 9.9 from Matthew's own wording.[52] Later Jewish literature from the Amoraic period does cite Zech. 9.9, and in each instance its application is messianic (*b. Ber.* 56b; *b. Sanh.* 98a, 99a; *Gen. Rab.* 75.6 [on Gen. 32.6]; 98.9 [on Gen. 49.11]; 99.8 [on Gen. 49.11]). The early Church Fathers use Zech. 9.9 in their argument of proof from prophecy about Jesus' earthly ministry and divine nature (Justin, *1 Apol.* 35.10-11; *Dial.* 88.6; Irenaeus, *Haer.* 3.19.2; 4.33.1, 12; *Epid.* 65). In addition, Justin connects Zech. 9.9 with Gen. 49.10-11 (like *Genesis Rabbah*), to

---

50. Luz, *Matthew 8–20*, II, p. 217.

51. J. Miler, *Les citations d'accomplissement dans L'Évangile de Matthieu: Quand Dieu se rend présent en toute humanité* (AnBib, 140; Rome: Editrice Pontifico Istituto Biblico, 1999), p. 224; P. Foster, 'The Use of Zechariah in Matthew's Gospel', in C. M. Tuckett (ed.), *The Book of Zechariah and its Influence* (Burlington, VT: Ashgate, 2003), pp. 65–85, esp. 74.

52. Massaux, *The Influence of the Gospel of Saint Matthew*, II, p. 91.

show that Jesus is the one 'for whom the kingdom was reserved' (*1 Apol.* 32.6) and to construe the two donkeys, according to his reading of Mt. 21.9, as allegorical symbols for Jews and Gentiles (*Dial.* 53.2-4).

In Mt. 21.5, the evangelist attests to Jesus' entry into Jerusalem as the coming king who brings salvation to the nations by citing Zech. 9.9 (cf. Jn 12.15).[53] The first three lines of the citation correspond well with the LXX, but the last line, in which the evangelist describes the donkey, uses terminology closer to the MT. Since the citation begins with wording that comes from Isa. 62.11, it alters the application of Zech. 9.9 from invitation ('Rejoice greatly') to proclamation ('Tell'). It also omits the description of the king as 'triumphant and victorious' found in Zech. 9.9, perhaps to accentuate the depiction of Jesus' entry as 'humble'. If this humble character is further emphasized in the description of the donkey according to the wording of the MT, the rendering may suggest that the citation, read in view of similar wording used in Gen. 49.11, identifies Jesus as the legitimate Davidic heir.[54]

Zech. 13.7 in Mt. 26.31

'I will strike the shepherd, and the sheep of the flock will be scattered'.

At the conclusion of Jesus' Passover celebration with his disciples (Mt. 26.17-30), Jesus predicts the desertion of all the disciples (26.31-35). This prediction is substantiated with an explicit citation from Zech. 13.7, introduced by the introductory formula (γέγραπται) used with citations from characters within the narrative (cf. Mt. 2.6). The citation in Mt. 26.31 has a parallel in Mk 14.27, suggesting that, if the evangelist has used Mark, he may have derived the citation from that source.[55] Although the wording of the citation differs in Mark and Matthew, both Gospels include the citation in the same context and for a similar literary purpose that accounts for the flight of the disciples at the death of Jesus. Zech. 13.7-9 is a prophecy of salvation, which portrays Yahweh as summoning the sword against the shepherd whose death scatters the flock but results in their subsequent refinement into the people of Yahweh.

Among the earliest known Jewish literature, only the *Damascus Document* (B XIX, 7–9) quotes Zech. 13.7, but its interpretation is complicated by the omission of the citation in manuscript A. The sectarians may have applied the text to the death of their leader, the

53. Ham, *The Coming King and the Rejected Shepherd*, pp. 39–44.
54. W. Weren, 'Jesus' Entry into Jerusalem: Matthew 21,1-17 in the Light of the Hebrew Bible and the Septuagint', in C. M. Tuckett (ed.), *The Scriptures in the Gospels* (BETL, 131; Leuven: Leuven University Press – Peeters, 1997), pp. 117–41, esp. 132–3.
55. Menken, *Matthew's Bible*, p. 221.

Teacher of Righteousness, and their persecution following his death, but this cannot be concluded with certainty.[56] The Early Church Fathers use Zech. 13.7 in reference to the suffering of Jesus and the Jewish responsibility for his death (e.g. *Barn.* 5.12). Justin sees in the crucifixion of Jesus and the desertion of the disciples a fulfilment of Zech. 13.7, although Justin may quote the verse from another source than Matthew (*Dial.* 53.6; cf. Irenaeus, *Epid.* 76).[57]

In Mt. 26.31, the citation of Zech. 13.7 appears on the lips of Jesus as an explanation of his prediction about the disciples' desertion.[58] In response, Peter expresses his willingness to die with Jesus (Mt. 26.35), suggesting that 'strike' in the citation refers to the death of Jesus, and 'shepherd' to Jesus himself. Thus, the metaphoric use of the citation corresponds with the historical reality:[59] the death of Jesus results in the defection of the disciples. More importantly, the citation identifies Jesus as the rejected shepherd, who suffers a punishment deserved by other royal and prophetic leaders (Zech. 13.1-6), portrayed, for example, as the worthless shepherd in Zech. 11.15-17.[60]

Zech. 11.12-13 in Mt. 27.9-10

'And they took the thirty pieces of silver, the price of the one on whom a price had been set, on whom some of the people of Israel had set a price, and they gave them for the potter's field, as the Lord commanded me'.

The account of Judas's death (Mt. 27.3-10) interrupts the narrative of Jesus' trial before Pilate (Mt. 27.1-2, 11–26). The report relates Judas's attempt to return the thirty pieces of silver he had received for handing Jesus over (Mt. 27.3-5; cf. 26.14-15) and the determination of the chief priests to use this 'blood money' to purchase the potter's field as a burial plot (27.6-8). To explain these actions, the evangelist presents the last of the ten formula quotations; this one, introduced by his characteristic formula, is allegedly from 'Jeremiah'.[61] However, the wording of the

---

56.   J. de Waard, *A Comparative Study of the Old Testament Text in the Dead Sea Scrolls* (STDJ, 4; Leiden: Brill, 1965), pp. 40–1.

57.   O. Skarsaune, *The Proof from Prophecy: A Study in Justin Martyr's Proof-Text Tradition: Text-Type, Provenance, Theological Profile* (NovTSup, 56; Leiden: Brill, 1987), p. 121.

58.   Ham, *The Coming King and the Rejected Shepherd*, pp. 78–83.

59.   H. Frankemölle, *Matthäus: Kommentar* (2 vols; Düsseldorf: Patmos, 1994–97), II, p. 453; cf. the citation's function in Mt. 26.31 with the possible use of Zech. 13.7 in CD B XIX, 7–9.

60.   M. J. Boda, *Haggai, Zechariah* (NIV Application Commentary; Grand Rapids: Zondervan, 2004), p. 515.

61.   On the attribution of the citation to Jeremiah, see M. Knowles, *Jeremiah in Matthew's Gospel: The Rejected-Prophet Motif in Matthaean Redaction* (JSNTSup, 68;

citation indicates that it derives from Zech. 11.12-13 with allusion to Jer. 19.1-13 (or less likely, Jer. 18.1-2 or 32.7-9). Zech. 11.4-14 depicts a prophetic symbolic action, in which Yahweh instructs the prophet to act as a shepherd. The prophet does so, but after some time decides to quit acting as a shepherd for the people, breaks his two staffs, and requests from the people a wage for his service.

Use of Zech. 11.12-13 in the early Jewish and Christian literatures does not assist with its application in Matthew. The evidence in known early Jewish sources is entirely nonexistent. Later rabbinic sources contemplate the allegorical interpretation of the thirty pieces of silver, whether the amount refers to thirty righteous Jews or thirty commands for Gentiles (*b. Hull.* 92a and *Gen. Rab.* 98.9 [on Gen 49.11]; cf. *Tg. Zech.* 11.12-13). Likewise, early Christian sources apparently ignore the text, except for Irenaeus (*Epid.* 81.7), who also attributes the citation to Jeremiah. Irenaeus refers to the amount as 'thirty *staters*' (στατῆρες), silver coins equal to four days' wages (cf. Mt. 17.27); this variation also appears in several New Testament manuscripts at Mt. 26.15.

In Mt. 27.9-10, the evangelist cites Zech. 11.12-13 to explain the actions of Judas following his betrayal and of the chief priests after Judas's suicide.[62] While the citation comes primarily from Zechariah, it is attributed to Jeremiah, perhaps drawing attention to an allusion from Jeremiah. The more likely text for the allusion is Jer. 19.1-13, since it shares with Mt. 27.3-10 a judgement against those who are guilty in relation to 'innocent blood'. Furthermore, the citation ends with a Pentateuchal formula generally relating to a command given to Moses in, among other places, Exod. 9.12. This creative combination of citation and allusion makes it difficult to determine whether the evangelist has followed the MT or the LXX, although the wording does not agree with the LXX against the MT at any point. Some wording has been altered to fit the narrative; most notable is the modification that silver is not thrown to the potter[63] but used to purchase a potter's field. The citation

Sheffield: Sheffield Academic Press, 1993), pp. 60–7. Here the introductory formula begins with 'then' (τότε) instead of 'so that' (ἵνα) and is identical to the formula used with the only other formula quotation from Jeremiah (Mt. 2.17); this modification, according to D. Senior, 'The Fate of the Betrayer: A Redactional Study of Mt. XXVII, 3–10', *ETL* 48 (1972), pp. 372–426, esp. 393–5, avoids ascribing fulfilment of the event to a divine plan but rather locates the source of this evil opposition in human action.

62.   Ham, *The Coming King and the Rejected Shepherd*, pp. 60–9.

63.   The rendering 'treasury' in NRSV and NJPS follows the suggestion of C. C. Torrey, 'The Foundry of the Second Temple at Jerusalem', *JBL* 55 (1936), 247–60, esp. 256–7 that יוֹצֵר should be taken as a technical term for 'founder' (cf. 'furnace' in the LXX); however, the notion does not fit well with the symbolic action in Zech. 11.4-14 or, according to M. Delcor, 'Deux passages difficiles: Zacharie 12.11 et 11.13', *VT* 3 (1953), 67–77, esp. 73–7, the irony of the monetary amount as a despicable sum. On the possible Sumerian origin of the phrase 'thirty pieces of silver', see E. Reiner, 'Thirty Pieces of Silver', *JAOS* 88 (1968), 186–90, esp. 189–90.

itself focuses on the use of thirty pieces of silver to purchase this field by the chief priests, who, in so doing, repudiate Jesus as the divinely chosen leader and incriminate themselves in his death that occurs according to the Lord's command.[64]

Conclusion

Ten times the Gospel of Matthew cites from the Minor Prophets. Three are among the so-called formula quotations introduced by the evangelist (Mt. 2.15; 21.5; 27.9-10); seven appear on the lips of characters in the narrative, six attributed to Jesus (9.13; 10.35-36; 11.10; 12.7, 40; 26.31) and one attributed to the chief priests and scribes (2.6). Two come within the birth narrative (2.6, 15), and two, within the passion narrative (26.31; 27.9-10); five are clustered in the middle of the Gospel, generally in contexts of controversy and opposition (9.13; 10.35-36; 11.10; 12.7, 40), and one appears in the material leading up to the passion narrative (21.5). Half of these citations are also found in other Gospels (10.35-36; 11.10; 12.40; 21.5; 26.31), and half, only in Matthew (2.6, 15; 9.13; 12.7; 27.9-10). These ten citations are drawn from five of the twelve Minor Prophets: Hosea, Jonah, Micah, Zechariah, and Malachi. Collectively, these ten account for approximately one out of every five citations from the Old Testament in Matthew's Gospel, suggesting that for Matthew the only prophetic book other than the Twelve with similar standing is Isaiah. The Gospel, however, does not appear to demonstrate a coherent strategy for reading the Twelve as one document, in spite of the textual evidence for their publication on one scroll and in distinction from modern efforts to read them as a literary and theological unit. Nonetheless, the Gospel grants the collection a prominence among those Old Testament texts it cites in order to present Jesus as one who teaches Scripture correctly and one who fulfils Scripture as the divinely appointed ruler, the new Israel, the legitimate Davidic heir, and the rejected shepherd.

---

64.   R. E. Brown, *The Death of the Messiah: A Commentary on the Passion Narratives in the Four Gospels* (ABRL; New York: Doubleday, 1994), p. 652.

Chapter 4

THE MINOR PROPHETS IN LUKE–ACTS

Huub van de Sandt

A comparison of the lists provided by Helmut Utzschneider[1] and the 27th edition of Nestle-Aland (1993) reveals that Luke–Acts contains seven quotations that could be ascribed to the Minor Prophets:

Lk.	7.27	= Mal. 3.1	from Q; cf. Mt. 11.10 (and Mk 1.2)
	12.53	= Mic. 7.6	from Q; cf. Mt. 10.35-36
	23.30	= Hos. 10.8	
Acts	2.17-21	= Joel 3.1-5 (ET 2.28-32)	
Acts	7.42-43	= Amos 5.25-27	
Acts	13.41	= Hab. 1.5	
Acts	15.16-17	= Amos 9.11-12	

In this study, attention will be given to the analysis of the original Old Testament contexts of Luke's quotations. I will demonstrate that ignoring the contexts from which these quotations originate is to miss important intertextual echoes. The focus will be on describing the meaning generated by Luke's use of Scripture and posing the question: What is the significance of a link between the old and new context with regard to exegesis?

One particular observation of the scriptural text used by Luke is worth noting at the outset. Today, there is general agreement among scholars that the LXX is the source of scriptural texts cited by Luke.[2] However, there are various differences between the explicit quotations from the

---

1.   H. Utzschneider, 'Flourishing Bones: The Minor Prophets in the New Testament', in W. Kraus and R.G. Wooden (eds), *Septuagint Research: Issues and Challenges in the Study of the Greek Jewish Scriptures* (SBLSCS, 53; Atlanta: SBL, 2006), pp. 276–8.

2.   See T. Holtz, *Untersuchungen über die alttestamentlichen Zitate bei Lukas* (TU, 104; Berlin: Akademie-Verlag, 1968), p. 166; J. Dupont, 'L'utilisation apologétique de l'Ancien Testament dans les discours des Actes', in his *Études sur les Actes des Apôtres* (LD, 45; Paris: Cerf, 1967), pp. 245–82, esp. 256–7; published previously in *ETL* 39 (1953), 289–327; G. J. Steyn, *Septuagint Quotations in the Context of the Petrine and Pauline Speeches of the Acta Apostolorum* (CBET, 12; Kampen: Kok Pharos, 1995), pp. 4–21.

Minor Prophets as rendered in Acts and the actual text of the LXX. As a rule one must be cautious about concluding that Luke altered the text for it is also possible to explain these differences by arguing that he had available various scrolls containing Greek translations of scriptural texts. This assumption does not apply, however, to Luke's use of the Minor Prophets in Acts since these quotations are clearly traceable back to a particular version of the LXX that was similar to that of the Alexandrian text group.[3]

In addition, Utzschneider pointed out that it is especially the long quotations in Acts – Joel 3.1-5 in Acts 2.17-21 (91 words); Amos 5.25-27 in Acts 7.42-43 (37 words); Amos 9.11-12 in Acts 15.16-17 (43 words), and Hab. 1.5 in Acts 13.41 (24 words) – that differ from the text of the 'Old Greek' version. He showed that certain characteristics of each of these four citations correspond to variants derived from the Alexandrian tradition and concluded: 'All these features taken together indicate, in my opinion, that the citations go back directly to a written Septuagint version of the Alexandrian manuscript group'.[4] This observation is vital to our argument. If, in fact, Luke used a copy of the Septuagint for Minor Prophets that exactly, or very closely, followed the A-group of the Septuagint tradition, we can achieve an adequate understanding of the original text and contexts of Luke's quotations.[5]

The Gospel of Luke

The first part of this study will focus on Luke's Gospel. By and large, our findings will suggest that here, the original texts of the Minor Prophets are of minor relevance. In two cases, Lk. 7.27 and 12.52, quotations appear to reflect a re-adaptation of the Q source rather than an underlying scriptural text. The Hosea quotation in Lk. 23.30 belongs to special Lukan material and reflects an Alexandrian form of the LXX. This suggests that the Gospel writer himself may have drawn on a written document of the LXX.

Mal. 3.1 (and Exod. 23.20) in Lk. 7.24-30

In Lk. 7.24-30 Luke has Jesus proclaim the greatness of John the Baptist. He is perceived to be a prophet and more than a prophet. According to v.

---

3.   Holtz, *Untersuchungen*, pp. 5–27 and Steyn, *Septuagint Quotations*, pp. 250–4.
4.   Utzschneider, 'Flourishing Bones', pp. 288. See also P. Mallen, *The Reading and Transformation of Isaiah in Luke–Acts* (LNTS, 367; London: T & T Clark, 2008), pp. 4–5.
5.   There are also many allusions to the Minor Prophets in Luke–Acts but space does not permit a discussion of these scriptural references.

27, John enjoys a high rank in the history of salvation as he is claimed to be responsible for the fulfilment of an Old Testament prophecy. The verse contains a mixed citation: 'This is the one about whom it is written, "See, I am sending my messenger ahead of you, who will prepare your way before you"' (Exod. 23.20; Mal. 3.1). In this quotation John is recognized as the messenger of 'you' which, in this Lukan context, can only refer to Jesus himself. Luke sees John as the messenger sent ahead of Jesus.

The wording of Jesus' testimony about John in Lk. 7.24-30 is largely similar to Mt. 11.7-15 and must therefore have been derived from the Q source.[6] The combined quotation from Exod. 23.20 LXX and Mal. 3.1 LXX in Lk. 7.27 is also found in Mt. 11.10 (and in an almost identical form in Mk 1.2 as well). Questions regarding the reception of the Minor Prophets in the Q source are not dealt with in this chapter. It goes without saying, however, that by identifying John with the messenger of Mal. 3.1 (who is recognized as 'Elijah' in Mal. 3.23 [ET 4.5]) Q recognizes that the Baptist was Jesus' precursor. In his Gospel Luke also identifies John the Baptist with Elijah (see Lk. 1.17, 76; 3.4-6, 15–16). However, although Luke could have decided to change the Malachi quotation since he is likely to have had independent knowledge of the Minor Prophets, he does not show any interest in modifying the Q source in accordance with Mal. 3.1 LXX.[7]

Mic. 7.6 in Lk. 12.49-53

Just like the quotation in Lk. 7.27, the beginning of the pericope of 12.49-53 recalls Elijah. The phraseology of Lk. 12.49 brings to mind this prophet who brought fire from heaven against the prophets of Baal (1 Kgs 18.36-40) and the soldiers of king Ahaziah (2 Kgs 1.10, 12, 14). In this passage, Jesus seems to express a longing for the eschatological judgement that was announced by John in Lk. 3.9, 17. The sayings in Lk. 12.51-53 deal with dissension within the family due to conflicting responses to Jesus. The fact that v. 51 and the Mic. 7.6 quotation in v. 53 have counterparts in Mt. 10.34-36 indicates that both verses come from Q:

> Do you think that I have come to bring peace to the earth? No, I tell you, but rather division! From now on five in one household will be divided, three against two and two against three; they will be divided: father against son and son against father,

---

6.   See also D. Rusam, *Das Alte Testament bei Lukas* (BZNW, 112; Berlin and New York: de Gruyter, 2003), pp. 163–4.

7.   The shift from 'me' to 'you' may have occurred as early as in Q under the influence of Exod. 23.20 LXX in order to adapt the quotation to new circumstances; cf. J. A. Fitzmyer, *The Gospel According to Luke* (AB, 28; Garden City, NY: Doubleday, 1981), p. 674.

mother against daughter and daughter against mother, mother-in-law against her daughter-in-law and daughter-in-law against mother-in-law (Lk. 12.51-53).

It is likely that the Micah quotation in the Q source is derived from the LXX.[8] Micah relates the collapse of solidarity and peacefulness in the family as a symptom of the moral degeneration of society. Individualism, harsh rebellious behaviour and hateful enmity broke down households. Since parents were expected to discipline their children, it seemed as if the world was turned upside down. The early Q community emphasizes the sharp distinction between those following Jesus and those rejecting him by alluding to Mic. 7.6 LXX. Since Q 12.53 is one of the logia concerning the threat of apocalyptic judgement (Q 12.39-59), the division within families generated by Jesus is considered an impending eschatological conflict.[9]

Returning to Luke's Gospel, it can be established that – in addition to v. 52 – he also inserted supplementary clauses in the quotation from Mic. 7.6. Each negative relationship of the younger generation to the older (son, daughter, daughter-in-law) is preceded by a negative relationship of the older to the younger. The inclusion of these phrases makes Luke's text considerably different from Q and, indirectly, also from the LXX. In Luke's report it is not just rebellious conduct on the part of young people but also a vigorous antagonism of older generations which is highlighted.[10] An additional Lukan modification to Q 12.53 is the way he shifts the conflict from the eschaton to the present. He moves the epoch of disagreement and friction from the 'End' to the period starting 'now': 'From now on five in one household will be divided' (v. 52). The era of inevitable loyalty conflicts – the discord compelling people to take sides and break family ties – is the immediate effect of Jesus' ministry.

Hos. 10.8 in Lk. 23.26-32

Verses 27–31 of the pericope in Lk. 23.26-32 recounting Jesus' journey to the place of crucifixion are exclusive to Luke. He may have had access to an alternative account of the crucifixion story. Nevertheless, there are two reasons why it is highly likely that it was Luke himself who inserted vv. 29–30 referring to the destruction of Jerusalem. First, Jesus wept over

---

8.   See C. Heil, 'Die Rezeption von Micha 7,6 LXX in Q und Lukas', *ZNW* 88 (1997), 211–22, esp. 217.

9.   J. S. Kloppenborg, *The Formation of Q: Trajectories in Ancient Wisdom Collections* (SAC; Philadelphia: Fortress, 1987), pp. 148–54; see also Heil, 'Die Rezeption', 219.

10.   A. D. Jacobson, 'Divided Families and Christian Origins', in R. A. Piper (ed.), *The Gospel Behind the Gospels: Current Studies on Q* (NovTSup, 75; Leiden: Brill, 1995), pp. 361–80, esp. 365.

the city earlier in the Gospel (in 19.41-44 and 21.20-36). In the latter case, v. 23 even has a special connection with Lk. 23.29: 'Woe to those who are pregnant and to those who are nursing infants in those days! For there will be great distress on the earth and wrath against this people'. Second, the Hos. 10.8 quotation in Lk. 23.30 inverts the order of the imperatives 'cover us' and 'fall on us'. This order is also found in the Alexandrian manuscript group of the LXX. Since Luke used a text that was similar to the one documented in the Alexandrian manuscripts, the quotation may be from Luke's hand[11] and reflect certain aspects of the evangelist's use of Scripture.

As many critics have noted, Hos. 9.10 is the beginning of a new phase in the book characterized by a reflection on Israel's early traditions.[12] Limiting ourselves to the LXX version we call attention to just a few relevant elements. The clause 'like grapes in the wilderness' in 9.10 corresponds to 'Israel is a luxuriant vine' in 10.1. The passage in Hos. 9.10-17 has a circular structure: God's discovery of Israel in the wilderness (v. 10) is reversed by his rejection of Israel (v. 17). As soon as the ancestors reached the edge of cultivated land, they fell for its sexual and numinous temptations. Glory is stripped away from Israel as its reproductive functions are reduced (v. 11), parents are deprived of their offspring (v. 12) and their children surrendered to slaughter (v. 13). In v. 14 the prophet's voice is different from God's who, up to that point, had spoken through him. He says his own prayer and asks for an apparently mild punishment: 'Give them, O Lord, (...) a miscarrying womb and dry breasts'. In spite of their tradition in which childbirth is a vital sign of God's blessing (Gen. 15.5; Deut. 30.5-10), this is a light punishment compared to the horrors awaiting them. Verse 16, then, harks back to the menace recounted in vv. 12 and 13: 'Ephraim is sick, he is dried up at his roots, he shall no longer bear any fruit: therefore even if they give birth, I will kill the desired (fruits) of their womb'. Women's inability to become pregnant, their childlessness and the murder of their children are represented by sterile images of a dry tree and killing which begins in the womb.

Subsequent verses (Hos. 10.1-8) also form an independent unit. Verses 1–2 are about the destruction of the altars and pillars representing local cults which reappear in v. 8 in parallel to the devastation of 'the altars of On'. The first part of the pericope exposes Israel's guilt (1–2a, 3–5)

11.   *Pace* L. T. Johnson who points out that the substantives are reversed in this citation from the LXX; see his *The Gospel of Luke* (Sacra Pagina Series, 3; Collegeville, MN: Liturgical Press, 1991), p. 373.

12.   For the following, see H. W. Wolff, *Dodekapropheton 1: Hosea* (BKAT, 14.1; Neukirchen-Vluyn: Neukirchener Verlag, 2nd edn, 1965), pp. 207–32; F. Landy, *Hosea* (Readings: A New Biblical Commentary; Sheffield: Sheffield Academic Press, 1995), pp. 111–31.

whereas the portents of the punishment (v. 2b) are elaborated in vv. 6–8. Instead of being honest, faithful and righteous, Israel worshipped the calf of the house of On and its priests had become idol priests. The last two verses of this unit specify their consequent desolation and shame (vv. 7–8). The capital of Samaria and its king were to be wiped out, its altars to be destroyed. The culmination of this passage can only be envisaged through the voices of the victims: 'And they shall say to the mountains, Cover us, and to the hills, Fall on us'. Israel cries for relief from punishment for its apostasy from YHWH by calling for a great earthquake so that mountains and hills fall upon and cover them.

In Lk. 23.27-31, Luke seems to connect the present event of Jesus' crucifixion with the catastrophe that struck Jerusalem by alluding to the Hosea text in his version of the LXX. The Lukan composition anticipates dreadful and appalling punishment for the contemporary sin committed against Jesus. The passage not only cites from Hos. 10.8 but also contains various additional elements present in Hosea 9–10. First, the violence committed against the innocent Jesus will be visited on those who inflicted it in a terrible manner; even their guiltless children will suffer (see Hos. 9.11-13). Second, the passage acts as a menacing statement against Jerusalem. The city's coming fate is equated with that of Samaria in the Hosean counterpart (Hos. 10.7). Third, the horror and disaster to be visited upon the inhabitants of Jerusalem will be so awful that people will consider childless women 'blessed' (v. 29; see Hos. 9.14).[13] The dreadfulness is so great that people will seek catastrophic relief from it (v. 30), just as in the quotation from Hos. 10.8. Finally, v. 31 contains an *a minori ad maius* argument claiming that what is known about something small can be known 'all the more' about something big: 'For if they do this when the wood is green, what will happen when it is dry?' If the fire is now hot enough to agonize, torment and crucify the blameless Jesus, how much worse will be the fate of the guilty who, 'dried up at his roots' (Hos. 9.16), is ripe for the impending judgement.

Acts

The second part of this study deals with quotations from the Minor Prophets in Acts. In Acts, Luke was able to shape his story more autonomously than in the Gospel. He was independent and his narrative was not tied to previous accounts. This allowed him to rewrite the stories of the early church and update them more freely in the light of certain parts of the LXX. We will see that it is precisely the form of Luke's quotations in Acts that reveals his understanding of the biblical text and

---

13. This saying exactly reverses the macarism of the woman from the crowd in Lk. 11.27: 'Blessed is the womb that bore you and the breasts that nursed you!'

the things he tried to communicate to his audience. The four quotations discussed below are evidently based on a Bible text that closely resembled the Alexandrian form of the LXX. We are in a position, therefore, to determine Luke's changes.

Joel 3.1-5 (ET 2.28-32) in Acts 2.17-21

The prophecy of Joel 3.1-5a (= 2.28-32a) is quoted in Acts 2.17-21 and the immediate context in which Luke situates Joel's prophecy is the Pentecostal event. The words 'this is what was spoken' in Acts 2.16 imply that the quotation primarily interprets the events that were described previously in Acts 2.1-11. It throws light on the gift of the Spirit and its consequences. A biblical prophecy is fulfilled there and then, within the community to which Peter is preaching.

> No, this is what was spoken through the prophet Joel: 'In the last days it will be, God declares, that I will pour out my Spirit upon all flesh and your sons and your daughters shall prophesy, and your young men shall see visions, and your old men shall dream dreams. Even upon my slaves, both men and women, in those days I will pour out my Spirit; and they shall prophesy. And I will show portents in the heaven above and signs on the earth below, blood, and fire, and smoky mist. The sun shall be turned to darkness and the moon to blood, before the coming of the Lord's great and glorious day. Then everyone who calls on the name of the Lord shall be saved.' (Acts 2.16-21)

In the initial phrase of the quotation Luke consciously deviates from the LXX reading by substituting 'in the last days' for 'afterward'. Since the first part of the prophecy is considered fulfilled by recent events, Luke assumes his own time is part of the end time. He clearly provides Joel's message with an eschatological understanding, thus underscoring that the 'last days' had dawned in his time. Luke was truly convinced that he was living in the last days of the present age.[14]

Luke's quotation from Joel is primarily presented as an apologetic defence against the idea of drunkenness (Acts 2.13, 15). It was not intoxication but the outpouring of the Spirit upon the disciples which caused prophetic activity and visions. The Galileans acted in accordance with the eschatological promise. For this reason the author of Acts added the clause 'God declares' in 2.17a which did not belong to the LXX or the

---

14. 'In Acts as *a whole* the eschatological element is strong' (original italics); see W. C. van Unnik, 'The "Book of Acts": the Confirmation of the Gospel', in his *Sparsa Collecta: The Collected Essays of W. C. van Unnik* (NovTSup, 29; Leiden: Brill, 1973), I, pp. 340–73, esp. 359 (published previously in *NovT* 4 [1960], pp. 26–59) – 'The very fact that the church lives in the end of times and awaits the consummation in the near future is simply a *conditio sine qua non*', see J. Jervell, *The Theology of the Acts of the Apostles* (New Testament Theology; Cambridge: Cambridge University Press, 1996), p. 115.

MT text traditions of Joel. The phrase was inserted in order to accentuate the quotation's Divine origin and to emphasize that it represented God's direct speech.[15]

The quotation also serves another purpose. It underlines Peter's speech in Acts 2.22-40. In that passage Peter elaborates on Joel 3.1-5a while preaching to those 'dwelling in Jerusalem'. He explains that not God (ἐκχεῶ in Joel 3.1 = Acts 2.17) but the exalted Lord has poured out the Spirit (ἐξέχεεν in Acts 2.33). The name to be called upon (τὸ ὄνομα κυρίου in Joel 3.5a = Acts 2.21) is identified as that of Jesus (Acts 2.38) whom God has made both Lord and Christ (Acts 2.36). It can therefore be concluded that the quotation from Joel dominates Acts 2. On the one hand it places the preceding events (Acts 2.1-13) in their proper perspective; on the other it serves as a starting point for extensive commentary (Acts 2.22-40).

The Joel quotation is also strongly related to the subsequent chapters in Acts. It contains words and themes that appear repeatedly, such as 'Spirit', 'visions', 'prophesying', 'portents and signs', the 'calling on the name', 'being saved', etc.[16] In this respect Joel 3.1-5a is significant for the whole of Acts. It is the book's guiding text which outlines the programme followed in the next chapters of the narrative. The mission to the Gentiles is central to Acts.[17] That is why Luke breaks from Joel 3 after v. 5a. He wanted to make clear that salvation is not merely found in Zion and Jerusalem and does not exclusively apply to Jews.[18]

---

15. See J. Strazicich, *Joel's Use of Scripture and the Scripture's Use of Joel: Appropriation and Resignification in Second Temple Judaism and Early Christianity* (BIS, 82; Leiden: Brill, 2007), p. 278. For details of the textual differences between Joel LXX 3.1-5 and its rendering in Acts 2.17-21, see Steyn, *Septuagint Quotations*, pp. 74–90.

16. See A. Kerrigan, 'The "sensus plenior" of Joel, III, 1–5 in Act, II, 14–36', in J. Coppens, A. Descamps and É. Massaux (eds), *Sacra Pagina: Miscellanea biblica congressus internationalis de re biblica, vol. II* (BETL, 13; Paris and Gembloux: Lecoffre-Duculot, 1959), pp. 295–315.

17. See, e.g., J. Dupont, 'Le Salut des Gentils et la signification théologique du Livre des Actes', in his *Études*, pp. 393–419 (published previously in *NTS* 6 [1959–60], 132–55); B. J. Koet, 'Paul and Barnabas in Pisidian Antioch: A Disagreement over the Interpretation of the Scriptures (Acts 13, 42–52)' and 'Paul in Rome (Acts 28, 16–31): A Farewell to Judaism?' in *Five Studies on Interpretation of Scripture in Luke–Acts* (SNTA, 14; Leuven: Peeters, 1989), pp. 97–118 and 119–39.

18. See Kerrigan, 'The "sensus plenior"', p. 298 and Steyn, *Septuagint Quotations*, pp. 89–90. Luke is likely to have been familiar with the original context of the quotation he presents in Acts 2.17-21. However, when we compare the original context of the Joel quotation with its new context in Acts, a problem arises. If Joel 3.1-5a sets the tone for the Book of Acts as a whole, how could Luke reconcile the catastrophic disaster for the Gentiles (described in Joel 4) with the fact that the Gospel is preached to them in Acts? Space does not allow me to go into this matter here, but see H. van de Sandt, 'The Fate of the Gentiles in Joel and Acts 2: An Intertextual Study', *ETL* 66 (1990), 56–77, esp. 67–77.

Amos 5.25-27 in Acts 7.42-43

The Amos quotation in Acts 7.42d-43 is found in the narrative of the golden calf which in turn is part of the Stephen speech (7.2-53). The people have made themselves a golden calf and offer sacrifices to the idol. God's reaction to this apostasy is one of rejection and He hands over his people to the worship of heavenly bodies. The text is formulated thus:

> [42] [(a)]'But God turned away [(b)]and handed them over to worship the host of heaven, [(c)]as it is written in the book of the prophets'.

Then Amos 5.25-27 is quoted from the LXX:

> [42] [(d)]Did you offer to me slain victims and sacrifices, [(e)]forty years in the wilderness, [(f)]O house of Israel? [43] [(a)]And you took the tent of Moloch [(b)]and the star of the god Rephan, [(c)]the images which you made to *worship them* [(d)]so I will remove you beyond *Babylon* (Amos 5.25-27).

The present study does not deal with specific textual problems in this citation[19] and only the major differences between Acts and the LXX source are printed in italics: the addition of 'to worship' (προσκυνεῖν), the modification of ἑαυτοῖς into αὐτοῖς and the replacement of Damascus by Babylon at the end of the quotation.

In Stephen's speech vv. 35–50 form a historic–thematic section. The eulogy on Moses (vv. 35–38a) is followed by the account of the sin of the calf (38b–43), composed of the apostasy itself and its punishment, and a survey of Israel's history from the tent of testimony in the desert through to Solomon's building of the temple (vv. 44–50). Verse 44 marks the scene transition. It is connected to the preceding section by the repeated use of elements from the Amos quotation, such as 'tent' (σκηνήν), 'wilderness', 'to make' and 'image'. At the same time, reference to the 'tent of testimony' introduces a new theme which is developed in the subsequent verses.

1. Acts 7.38b-43 in light of Exodus 32–34

The calf story rendered in Acts 7.38b-43 is largely based on the narrative in Exod. 32.1-6, with v. 40 almost literally quoting Exod. 32.1 (cf. also 32.23) and v. 41 summarizing Exod. 32.4-6.[20] In the Exodus account we note that the apostasy with the calf results in the breaking of the covenant. In the remaining part of Exodus 32 and the beginning of Exodus 33 the incident causes God to withdraw his presence and to send an angel to guide his people in his place. When this punishment

---

19. For these, see e.g., Holtz, *Untersuchungen*, pp. 14–19.
20. The same story also occurs in Deut. 9.7-21 but no quotation from or allusion to this pericope is found in Acts 7.38b-43.

is announced people start mourning in vv. 4–6. This theme is suddenly interrupted,[21] however, by the mention of the 'tent of testimony' in Exod. 33.7 as the place where 'everyone who sought the Lord' (πᾶς ὁ ζητῶν κύριον) could go. In the following verses, this tent serves as a setting God periodically visits to announce his will. Considering that the 'tent of testimony' occurs in a similar, unexpected way in Acts 7.44 directly following the Amos quotation describing the punishment for the sin of the calf, it seems that Luke at this point resumes the text of Exodus 32–34 and refers to the tent section of Exod. 33.7-11. Luke leaves out the text between Exod. 32.7 and 33.6 in which Moses intercedes and God partially forgives his people (Exod. 32.14). Instead, in Acts 7.42-43 he inserts an account of God completely turning away from his people and surrendering them to the cult of the celestial host and to exile.

2. Acts 7.38b-43 in Light of Deut. 4.1-28

It is important to note that Luke's account of the golden calf was strongly influenced by Deut. 4.1-28. He combined the passage in Exod. 32.1-6 with Deut. 4.1-28, interpreting the construction of the calf as a transgression of the prohibition of images in Deut. 4.1-28. To illustrate this, a brief outline of this Deuteronomy section is presented here. Two themes are central to Deut. 4.1-28: the summons to be obedient to the law (vv. 1–14) and the prohibition against images (vv. 15–28). The main reason for the prohibition of images is stated in Deut. 4.15 (for at Horeb / Sinai 'you saw no form') and in 4.12 ('and you saw no form, only a voice').[22] The prohibition itself is rendered in 4.16-18:

> (Beware) lest you act lawlessly, and make for yourselves a graven image, a form of any figure, the image of male or female, the image of any beast of those that are on the earth, the image of any winged bird, which flies under heaven, the image of any reptile which creeps on the earth, the image of any fish of those which are in the waters under the earth. (Deut. 4.16-18)

The following verse, Deut. 4.19, connects Deut. 5.7 (the prohibition of other gods = Exod. 20.3) with 5.9 (the prohibition of serving other gods = Exod. 20.5):

> and (beware) lest you look up to the sky, and when you see the sun and the moon and the stars, and all the order of heaven, you should go astray and worship them, and serve them (...), things which the Lord your God has allotted to all the nations under heaven. (Deut. 4.19)

---

21.   Cf. B. S. Childs, *Exodus: A Commentary* (OTL; London: SCM Press, 1974), pp. 589–91; R. W. L. Moberly, *At the Mountain of God: Story and Theology in Exodus 32–34* (JSOTSup, 22; Sheffield: JSOT Press, 1983), pp. 48–53; M. Noth, *Das zweite Buch Mose: Exodus* (ATD, 5; Göttingen: Vandenhoeck & Ruprecht, 1968), pp. 209–10.

22.   This assertion may be reflected in the designation of the one 'who speaks' (τοῦ λαλοῦντος / ὁ λαλῶν) in Acts 7.38 and 44.

Because this verse warns against the cult of the stars which, according to 4.19b, God has allotted to all (other) peoples to serve, the heavenly bodies referred to in this passage may be considered identical with the 'other gods' mentioned elsewhere.

In Deut. 4.16-20 the first and second commandments of the Decalogue are presented as a single unit. The prohibition of images is inculcated, referring to all living beings in the whole of the universe (Deut. 4.16-18), and the interdiction to have other gods (Deut. 5.7) and serve them (Deut. 5.9) is expressed in the interdiction to serve heavenly bodies.[23] It can be provisionally established that Amos 5.25-27, which is quoted in Acts 7.42-43, is another Old Testament passage in which heavenly bodies are identified with 'other gods'.

In Deuteronomy 4 Moses emphatically assures the people that they will fare badly if they disregard the prohibition against making images. The promised land will be taken away from them and utterly destroyed. Adversities follow in vv. 27–28 which, in contrast to v. 26, are explicitly ascribed to God:[24]

And the Lord will scatter you among all nations, and you will be left few in number among the nations, to which the Lord will bring you. And there you will serve other gods, the works of men's hands, wood and stone, which cannot see, nor can they hear, nor eat, nor smell. (Deut. 4.27-28)

This prediction in Deuteronomy has a hortatory function: the future consequences of Israel's behaviour are pictured in order to show that only an obedient people will be saved.

3. The Quotation of Amos 5.25-27 in Acts 7.42-43

This brings us to Acts 7.40-43. Leaving aside other similarities between Deut. 4.1-28 and Acts 7.38-44,[25] we will establish that according to Luke the prediction of Deut. 4.27-28 is fulfilled in the Amos verses quoted in Acts 7.42b-43. In his opinion Israel has violated the prohibition against making images in Deut. 4.16-20 by constructing the calf (Acts 7.40-41).[26] This idea was not new. In Ps. 105.19-20 LXX the glory in which God

---

23. Cf. D. Knapp, *Deuteronomium 4: Literarische Analyse und theologische Interpretation* (GTA, 35; Göttingen: Vandenhoeck & Ruprecht, 1987), pp. 71–4 (Knapp is convinced that the composer of Deuteronomy 4 used the Decalogue), and G. Braulik, *Die Mittel deuteronomischer Rhetorik: Erhoben aus Deuteronomium 4,1-40* (AnBib, 68; Rome: Biblical Institute Press, 1978), pp. 36–43.

24. Braulik, *Mittel*, p. 55.

25. For more details, see H. van de Sandt, 'Why is Amos 5,25-27 Quoted in Acts 7,42f.?', *ZNW* 82 (1991), 67–87, esp. 71–83.

26. This suggestion is supported by M. Stowasser, 'Am 5,25-27; 9,11 f. in der Qumranüberlieferung und in der Apostelgeschichte: Text- und traditionsgeschichtliche Überlegungen zu 4Q174 (Florilegium) III 12 / CD VII 16 / Apg 7,42b-43; 15,16-18', *ZNW* 92 (2001), 47–63, esp. 57, n. 56. See also Rusam, *Das Alte Testament*, pp. 140–1.

showed himself to Israel was also said to have been exchanged for 'the image of a calf that eats grass'.[27]

We suggested above that the formulation 'tent of testimony' links up with the same wording in Exod. 33.7. One might ask why, after his rendering of the calf story in Exod. 32.1-6 and the punishment in Amos 5.25-27, Luke suddenly jumped to Exod. 33.7. The change of subject from the Babylonian exile back to the wilderness period is at least surprising. This transition, however, is explained by the assumption that Luke took the punishment stated in the Amos quotation to be the equivalent of Deut. 4.27-28. Returning to Deuteronomy 4, we see that the verses following vv. 27–28 offer a new prospect:[28]

> And there (i.e. among all the nations, cf. v. 27) you will seek (ζητήσετε) the Lord your God, and you will find (him) whenever you seek him with all your heart, and with all your soul in your affliction. And all these things will come upon you in the last days (ἐπ᾿ ἐσχάτῳ τῶν ἡμερῶν) and you will turn to the Lord your God ... (Deut. 4.29-30)

The unexpected transition from exile and idolatry (Amos 5.26-27 = Acts 7.43 = Deut. 4.27-28) to the tent of testimony in the wilderness (Acts 7.44) is due to the wording 'seek (ζητήσετε) the Lord your God' in Deut. 4.29, coupled with the 'last days'. Deut. 4.29-30 is the only place in the Pentateuch where the phrase 'seek the Lord your God' occurs in combination with the 'last days'. In the first section we have seen that Luke probably replaced 'afterward' in the Joel quotation by 'in the last days', being convinced that he himself lived in that age. Acts 7, however, does not deal with the eschatological events represented by Deut. 4.29-30 but with Israel's history. Therefore, Luke did not follow the sequel of his source but instead shifted his frame of reference. In Acts 7.44, he linked up with Exod. 33.7, the only other place in the Pentateuch where the verb 'to seek' is found in combination with the accusative 'Lord' but without reference to the 'last days'. Writing about Israel's past, Luke continues his account with the 'tent of testimony' in the wilderness period, the subject of Exod. 33.7-11.

4. Why was Deut. 4.27-28 replaced by Amos 5.25-27 in Acts 7.42-43?

What considerations led Luke to substitute Amos 5.26-27 for Deut. 4.27-28? We established above that the interpretation of the first two commandments of the Decalogue in Deut. 4.16-20 must have attracted

27.   Cf. L. Jacquet, *Les Psaumes et le coeur de l'Homme: Etude textuelle, littéraire et doctrinale. Psaumes 101 à 150* (Gembloux: Duculot, 1979), p. 144. For the method used here, which was probably based on the principle of analogy, see Van de Sandt, 'Why is Amos 5,25-27 Quoted', 76–7, n. 32.

28.   C. Begg, 'The Literary Criticism of Deut. 4, 1–40: Contributions to a Continuing Discussion', *ETL* 56 (1980), 10–55, esp. 49 and Knapp, *Deuteronomium 4*, pp. 39 and 91–3.

Luke's attention. Because these verses suggested that 'other gods' referred to heavenly bodies, he might have attached the same meaning to the 'other gods' in Deut. 4.28. This explanation is problematic, however, because it is difficult to imagine heavenly bodies as being 'works of men's hands'. Nevertheless, if the prohibition of images in Deuteronomy 4 is transgressed through the construction of the calf, this punishment must be feasible. The text in Amos offers the solution to this problem: 'And you took up the tent of Moloch and the star of your god Raiphan, the figures (of them) which you made'. Amos 5.26 not only enables Luke to understand the heavenly bodies as 'works of men's hands' but also links this identification with a specific period in Israel's history.

This brings us to a second possible reason why Luke replaced Deut. 4.27-28 with Amos 5.25-27. In Deut. 4.25 the transgression of the prohibition of images takes place after Moses' death (4.22) and in the promised land (4.25) whereas according to Exod. 32.1-6 (and Deut. 9.7-21) the sin of the calf occurred in the wilderness while Moses was still alive. Again, it is Amos who provides the answer: 'Did you offer to me slain beasts and sacrifices, forty years in the wilderness, O house of Israel? And you took up the tent of Moloch' (5.25-26). God, speaking here in the first person, confirms the unfaithfulness of Israel in the wilderness as well as the execution of the sentence in Deut. 4.27-28. The Amos quotation thus corroborates and strengthens Luke's interpretation of Deuteronomy 4.

Luke's interpretation of the sin of the calf in light of Deuteronomy 4 makes him resort to Amos 5.25-27. His rendering of this quotation in Acts 7.42d-43, however, is clearly influenced by his reading of Deut. 4.27-28. Because Deut. 4.27 ('and the Lord will scatter you among all nations') refers to Israel's exile, Luke replaced 'Damascus' with 'Babylon'. Moreover, Deut. 4.28 explicitly mentions the cult of the other gods ('you will serve other gods'). This is why Luke interpolated the words 'to worship them' (προσκυνεῖν αὐτοῖς), probably derived from Deut. 4.19, in his quotation.

If Luke wanted the Amos quotation to reflect Deut. 4.27-28, Amos 5.26 would also have to be presented as part of the punishment described in that particular passage. In order to promote this reading of the verse he provided his quotation with a key for its interpretation. The phrase 'and (he) handed them over to worship the host of heaven' in the introductory verse (Acts 7.42b) has a hermeneutical function. It explains that God's initiative does not begin in Amos 5.27 but in 5.26. In addition to the exile, the worship of celestial bodies is also presented as part of the punishment. In effect, the content of the punishment is extended to v. 26 (Acts 7.43a-c) and its cause is reduced to v. 25 (= Acts 7.42d-f). The cult of God was replaced by the worship of the calf.

Hab. 1.5 in Acts 13.41

The middle part of the report of the first missionary journey undertaken by Paul and Barnabas (Acts 13.1–14.28) deals with their visit in Pisidian Antioch (vv. 14–52). Their sojourn in this small diaspora city is marked by two important events: Paul's address in vv. 16–41 and, after having met with opposition, his decision to turn to the Gentiles (vv. 42–52). The address ends in vv. 38–41. The concluding conjunction 'therefore' (οὖν) leads to a concrete offer of salvation to the Antiochians whereas the second 'therefore' introduces an admonition coupled with the quotation from Hab. 1.5. The preceding warning ('Beware, therefore, that what the prophets said does not happen to you') expresses the threatening character of the quotation:

> Look, you scoffers! Be amazed and perish, for in your days I am doing a work (ἔργον), a work that you will never believe, even if someone tells you (ἐκδιηγῆται). (Hab. 1.5)

1. Hab. 1.1-11

The quotation is adopted from God's first reply (Hab. 1.5-11) to Habakkuk's complaint (1.1-4), which probably describes the religious and moral abuses in Judah during the reign of king Jehoiakim (608–598). Verses 1–11 are considered a coherent unit because in Hab. 1.12 a new passage starts in which God is addressed again.[29]

> The burden, which the prophet Ambacum saw. How long, O Lord, shall I cry and will you not listen? (How long) shall I, while being injured (ἀδικούμενος), cry out to you and will you not save? Why did you show me troubles and griefs, to look upon misery and ungodliness? Before me a trial is held, and the judge receives (a reward). Therefore the law is thwarted and judgement does not come forth effectually, because the ungodly one oppresses the righteous one: therefore judgement will come out perverted. Behold, you scoffers, and look and be greatly amazed and vanish, for I am doing a work in your days, which you will never believe if one declares it to you. Because, behold, I arouse the Chaldeans, the warriors,[30] the bitter and hasty nation that marches upon the breadth of the earth to inherit tents not its own: it[31] is terrible and famous, from itself shall

---

29.   For the exegesis of Hab. 1.1-11 – as far as is relevant for the LXX version – we used A. S. van der Woude, *Habakuk–Zefanja* (POut; Nijkerk: Callenbach, 1978), pp. 9–26; A. Weiser, *Das Buch der zwölf kleinen Propheten. I: Die Propheten Hosea, Joel, Amos, Obadja, Jona, Micha* (ATD, 24; Göttingen: Vandenhoeck & Ruprecht, 5th edn, 1967), pp. 27–34; W. Rudolph, *Micha – Nahum – Habakuk – Zephanja* (KAT, 13.3; Gütersloh: Mohn, 1975), pp. 200–8; J. D. W. Watts, *The Books of Joel, Obadiah, Jonah, Nahum, Habakkuk and Zephaniah* (CBC; Cambridge: Cambridge University Press, 1975), pp. 121–8.

30.   The text of the Septuaginta in the Göttingen series is followed here. It holds 'the warriors' to be the original text. Cf. J. Ziegler, *Duodecim prophetae* (Septuaginta, 13; Göttingen: Vandenhoeck & Ruprecht, 2nd edn, 1967).

31.   Referring back to ἔθνος, the LXX does not adhere to the neuter gender.

come forth its judgement,[32] and its dignity [burden] shall come out of itself ... (Hab. 1.1-7)

Subsequent verses describe the capacities of their horses and horsemen (v. 8), the destruction and captivity of ungodly men (v. 9), the kings and rulers who are left at the mercy of these fighters and the insufficiency of their fortresses (v. 10). After describing the violence and terror the pericope concludes as follows: 'Then it shall change its spirit and it shall pass through and it will make atonement (saying): this strength (belongs) to my god' (v. 11).

The singular 'while being injured' (ἀδικούμενος) in v. 2 indicates that the LXX translator interprets the injustice as being inflicted upon the prophet himself. It is obviously not the first time he complains of the misery brought upon him by his compatriots ('How long' in v. 2). He asks why God does not intervene and allows harm and grief (v. 3). People do not take their responsibility to act socially and justly seriously: the judge accepts bribes. The prophet concludes his complaint with 'Therefore' (v. 4a) to summarize the cause of these abuses: because the ungodly one overpowers the righteous one (v. 4b) the law cannot warrant justice (v. 4a), which results in the perverted law of the strongest (v. 4c). When the law remains silent, the innocent fall victim to unjust judgement. In v. 5 God addresses the oppressors, the scoffers who harass their own people and do not believe that God has the power to procure justice for the righteous. The verse stresses their amazement rather than the harsh fate that will befall them. The Lord announces that they will live to see the unbelievable in their days, something which will astonish them and which they did not expect from God. The subsequent lines indicate that the punishment will be inflicted by a formidable Gentile nation that only obeys its own laws and is bent on violence. After the description of these horrors, however, the LXX version provides a totally different description of this nation: in v. 11 its disposition suddenly changes; it does penance and confesses that its power derives from God.

2. *The Quotation from Hab. 1.5 in Acts 13.41*

In Acts 13.41 Hab. 1.5 LXX appears in a slightly altered form.[33] Many scholars have wondered why Luke interpolated the word 'work' into its conclusion. It is likely that this repetition was inserted intentionally. In Acts the singular 'work' (ἔργον) appears more than once (13.2; 14.26; 15.38). Because the word ἔργον is each time used in reference to the mission to the Gentiles,[34] Luke's duplication of the term in the Habakkuk

32. They do as they please, establishing their own law (without the Torah; cf. v. 4).

33. For textual differences, see Holtz, *Untersuchungen*, p. 20; Steyn, *Septuagint Quotations*, pp. 190–2.

34. In Acts 5.38 – belonging to Gamaliel's speech – the term ἔργον refers to God's work of gathering the followers of Jesus.

quotation also has this connotation: astonishment about God's work is connected with the mission to the Gentiles.[35] There is an additional reason for this supposition: apart from this passage, the verb ἐκδιηγέομαι ('to declare, tell, narrate') only occurs in Luke–Acts in Acts 15.3 when the success of the mission to the Gentiles is its object. Barnabas and Paul travel through Phoenicia and Samaria and bring great joy to all the brethren by 'reporting (ἐκδιηγούμενοι) the conversion of the Gentiles'.

In the original text of Hab. 1.5, the actions of the 'warriors' described in vv. 6–11 would have been startling to the prophet's readers. The addition of the 'terminus technicus' ἔργον to the quotation in Acts, however, shows that for Luke, God's unexpected intervention refers to the conversion of the Gentiles. Luke may not have shared the surprise at the punishment of the scoffers described in vv. 6–10 but he must have been amazed by the unique statement in v. 11. This violent people returned to the Lord! It is also the position of this verse that may have attracted Luke's attention, because it does not fit into the context.[36]

Luke therefore links Hab. 1.5 to 1.11. The astonishment at God's work in Hab. 1.5 is not related to the arrival of the all-destroying fighters initiated by God described in vv. 6–10, but to the incident referred to in v. 11: the way the mentality of these fighters suddenly changed. This interweavement, however, not only transforms the content of the ἔργον in v. 5 but also the meaning of v. 11: the conversion of the Gentiles does not emanate from these Gentiles themselves but it is God's work. In this context, it is clear why in Acts 13.40 Luke introduces the quotation with an admonition for those who do not 'believe' (13.39), the scoffers (13.41). For him the 'vanishing', which is maintained in the quotation from Hab. 1.5, is the essence of God's punishment as described in Hab. 1.6-10. This penalty is not dwelled upon as much as in Habakkuk but it implies the same: God's work for the Gentiles may result in the disappearance of Israel.

3. The Relevance of the Quotation from Hab. 1.5 in Acts 13.41

Why does Luke consider this quotation to be relevant to his own time? And why should it apply to the Jesus movement? In order to answer these questions, it is necessary to consider the verse preceding the quotation

---

35.   E.g. J. Roloff, *Die Apostelgeschichte* (NTD, 5; Göttingen: Vandenhoeck & Ruprecht, 1981), p. 208; E. Haenchen, *Die Apostelgeschichte* (KEK, 3; Göttingen: Vandenhoeck & Ruprecht, 5th edn, 1965), p. 355; U. Wilckens, *Die Missionsreden der Apostelgeschichte* (WMANT, 5; Neukirchen-Vluyn: Neukirchener Verlag, 3rd edn, 1974), p. 52; Rusam, *Das Alte Testament*, p. 411.

36.   The rendering of the LXX, which takes this verse to indicate a radical change in the mentality of the cruel conquerors, does not do justice to the context because it makes the prophet's subsequent objection (1.12-17) seem superfluous. In these verses, the prophet asks the question why the holy and righteous God should choose these robbers, who are no better than their victims, to carry out his punishment.

in the original context: 'Therefore the law is thwarted and judgement does not come forth effectually, because the ungodly one oppresses the righteous one (τὸν δίκαιον)' (1.4a-b). When the righteous are ill-treated, violence replaces justice.

In Luke–Acts the adjective 'righteous' (δίκαιος) and the noun 'righteous one' (ὁ δίκαιος) apply to the suffering and persecuted Jesus.[37] This can be concluded from the words of the centurion confessing beneath the cross in Lk. 23.47: 'Certainly this man was (a) righteous (one) (δίκαιος ἦν)'. The term '(a) righteous (one)' replaces the predicate 'the Son of God' from Mt. 27.54 and Mk 15.39. In Acts 3.14 the murderer Barabbas is set against the 'righteous one': 'But you denied the holy and righteous one (δίκαιον), and asked for a murderer to be granted to you'. In Acts 22.1-21 Paul addresses the people to tell them about his Damascus vision. The pious Jew Ananias rephrases the words Jesus speaks to Paul in the two other reports of this event (cf. 9.15, 17 and 26.16-18): 'The God of our fathers appointed you to know his will, to see the just one (τὸν δίκαιον) and to hear a voice from his mouth; for you will be a testimony for him to all men' (22.14-15a). The preceding v. 8 makes it clear that the term 'righteous one' refers to Jesus as the 'persecuted one'.

These passages suggest that Luke identified the 'righteous one' from Hab. 1.4 (cf. 1.13) as Jesus. The complaint of Hab. 1.4 is reflected in Acts 13.27-28 in which the prosecution and execution of the righteous Jesus results in a perversion of justice: 'Though they could charge him with nothing deserving death, yet they asked Pilate to have him killed' (see also Acts 7.52).[38]

Amos 9.11-12 in Acts 15.16-17

The primary issue addressed at the Jerusalem Conference (Acts 15.6-21) was whether converted Gentiles are redeemed if they remain uncircumcised and do not keep the law. The discussion consists of two parts. The introduction in vv. 6–7a is followed by Peter's speech (vv. 7b-11), which, after a short observation (v. 12), is followed by an address by James (vv. 13–21). James summarizes Peter's words and mentions how God 'first visited the Gentiles' (v. 14), a statement which he underscores by referring to the prophecy from Amos (vv. 16–17). He then goes into the consequences of this divine initiative, points out the line of conduct

37.   See L. Ruppert, *Jesus als der leidende Gerechte? Der Weg Jesu im Lichte eines alt- und zwischentestamentlichen Motivs* (SBS, 59; Stuttgart: Katholisches Bibelwerk, 1972), pp. 47–8 and n. 17.

38.   For a more elaborate discussion of this Habakkuk quotation in Acts, see H. van de Sandt, 'The Quotations in Acts 13,32-52 as a Reflection of Luke's LXX Interpretation', *Bib* 75 (1994), 26–58, esp. 42–50.

towards the Gentile Christians (vv. 19–20) and concludes with a reference
to Moses' authority (v. 21).

1. The close relationship of the two Amos quotations in Acts

The quotation from Amos 9.11-12 in Acts 15.16-17 and the one from
Amos 5.25-27 in Acts 7.42b-43 are closely related.[39] In addition to the
fact that these are the only Amos quotations in Luke–Acts, the passages
and their contexts are closely interconnected in other respects as well.
Themes like the 'tent' (σκηνή in 7.43, 44 and 15.16), 'David' (7.45-46 and
15.16) and 'to build/rebuild' (7.47, 49 and twice in 15.16) are related.
Moreover, among all the explicit quotations in Acts, only these two are
introduced with the formula 'as it is written'.[40] In Acts 7.38-43 Stephen
recalls Israel's construction and cult of the golden calf, a sin for which
God abandoned the people to star worship and exile, as mentioned in
the Amos quotation (Acts 7.42b-43). God's punishment of this apostasy
is introduced in 7.42a with the words 'but God turned away from them
(ἔστρεψεν δὲ ὁ θεός)'. In Acts 15.16 the beginning of the Amos quotation
is changed. The phrase 'on that day' in Amos 9.11 is replaced by 'After
this I will return (μετὰ ταῦτα ἀναστρέψω)'.

> After this I will return, and I will rebuild the tent of David, which has fallen; from its
> ruins I will rebuild it, and I will set it up, so that all other peoples may seek the Lord
> – even all the Gentiles over whom my name has been called. Thus says the Lord, who
> has been making these things known from long ago. (Acts 15.16-18)[41]

The mention of God's 'return' agrees with his 'turning away' in the
introduction of the citation in Acts 7.42.[42] Whereas Luke cites Amos
5.25-27 in his treatment of Israel's history, he uses Amos 9.11-12 to
characterize his own period, marked by the renewal of Israel.

We established above that Luke's account of the golden calf (Acts
7.38-43) was strongly influenced by the LXX version of Deut. 4.1-28. He
considered the quotation from Amos 5.26-27 substantially equivalent to

---

39.   E. Richard, 'The Creative Use of Amos by the Author of Acts', *NovT* 24 (1982),
37–53, esp. 49–50.

40.   Cf. P. A. Paulo, *Le Problème ecclésial des Actes à la lumière de deux Prophéties
d'Amos* (Paris: Cerf, 1985), pp. 29 and 47.

41.   For a discussion of the textual differences from the LXX, see Rusam, *Das Alte
Testament*, pp. 423–7 and R. T. McLay, *The Use of the Septuagint in New Testament
Research* (Grand Rapids: Eerdmans, 2003), pp. 17–27. The end of the quotation in Acts
15.18 does not occur in Amos: '(..., who has been making these things) known from long
ago'. This clause is generally taken to be an allusion to Isa. 45.21. For the significance
of this allusion, see H. van de Sandt, 'An Explanation of Acts 15.6-21 in the Light of
Deuteronomy 4.29-35 (LXX)', *JSNT* 46 (1992), 73–97, esp. 81–6.

42.   Cf. Richard, 'The Creative Use', 49–50 and Paulo, *Le Problème ecclésiale*, p.
79. See also J. Dupont, '"Je rebâtirai la cabane de David qui est tombée" (Ac 15,16 = Am
9,11)', in E. Grässer und O. Merk (eds), *Glaube und Eschatologie* (Tübingen: Mohr, 1985),
pp. 19–32, esp. 27, n. 31.

Deut. 4.27-28 and replaced the latter with the former. Based on the large number of agreements between Acts 15.16-17 and the calf story in Acts 7, it can be suggested that this substitution provides us with directions for the interpretation of Amos 9.11-12 in the light of Deut. 4.29-30 in Acts 15.16-17. After all, when he resumes his discussion of Israel's history in Acts 15.16 Luke again quotes from Amos to announce a new period, the restoration of David's tent.

The passage in Deut. 4.29-30 was discussed above. We have established that a new theme is introduced in that particular passage ('And there you will seek [ζητήσετε] the Lord your God') which no longer refers to the prohibition of images. Israel need not live without God forever. God's promise to let himself be found is the answer to Israel's search. The verb 'to seek' (ζητέω) also occurs in the Amos quotation in Acts 15.17 and the object 'the Lord' (τὸν κύριον) is found in the Alexandrian Amos texts.[43] The expression 'to seek the Lord / God' was important to Luke as becomes clear in the Areopagus-speech in Acts 17.27. In that speech Paul states: 'And he [God] made from one every nation of men ... that they should seek (ζητεῖν) God, in the hope that they might feel after him and find him'. As in the Amos quotation in Acts 15.17 these words also refer to non-Jews who seek God.

We explained above that Deut. 4.29-30 is the only place in the Pentateuch where the wording 'seek (ζητήσετε) the Lord' occurs in combination with the reference to 'last days'. Even though this temporal notion is not found in Acts 15.16-17 it can be assumed that Luke was certain he was living in the last days of the present age. In this new era, marked in the Joel quotation by the outpouring of the Spirit 'on all flesh', the mission to the Gentiles was to be conducted and completed.[44] Thus, the fact that the twofold quotation from Amos in Acts 7.42-43 and 15.16-18 substitutes Deut. 4.27-28 and 4.29-31 indicates that these passages are closely linked.

2. *Amos 9.11-12 (LXX) in Acts 15.16-17*

The first quotation from Amos (5.25-27) in Acts 7.42-43 mentions God's punishment for the construction and worship of the calf. In the Book

43. Cf. Steyn, *Septuagint Quotations*, pp. 252–3; Utzschneider, 'Flourishing Bones', p. 288.

44. 'It is generally recognized that Luke was concerned to show the spread of Christianity from its beginnings "in Jerusalem and in all Judea" through the world "to the end of the earth". But it is not so widely recognized that his mission had *eschatological* importance of the highest order, for it was understood that this mission must take place before the end of the age'; cf. R. H. Hiers, 'The Problem of the Delay of the Parousia in Luke–Acts', *NTS* 20 (1974), 145–55, esp. 154. See also E. Kränkl, *Jesus der Knecht Gottes: Die heilsgeschichtliche Stellung Jesu in den Reden der Apostelgeschichte* (Biblische Untersuchungen, 8; Regensburg: Pustet, 1972), pp. 191–2; J. T. Carroll, *Response to the End of History: Eschatology and Situation in Luke–Acts* (SBLDS, 92; Missoula, MT, 1986), pp. 132–5.

of Amos itself these verses occur in a similar context. The punishment in 5.27 results from God's aversion to Israel's cult (5.21-23). His accusations against the feasts, assemblies, offerings and accompanying music are formulated in sharp words ('I hate', 'I reject', 'I will not accept', 'Remove from me'). Announcements of horror and death, as well as additional charges (6.3-6, 8; 8.4-6 etc.), continue in Amos. It seems that Israel's future will be nothing but an ordeal. Moreover, God's dominion extends beyond Israel's borders. His supreme and sovereign power is revealed and as He made himself known to Israel, He will also make himself known to other nations. Amos 9.7 in particular indicates that God's mercy no longer exclusively applies to Israel. The migration of the Philistines from Cappadocia and the Syrians from 'the ditch' are cited as events from the past, comparable to the Exodus of Israel: 'Did I not bring Israel up out of the land of Egypt, and the Philistines from Cappadocia and the Syrians out of the ditch?'

What follows from Amos 9.7 is that Israel's relationship with God creates no self-security or privileges. Its election does not guarantee automatic salvation and God's act in the Exodus does not establish 'Israel in a special status *vis-à-vis* the other nations'.[45] Then, after proclamations of only judgement and doom God speaks of the restoration of the Davidic kingdom in 9.11-12. This is the very oracle of salvation, reflecting the new possibilities for Israel referred to in Deut. 4.29-31 which Luke adopted in his second quotation from Amos in Acts 15.16-17. It is interesting, however, that the LXX translation Luke followed interprets the Hebrew text of Amos 9.12 in a universal perspective of salvation.[46] Out of the promise that Israel would possess the lands of the Gentiles in the Hebrew version, the LXX envisages the conversion of the Gentiles.

The change of the Gentiles' status appears from the following clause in Amos 9.12 LXX: '(and all the Gentiles) upon whom my name is called'. In the Old Testament the divine name is called over a thing (the temple, the ark, Jerusalem) or person(s) (e.g. Israel), indicating the establishment of a relationship of dominion and possession towards God (1 Kgs 8.43; 2 Sam. 6.2; Dan. 9.19; 2 Chron. 7.14; Jer. 14.9 etc.).[47] However, it is striking that Amos 9.12 is the only place where the divine name is called

---

45. See J. L. Mays, *Amos: A Commentary* (OTL; London: SCM Press, 1969), p. 158.

46. The original Hebrew text runs as follows: '"In that day I will raise up the booth of David that is fallen and repair its breaches, and raise up its ruins, and rebuild it as in the days of old; that they may inherit (יירשו) the remnant of Edom (את שארית אדום) and all the nations who are called by my name", says the Lord who does this'. The change of meaning in the LXX rendering of v. 12 is due to two main changes. The translators read יירשו as ידרשו (= 'they will seek') and the object אדם as אָדָם. By omitting את they held שארית אדם to be the subject of the verb and translated it as 'the rest of men'.

47. Cf. H. A. Brongers, 'Die Wendung *bešēm jhwh* im Alten Testament', ZAW 77 (1965), pp. 1–20, esp. 13.

over the Gentile nations.[48] Because Luke reserved the term 'seeking of the Lord' for a form of communion with God that was available for Jews as well as Gentiles in his own time, he replaced Deut. 4.29-30 with Amos 9.11-12. In the Amos quotation Luke refers to God's *oratio directa*, thus suggesting that converted Gentile nations have become a people of God's possession.

However, between the first Amos quotation (punishment of Israel) in Acts 7 and the second (new perspective for the Gentiles) in Acts 15, many chapters are needed to gradually introduce Luke's view that the Gentiles will be saved as Gentiles. Through his accounts in chapters 8 (the actual start of missionary activities aimed at non-Jews), 9 (Paul's call), 10–11 (Cornelius' story), and 13–14 (the extended mission among the Gentiles), Luke shows how in his time, salvation had come within reach of the nations. In order to substantiate this view, he presents Peter and James in Acts 15 as interpreters of events that recently happened to the Gentiles. The realization of the promise in Amos 9.11-12 was guaranteed by the events taking place in his time. The converted Gentiles are accepted as Gentiles in the restored 'tent of David' and will participate in the promises to Israel.

Conclusion

More than Luke's Gospel, the Book of Acts provides evidence that the original contexts of the quotations from the Minor Prophets were thematically and verbally important to Luke. This could be due to the fact that Luke had fewer sources at his disposal when writing his second volume. Apart from the 'we' sections, it is difficult to identify certain sources for Acts. He was in a position to allow himself more literary freedom. He used the LXX as a framework to reinterpret contemporary events and carefully selected the LXX passages. Indeed, this sometimes explains the rationale behind the grouping of Luke's materials from the Minor Prophets.

One of Luke's main preoccupations was to nullify the demarcation between Jewish and Gentile Christians. In his view the basis for an adequate understanding of God's intentions toward Gentiles was found in the Bible, that is, his version of the LXX. Since he regarded the traditional contrast between Israel and the nations as a thing of the past, he set himself the task of writing the continuation of his Gospel story so as to defend the ways of God in the world.

48.   Cf. J. Dupont, 'Un peuple d'entre les nations (Actes 15.14)', *NTS* 31 (1985), 321-35 (324).

Chapter 5

THE MINOR PROPHETS IN JOHN'S GOSPEL

Maarten J. J. Menken

Introduction

In the New Testament period, the twelve Minor Prophets were considered to constitute one biblical book. This is evident from, for instance, Acts and Josephus. The author of Acts indicates the source of a quotation from Amos 5.25-27 as 'the book of the prophets' (7.42), he characterizes Hab. 1.5 as 'what the prophets said' (13.40), and Amos 9.11-12 belongs to 'the words of the prophets' (15.15). To this author, 'the prophets' denotes the Dodecapropheton. In listing the holy books of his people, Josephus (*Ag. Ap.* 1.39-41) speaks of thirteen prophetic books; his count is not completely clear, but it implies in any case that the twelve Minor Prophets are counted as one book.

We may assume that the fourth evangelist also saw the collection of the Minor Prophets as one book, but in his actual use of this book he is selective in that he shows a clear preference for Zechariah, and then especially for the collection of eschatological prophecies in Zechariah 9–14, commonly called Deutero-Zechariah. These chapters, often rather obscure, have drawn much interest in early Christianity, especially in connection with Jesus' passion and death.[1] John's Gospel contains two marked[2] quotations from the Minor Prophets, and both are from Deutero-Zechariah (Zech. 9.9 in Jn 12.15, and Zech. 12.10 in Jn 19.37). Besides, there are two marked Old Testament quotations in John in which words from one of the Minor Prophets constitute, so to speak, a secondary element: they have ended up in a quotation from another Old Testament source, either as an addition or as a replacement. This

---

1. See C. H. Dodd, *According to the Scriptures: The Sub-Structure of New Testament Theology* (London: Nisbet, 1952), pp. 64–7; D.C. Allison, *Scriptural Allusions in the New Testament: Light from the Dead Sea Scrolls* (The Dead Sea Scrolls & Christian Origins Library, 5; North Richland Hills, TX: Bibal, 2000), pp. 57–64.

2. That is, introduced or concluded by a formula that makes clear that the words in question come from Scripture.

has happened with Zech. 14.8 in Jn 7.38, and with Zeph. 3.16 in Jn 12.15. In the former case, we have again evidence of John's preference for Deutero-Zechariah.

John's allusions to the Minor Prophets are less easily established than his quotations. I have taken as my starting point the data in the lists of allusions in NA[27] and UBS[4], and have tried to sort these materials out in a critical way. Many of the presumed allusions then drop out because there is no specific verbal or conceptual link between allusion and Old Testament source. In these cases, there is often a link to an Old Testament *theme*, found in a range of Old Testament texts, but not to an individual Old Testament *passage*.[3] The allusions, which to my mind should be retained,[4] are as follows: to Mal. 3.23 (ET 4.5) in Jn 1.21, to Zeph. 3.13 in Jn 1.47, to Zech. 14.21 in Jn 2.16, to Mal. 3.1 in Jn 3.28, to Mic. 5.1 in Jn 7.42, to Mal. 2.10 in Jn 8.41, to Zech. 1.5 in Jn 8.52, to Jonah 1.12-15 in Jn 11.50, and finally to Zech. 13.7 in Jn 16.32. Among these nine allusions, three are to verses from Zechariah, and two from these three concern Deutero-Zechariah.

I shall start with a discussion of the textual form and the meaning of the two marked quotations from Zechariah in John. The two instances of secondary influence of a Minor Prophets passage on a quotation have to be discussed next; as one of these concerns influence on Zech. 9.9 in Jn 12.15, it is more logical and more convenient to incorporate it into the treatment of the quotation as a whole. Finally, I shall give attention to John's allusions to passages from the Dodecapropheton.

Quotations

Zech. 9.9 in Jn 12.15

According to John's story of the entry into Jerusalem (Jn 12.12-19), the crowd that has set out to meet Jesus welcomes him with the words of Ps. 118.25-26. Jesus then finds a donkey and sits down on it, and the evangelist considers this action as agreeing with the scriptural word:

---

3.   The same criticism applies to the references to the Minor Prophets offered in addition to those in NA[27] and UBS[4] by H. Hübner, *Vetus Testamentum in Novo 1,2: Evangelium secundum Johannem* (Göttingen: Vandenhoeck & Ruprecht, 2003). Hübner's collection of Old Testament materials is extremely useful, but the user should distinguish between quotations, allusions and thematic parallels.

4.   Debate, of course, always remains possible. For criteria to discern the presence of allusions, see R. B. Hays, '"Who Has Believed Our Message?" Paul's Reading of Isaiah', in idem, *The Conversion of the Imagination: Paul as Interpreter of Israel's Scripture* (Grand Rapids: Eerdmans, 2006), pp. 25–49, esp. 34–45. At least in John, NA[27] accepts many more allusions to the Minor Prophets than UBS[4].

Do not be afraid, daughter Zion.[5]
Look, your king is coming,
sitting on a donkey's colt! (12.15)[6]

The NRSV translation of Zech. 9.9 reads in slightly adapted form:

Rejoice greatly, daughter Zion,
Shout aloud, daughter Jerusalem.
Look, your king is coming to you;
triumphant and victorious is he,
humble and riding on a donkey,
on a colt, the foal of a donkey!

The Greek translation of Zech. 9.9 in Jn 12.15 differs at several points from the other versions that we know:

(a) John offers an abbreviated text. The second appeal, addressed to 'daughter Jerusalem' and parallel to the first appeal to 'daughter Zion', is missing. Of the four characteristics of the coming king, only one remains: that he is riding on a donkey. At the end, only one of the two parallel indications of the mount has been retained.

---

5.   The NRSV wrongly translates 'daughter of Zion' for 'Zion' is the name of the daughter, not of her parent. The NRSV translation of Zech. 9.9, on the other hand, is correct, with 'daughter Zion' and 'daughter Jerusalem'.

6.   On this quotation, see M. J. J. Menken, *Old Testament Quotations in the Fourth Gospel: Studies in Textual Form* (CBET, 15; Kampen: Kok Pharos, 1996), pp. 79–97 (with references to earlier literature); A. Obermann, *Die christologische Erfüllung der Schrift im Johannesevangelium: Eine Untersuchung zur johanneischen Hermeneutik anhand der Schriftzitate* (WUNT, 2/83; Tübingen: Mohr Siebeck, 1996), pp. 203–15; A. J. Köstenberger, 'John', in G. K. Beale and D. A. Carson (eds), *Commentary on the New Testament Use of the Old Testament* (Grand Rapids: Baker; Nottingham: Apollos, 2007), pp. 415–512, esp. 472–4. On John's use and evaluation of Scripture in general, see J. Beutler, 'The Use of "Scripture" in the Gospel of John', in R. A. Culpepper and C. C. Black (eds), *Exploring the Gospel of John* (FS D. M. Smith; Louisville, KY: Westminster John Knox, 1996), pp. 147–62; M. J. J. Menken, 'Observations on the Significance of the Old Testament in the Fourth Gospel', *Neot* 33 (1999), 125–43; K. Scholtissek, '"Die unauflösbare Schrift" (Joh 10,35): Zur Auslegung und Theologie der Schrift Israels im Johannesevangelium', in T. Söding (ed.), *Johannesevangelium – Mitte oder Rand des Kanons? Neue Standortbestimmungen* (Quaestiones Disputatae, 203; Freiburg: Herder, 2003), pp. 146–77; J. Clark-Soles, *Scripture Cannot Be Broken: The Social Function of the Use of Scripture in the Fourth Gospel* (Leiden: Brill, 2003); H.-J. Klauck, 'Geschrieben, erfüllt, vollendet: Die Schriftzitate in der Johannespassion', in M. Labahn, K. Scholtissek and A. Strotmann (eds), *Israel und seine Heilstraditionen im Johannesevangelium* (FS J. Beutler; Paderborn: Schöningh, 2004), pp. 140–57; M. Labahn, 'Jesus und die Autorität der Schrift im Johannesevangelium: Überlegungen zu einem spannungsreichem Verhältnis', in Labahn *et al.* (eds), *Israel und seine Heilstraditionen*, pp. 185–206; S. E. Witmer, 'Approaches to Scripture in the Fourth Gospel and the Qumran *Pesharim*', *NovT* 48 (2006), 313–28.

(b) The appeal addressed to daughter Zion, 'rejoice greatly', has become 'do not be afraid'.

(c) In the second line, 'to you' has been omitted.

(d) In the third line, 'riding' has been changed into 'sitting'.

(e) The final words of the verse ('a donkey's colt') do not agree precisely with either of the two descriptions of the mount in the Hebrew text or in any of the known Greek versions.

How do we explain this peculiar textual form of Zech. 9.9? Does it come from the LXX or from another version? Did John copy or edit it together with an existing form of the entry story, or did he create it himself? What does it mean?

Apart from the omissions and the changes, John's text of Zech. 9.9 agrees with the LXX, but this fact is not very telling, because the Greek translation is correct and obvious. John normally makes use of the LXX, and he will probably have done so here as well.

It is evident that the evangelist made use of traditional materials for his entry story: Jn 12.12-14 contains relatively few characteristics of Johannine style, and it has a parallel in the Synoptic Gospels (Mk 11.1-10 par.). The link between the entry story and Zech. 9.9 existed before John: Matthew has the same quotation in his entry story, although in another form and at another place in the narrative (Mt. 21.5), and Mark's entry story was already influenced by the verse from Zechariah (see Mk 11.2).[7]

It is also evident that the quotation in John has been abbreviated, both to adapt it to its present context (only the arrival of Jesus as king and his sitting on a donkey have been retained) and to eliminate the parallelisms at beginning and end. Comparable abbreviations, especially the suppression of parallelism, occur in nearly all other Old Testament quotations in John. The formula that introduces the quotation (καθώς ἐστιν γεγραμμένον, 'as it is written') looks Johannine (see esp. Jn 6.31; further 2.17; 6.45; 10.34), and the ensuing vv. 16–18 are, for reasons of grammar and content, almost certainly editorial.

All this suggests that John edited an existing entry story; either this story contained a quotation from Zech. 9.9, or the evangelist, knowing about the traditional link between Jesus' entry into Jerusalem and Zech. 9.9, added the quotation. The moot point remains the explanation of the changes introduced into the quotation (items b–d of the above list). How do we explain them?

---

7. To my mind, it is not very probable that John here directly depends on one of the Synoptic Gospels: there are substantial differences between the synoptic and the Johannine story, and the quotations from Zech. 9.9 in Matthew and John agree only where both agree with the LXX.

Why is, in John's text, 'daughter Zion' incited 'not to be afraid' instead of 'to rejoice greatly'? Among the Old Testament passages in which Israel or Jerusalem is addressed with 'do not be afraid', Isa. 40.9-11 and Zeph. 3.14-17 can easily be considered as analogous to Zech. 9.9 in the technical sense, that is, as having at least one word in common with Zech. 9.9 and having a similar content. Both passages concern the arrival of God, while Zech. 9.9 concerns the arrival of God's agent. Both passages share several words with Zech. 9.9, for instance, 'Zion' and 'Jerusalem'; in the LXX, Zeph. 3.14 and Zech. 9.9 even begin in exactly the same way ('rejoice greatly, daughter Zion, proclaim, daughter Jerusalem').[8] Because an analogous passage could be used not only for the exegesis but also for the rendering of the text with which it is analogous, as a substitute or as an addition, the words 'do not be afraid' in Jn 12.15 may come from either Isa. 40.9 or Zeph. 3.16.[9] A choice between the two verses is hardly possible, nor is it necessary. In favour of Zeph. 3.14 is the circumstance that the title 'the king of Israel' occurs in both Zeph. 3.15 and Jn 12.13; in favour of Isa. 40.9 is the importance of Isa. 40.1-11 in early Christianity.

So far, we have established that it was permitted to change 'rejoice greatly' into 'do not be afraid'; but what was the motive for the change? As far as I can see, a decisive motive can only be found at the level of Johannine redaction. In John, the entry narrative is closely linked to the sign of the raising of Lazarus (Jn 11.1-44). On the day before the entry (cf. 12.12) many people have come to the house of Lazarus and his sisters to see Jesus and Lazarus (12.9); now a large crowd, having heard about the raising of Lazarus (12.17-18), sets out to welcome him. So the acclamation of the crowd in 12.13 functions as the crowd's answer to the raising of Lazarus: because of this great sign they proclaim Jesus as 'the one who comes in the name of the Lord', 'the King of Israel'. John considers the raising of Lazarus as an impressive manifestation of God's power in Jesus (see 11.4, 40–42). Such a miracle may be expected to arouse fear in the audience who do not understand him, or only partly understand him (see, e.g., Mk 4.41 // Lk. 8.25; Mk 5.15 // Lk. 8.35; Lk. 7.16), so that the appeal 'do not be afraid' is fitting in such a context (see Mk 6.49-50 // Mt. 14.26-27; Mt. 17.6-7; 28.4-5; Lk. 5.9-10; Jn 6.19-20). In John, the crowd misunderstand Jesus, who has just raised Lazarus from the grave, by considering him to be a national king; this is evident from their use of palm branches, which had a nationalistic connotation since the Maccabean revolt (1 Macc. 13.51), and from the words εἰς ὑπάντησιν αὐτῷ, 'to meet him', which suggest

---

8. This agreement may also be the result of connection of analogous scriptural passages.

9. In the latter instance, it cannot come from the LXX, which has θάρσει, 'take courage'.

the welcoming of a king.[10] Jesus, on the other hand, mounts a donkey, to show that he is the peaceful king of Zech. 9.9-10 (for a comparable sequence, see Jn 6.14-15). The crowd misunderstand Jesus as a national king who does things that inspire fear; hence the change from 'rejoice greatly' into 'do not be afraid' in the quotation.

The explanation for the omission of 'to you' in the second line of John's quotation may also have been provided by analogous Old Testament passages. In Isa. 40.9-11, already taken into consideration in connection with the first line, it is said of God that he 'is coming' (v. 10; יבוא in MT, ἔρχεται in LXX, just as in Zech. 9.9), but it is not said to whom God is coming. Another relevant passage is Gen. 49.10-11, a part of Jacob's blessing. Already in pre-Christian Judaism, the mysterious *Shiloh* who is said to 'come' (v. 10; יבא in MT, ἔλθῃ in LXX) was interpreted as a Messianic figure.[11] So there is agreement of content between Gen. 49.10-11, read in a Messianic sense, and Zech. 9.9. Besides, the two passages have words in common: not only the verb 'to come', but also in the various indications of the mount of the Messianic figure (the end of Zech. 9.9 is about 'the foal of a donkey', in the MT עיר בן-אתנות, in the LXX πῶλον νέον; the beginning of Gen. 49.11 is about 'his foal' and 'his donkey's colt', in the MT עירה ... בני אתנו, in the LXX τὸν πῶλον αὐτοῦ ... τὸν πῶλον τῆς ὄνου αὐτοῦ).[12] I conclude that the verb 'coming', used absolutely, may well derive from either Isa. 40.10 or Gen. 49.10.

A cogent motive for the omission of 'to you' can again be found at the level of Johannine redaction. Throughout his gospel, John emphasizes that Jesus came from God into this world (see, e.g., 6.38; 17.8). Part of his terminology to convey this idea is the verb ἔρχεσθαι, 'to come' (see, e.g., 3.31; 8.14; 9.39; 11.27; 15.22; 18.37). Insofar as the destination of Jesus' coming is indicated, it is almost always 'the world' or 'this world' (1.9; 3.19; 6.14; 9.39; 11.27; 12.46; 16.28; 18.37; the only exception is 1.11). Against this background, we can assume that the evangelist has omitted 'to you' from the quotation because it could suggest that Jesus' coming would have been limited to 'daughter Zion'. Moreover, 'to you' in Zech. 9.9 has the connotation of a *dativus commodi*: the king comes 'to you' as well as 'in favour of you'. In the view of the fourth evangelist, Jesus has come to the world to save it insofar as it believes (cf. 3.16-17; 4.42; 6.33, 51; 12.47). His coming to the world starts with his coming 'to his own' (1.11), but at the stage of the development of John's plot

---

10.   See Josephus, *War* 7.100; *Ant.* 11.327, 329; 7.263.

11.   See Gen. 49.10 LXX; 4QpGen^a V 3–4.

12.   The connection between Zech. 9.9 and Gen. 49.10-11 is regularly made in early Jewish and early Christian literature; see Menken, *OT Quotations*, p. 89. On account of the verb 'to come', Ps. 118.26 ('Blessed is the one who comes in the name of the Lord'), quoted without marking in Jn 12.13, can also be considered to be analogous to Zech. 9.9; however, the verbal analogy with Isa. 40.10 or Gen. 49.10 is decidedly stronger.

where we meet the entry narrative, many of his people have already rejected Jesus, and in the context of the entry narrative, the evangelist draws attention to Jesus' universal significance (see 11.52; 12.19, 20, 32). At the same time, 'your king' in the quotation shows that in John's view, Jesus is and remains 'the King of Israel'. The omission of 'to you' is then best understood as an editorial change by the evangelist, to show the universal significance of Jesus' coming as king.

The next change to be discussed is that of 'riding' into 'sitting' in the final line. The rendering of the Hebrew verb רכב, 'to ride', by the Greek verb καθῆσθαι, 'to sit', is unusual. It was probably preferred here to draw attention to Jesus' royal dignity: the Greek verb is often used of royal throning (as in Mk 10.37 par., 40 par.; Acts 12.21; 2 Thess. 2.4; Rev. 3.21). More specifically, 1 Kgs (3 Kgdms) 1, the first part of the narrative of Solomon's accession to the throne, may have been influential. In this story, Solomon's sitting on David's mule functions as an anticipation of his sitting on David's throne. It is therefore not surprising that in the LXX version, we meet several occurrences of καθῆσθαι ἐπὶ τοῦ θρόνου or something similar ('to sit on the throne', vv. 13, 17, 20, 24, 27, 30, 35, 46, 48), and that רכב hiphil ('to cause to ride') is twice rendered with ἐπικαθίζειν, 'to seat' (vv. 38, 44). The parallels between 1 Kings 1 and the entry narrative are obvious: royal acclamation by a crowd in Jerusalem, riding as a king on a mule or a donkey, anxiety among the opponents. So it may be justified to ascribe the change of 'riding' into 'sitting' to the influence of 1 Kings 1. It is hard to decide at which literary level the change took place: on the one hand, the pre-Johannine entry story already depicted Jesus as king; on the other the fourth evangelist has an evident interest in Jesus' kingship (see 1.49; 6.15; 12.13; 18.33-19.22).

The words πῶλον ὄνου, 'a donkey's colt', at the end of the quotation deviate from the descriptions of the mount as we find them in the Hebrew text or in any of the known Greek versions. In the LXX version of Gen. 49.11, a verse which we already observed to be analogous to Zech. 9.9, we read τὸν πῶλον τῆς ὄνου αὐτοῦ, 'his donkey's colt'; it is the only place in the LXX where πῶλος ὄνου is used. So πῶλον ὄνου in Jn 12.15 very probably derives from Gen. 49.11 LXX; it serves to relate Zech. 9.9 and Gen. 49.10-11. The change can have taken place at either the pre-Johannine or the Johannine level.

I conclude that the peculiar form which Zech. 9.9 has taken in Jn 12.15 is largely due to the fourth evangelist, that he probably worked with a LXX text, and that he uses it to emphasize that Jesus comes as a peaceful king for the benefit of the world.

Zech. 12.10 in Jn 19.37

The fourth evangelist connects the piercing of Jesus' side after his death by a Roman soldier (19.34) with a clause from Zech. 12.10: ὄψονται εἰς ὃν ἐξεκέντησαν, 'They will look on the one whom they have pierced' (19.37).[13] The MT of this clause reads: וְהִבִּיטוּ אֵלַי אֵת אֲשֶׁר־דָּקָרוּ; in a literal English translation: 'And they will look on me whom they have pierced'. The LXX is very different: καὶ ἐπιβλέψονται πρός με ἀνθ᾽ ὧν κατωρχήσαντο, 'They will look on me because they have danced'.

It is immediately evident that we meet here a problem of textual form. An important observation to be made is that the textual form of John's quotation returns, with remarkable constancy, in the numerous other early Christian quotations from or allusions to this part of Zech. 12.10. The marked quotations in Justin, *1 Apol.* 52.12; *Dial.* 14.8; 32.2; the unmarked quotations in Rev. 1.7;[14] Justin, *Dial.* 64.7; 118.1, and the allusions in Mt. 24.30; *Barn.* 7.9, all offer, or are based on, the textual form that we find in John, with ὁρᾶν, 'to look', in the future (or with μέλλειν), with ἐκκεντεῖν, 'to pierce', and with avoidance of the grammatical obscurity of the Hebrew text (see below). As there is no convincing reason to assume that any of the authors of the writings just mentioned was directly dependent on any other of them in making use of this clause from Zech. 12.10, we have to suppose that it was current in early Christian circles in the textual form given in Jn 19.37, mainly as a testimony to Christ's second coming.

The clause in question has, in the Masoretic vocalization, either a double object ('me' and 'whom they have pierced') or an oddly construed relative clause (with the *nota accusativi* אֵת apparently at the wrong place[15]). In both cases, the Hebrew text remains rather obscure, and certainly in the second case it seems to contain a strong anthropomorphism: God is pierced. No wonder that several ancient translators tried to solve these problems, and especially to circumvent the anthropomorphism; to these belongs the LXX translator, who, by means of the exegetical device of letter transposition, read רִקְּדוּ,

---

13. See Menken, *OT Quotations*, pp. 167–85 (with references to earlier literature); Obermann, *Christologische Erfüllung*, pp. 310–25; M. C. Albl, 'And Scripture Cannot Be Broken': The Form and Function of the Early Christian Testimonia Collections (NovTSup, 96; Leiden: Brill, 1999), pp. 253–65; C. M. Tuckett, 'Zechariah 12:10 and the New Testament', in C. Tuckett (ed.), *The Book of Zechariah and its Influence* (Aldershot: Ashgate, 2003), pp. 111–22; Köstenberger, 'John', pp. 504–6.

14. See M. J. J. Menken, 'John's Use of Scripture in Revelation 1:7', *In die Skriflig* 41 (2007), 281–93.

15. One would expect אֲשֶׁר דָּקְרוּ אֹתִי. The construction also occurs in Gen. 31.32; Num. 22.6; Isa. 65.12; see P. Joüon and T. Muraoka, *A Grammar of Biblical Hebrew* (SubBi, 14; Rome: Biblical Institute Press, 1991), §158m, where more examples are given.

'they have pierced', as רקדו, 'they have danced'. All these translations presuppose a consonantal text and a vocalization like those of the MT.

The early Christian Greek translation of the clause from Zech. 12.10 is also based on this Hebrew text. The problem of the anthropomorphism has now been solved by eliminating the 'I' of God from the text: it seems that the translator has read, in the manner of a *pesher*, אלי not as אֵלַי, 'on me', but as אֱלִי, a poetic form of the preposition אֶל, 'on'.[16] He has further rendered the verb נבט hiphil, 'to look', not by ἐπιβλέπειν, as the other Greek translators did, but by ὁρᾶν. This is a somewhat weak translation (ὁρᾶν is usually translated as 'to see') but an acceptable and precedented one.[17] To my mind, it was preferred because early Christians predominantly interpreted the clause from Zech. 12.10 in an eschatological sense (people will look on the pierced Christ at his second coming) and ὁρᾶν was in use in early Christian literature for witnessing the *parousia* of Christ, or God, or the kingdom, at the eschaton (see, e.g., Mk 13.26 par.; Heb. 12.14; 1 Jn 3.2). Finally, the early Christian translation uses the Greek verb ἐκκεντεῖν, 'to pierce', for the Hebrew verb דקר. The Greek verb is a natural equivalent of the Hebrew one.[18]

I conclude that John's quotation from Zech. 12.10 represents an independent early Christian translation into Greek of the Hebrew text. The translation and its use as a Christological testimony must date back to a relatively early stage: it is used in a series of (at least on this point) mutually independent writings (among them Matthew, John, Revelation), and its Christological potential (the identification of Christ and God) is not yet exploited.

What does the quotation mean in its Johannine context? It follows another scriptural quotation: 'None of his bones shall be broken' (19.36). This is a combination of words from Ps. 34.21 and the prohibition not to break a bone of the paschal lamb of Exod. 12.10 (LXX); 12.46; Num. 9.12. It interprets the fact that the Roman soldiers did not break Jesus' legs (19.33); the quotation from Zech. 12.10 interprets the piercing of his side (19.34). The first quotation is introduced by the words, 'These things occurred so that the scripture might be fulfilled'; the second one by, 'And again another passage of scripture says'. So the first quotation is an unambiguous fulfilment quotation: the scriptural word has become reality in the fact that Jesus'

16.   See Job 3.22; 5.26; 15.22; 29.19.
17.   See LXX Num. 12.8; Job 6.19; Isa. 38.11; also Symmachus' translation of 1 Sam. 2.32.
18.   Aquila and Theodotion have it in their translations of Zech. 12.10; Symmachus has ἐπεκκεντεῖν. See further, e.g., LXX Judg. 9.54; 1 Chron. 10.4; Lam. 4.9.

legs were not broken. The second quotation seems to be subsumed under the fulfilment formula of 19.37, but at the same time it has its own introductory formula, without the verb 'to fulfil',[19] and this circumstance leaves open the possibility that the evangelist wants to say more than just emphasize that Zechariah's prophecy was realized in the piercing of Jesus' side by a Roman soldier (and indirectly also by those who commissioned him, 19.31).

Reading the quotation as a fulfilment quotation in the strict sense becomes problematic when we try to establish whom John considers to be the subject of the main clause; in John's narrative, nobody is explicitly said to look on the pierced Jesus.[20] One could think of the soldier who pierced Jesus' side, but that is not the only possibility: although in Zech. 12.10 those who will look and those who have pierced are the same, a first-century interpreter could easily distinguish between the two. Within the immediate context of the quotation, the eyewitness of 19.35 may be one who looks on the pierced Jesus (see below). We should not take, however, the 'looking on the pierced one' of which the quotation speaks, in a too narrowly literal sense; a very limited number of people actually saw Jesus hanging on the cross. We can and should read the quotation not only from the perspective of fulfilment in the strict sense but also from the perspective of fulfilment in the message of John's Gospel as a whole. This means that we have to ask whether other passages from John can be helpful in determining the subject, the precise object, the character, and the point in time of the 'looking' in 19.37.

A passage that almost immediately comes to mind is 3.14-15 (with parallels in 8.28 and 12.32): whoever believes, has eternal life in the Son of Man, lifted up on the cross (see 12.33) as the serpent was lifted up by Moses in the wilderness (see Num. 21.8-9). The link between the Zechariah quotation and 3.14-15 becomes still clearer when one realizes that the 'seeing' of the serpent from Numbers is paralleled in Jn 3.15 by 'believing'. The quotation can then be said to mean that people will look on the pierced Jesus, and that they should look with faith, toward their salvation. This explanation concurs with John's use of verbs of seeing for seeing Jesus with faith (6.40; 12.45; 14.9) or with unbelief (6.36; 15.24).

We can take a further step and interpret the looking on the pierced one on the basis of John's ideas on Jesus' resurrection. The positive reaction,

19.   For a similar sequence of Old Testament quotations, see Jn 12.37-40.

20.   That the only point of the quotation would be the fulfilment of the piercing announced by Zechariah is not very probable in view of the circumstance that John usually omits from his Old Testament quotations the elements he cannot use; see the discussion of Jn 12.15 above, and as the most telling example the extremely brief quotation from Ps. 69.5 (or 35.19) in Jn 15.25.

the 'looking on whom they have pierced' at which the evangelist aims, consists in seeing in the crucified Jesus the risen Lord, and vice versa. Only believers can see the risen Lord, 'the world' cannot (14.18-24; cf. 16.16-19), and the risen Lord who appears to his followers bears the marks of his crucifixion (20.20, 25, 27). So we can say that the quotation of 19.37 comes true in the appearance stories of John 20; one should especially notice that in ch. 20, the verb ὁρᾶν from the quotation is said of seeing the risen Jesus (vv. 18, 20, 25, 29). This Jesus says to Thomas: 'You have believed because you have seen me; blessed are those who have not seen, and believe' (20.29).[21] The macarism concerns the later generations, who did not physically see the risen Lord as the disciples saw him but who can only believe on the basis of their testimony. As believers who 'see' the risen Lord in the preaching of the church, they belong to those who 'will look on the one whom they have pierced'. We can consider the eyewitness mentioned in 19.35, 'who saw this [i.e., the events narrated in v. 34]' (ὁ ἑωρακώς) and who apparently also believed (his true testimony should lead to the belief of others), as the first person who 'looks on the one whom they have pierced'. He represents all believers, and his looking on the pierced Jesus is a representative fulfilment of Zechariah's prophecy.[22]

John seems to be an exception among early Christian interpreters of Zech. 12.10 in that he does not apply the prophecy to Christ's second coming but to his death and resurrection. However, within John's present eschatology, traditions that originally concerned Christ's *parousia* are applied to his resurrection (see, e.g., Jn 14.18; 16.16-22). The evangelist reinterpreted the traditional interpretation of Zech. 12.10: the future looking on the pierced one takes place when people look in faith on the crucified Jesus as the risen Lord.

Zech. 14.8 in Jn 7.38

According to Jn 7.37-38, Jesus invites on the last and greatest day of the Festival of Tabernacles the thirsty to come to him and drink, that is, to believe in him. He substantiates his invitation with a scriptural word: 'Rivers of living water shall flow from his inside' (v. 38).[23] This Old Testament quotation is problematic because the referent of 'his' in the quotation is uncertain (is it Jesus or the believer?), and because the

21. Here, I depart from the NRSV. Reading the first clause as a question ('Have you believed because you have seen me?') makes it a reproach, which it cannot possibly be in its context.

22. He is probably the beloved disciple (see 19.26-27), who functions in John as the ideal believer (also 13.21-30; 20.2-10; ch. 21).

23. The NRSV is not literal enough for my purposes here.

Old Testament source of the quotation is uncertain.[24] Within the limits of this essay, a thorough discussion of these problems is not possible. To my mind, it is best to consider Jesus to be the referent of 'his': in Johannine theology, Jesus is the one who gives life (or the Spirit, see v. 39), not the believer. The most probable source of the quotation is, in my view, Ps. 77(78).16, 20 LXX: no other Old Testament passage has more key words and themes in common with the quotation, and John quotes from v. 24 of the same psalm in 6.31. By means of the quotation, the Johannine Jesus presents himself as the true, eschatological rock from which water will flow. It is not coincidental that the evangelist makes Jesus do so on the final day of the Festival of Tabernacles: the water libation in the temple practised during this feast was associated with both the promise of water flowing from the temple and the past event of water flowing from the rock.[25]

However, Ps. 77(78).16, 20 LXX is not the only source of the quotation, because it leaves some elements of it unexplained. One of these elements is the epithet 'living' (ζῶν), said about 'water' (ὕδωρ). In the Old Testament, we find 'living water' (MT: מים חיים; LXX: ὕδωρ ζῶν) a few times in contexts that have some similarity to our Johannine passage (Cant. 4.15; Zech. 14.8; Jer. 2.13 l.v.). For several reasons, Zech. 14.8 (in a literal translation: 'And on that day living water shall go out of Jerusalem') best explains the final words of the quotation in Jn 7.38.[26] First, John considers Jesus' body to be the place of God's presence, the true temple (1.14, 51; 2.19-21; 4.21-24); by consequence, the Johannine Jesus can apply a prophecy on the eschatological living water from Jerusalem to himself. Second, Zech. 14.8 is analogous (in the technical sense) to Ps. 78.16, on account of identical words ('water',

---

24.   Many scholars relate the problem of the referent of 'his' to that of the punctuation of 7.37b-38: should one read a stop before or after ὁ πιστεύων εἰς ἐμέ, 'the one who believes in me'? However, these two questions are not necessarily connected, and I shall leave the punctuation problem aside. For a discussion of the various problems connected with Jn 7.38, see G. Balfour, 'The Jewishness of John's Use of the Scriptures in John 6:31 and 7:37-38', *TynBul* 46 (1995), 357–80, esp. 368–79; Menken, *OT Quotations*, pp. 187–203 (with references to earlier literature); J. Marcus, '"Rivers of Living Water" from Jesus' Belly (John 7:38)', *JBL* 117 (1998), 328–30; M. Daly-Denton, *David in the Fourth Gospel: The Johannine Reception of the Psalms* (AGJU, 47; Leiden: Brill, 2000), pp. 144–61; G. T. Manning, *Echoes of a Prophet: The Use of Ezekiel in the Gospel of John and in Literature of the Second Temple Period* (JSNTSup, 270; London: T&T Clark, 2004), pp. 172–86. Recent contributions to the punctuation debate and to the search for the scriptural background of Jn 7.37b-38a are M. A. Daise, '"If anyone thirsts, let that one come to me and drink": The Literary Texture of John 7:37b-38a', *JBL* 122 (2003), 687–99, and A. Pinto da Silva, 'Ancora Giovanni 7,37-39', *Salesianum* 66 (2004), 13–30.

25.   See *t. Sukkah* 3.3-18, where one meets within one context quotations from Ezek. 47.1-10; Zech. 14.8; 13.1; Num. 21.17-20; Ps. 78.20; 105.41; Zech. 14.17-18.

26.   Balfour, 'Jewishness', pp. 373–79, even considers Zech. 14.8 to be the primary source of the quotation.

'to go out') and identical subject matter. Third, Zech. 14.8 is connected with the Festival of Tabernacles, the occasion at which Jesus applies the quotation to himself. The verse is part of a vision of the future that reaches its climax in the remnant of the nations coming to Jerusalem to celebrate this feast (Zech. 14.16), and it is used in the interpretation of the water libation during the feast in *t. Sukkah* 3.8 (see above).[27] Finally, John's evident interest in Zechariah 9–14 makes a reference to a verse from these chapters plausible.

The addition of the word 'living' to the quotation in Jn 7.38 draws attention to Jesus as being life and giving life. These are obvious theological themes throughout the Fourth Gospel (see, e.g., 5.19-30; 6.27-58; 11.25; 14.6). Jesus partakes in God's own life (5.26; 6.57), and therefore he is able to mediate God's life to believers. In the first part of Jesus' dialogue with the Samaritan woman (4.7-15), Jesus has already been presented as one who is able to give 'living water', in the sense of water that gives eternal life (v. 14). The quotation resumes this topic, and announces the water flowing from the pierced side of the dead Jesus according to Jn 19.34. This water is probably best interpreted as symbolizing the salvation realized in Jesus' death, especially the gift of the Spirit (see 7.39).

Allusions

Mal. 3.23 (ET 4.5) in Jn 1.21, and Mal. 3.1 in Jn 3.28

One of the questions that envoys from Jerusalem ask John the Baptist about his role in salvation history is: 'Are you Elijah?' (Jn 1.21). This question alludes to Mal. 3.23 (4.5): 'Lo, I will send you the prophet Elijah before the great and terrible day of the Lord comes'. From this prophetic word derives the expectation of the eschatological return of Elijah (see Sir. 48.10). In the Synoptic Gospels, John the Baptist is identified with Elijah (see Mk 9.11-13 par.; Mt. 11.14; Lk. 1.17); the fourth evangelist makes him deny that he is Elijah. The evangelist does not go directly back to Malachi, but makes use of the early Christian view of the Baptist as we find it in the synoptic tradition.

He does so again in 3.28, when he has John the Baptist say on his relation to Jesus: 'I have been sent ahead of him' (ἀπεσταλμένος εἰμὶ ἔμπροσθεν ἐκείνου). Here, he alludes to the divine oracle of Mal. 3.1: 'I am sending my messenger ... before me' (LXX: ἐγὼ ἐξαποστέλλω τὸν ἄγγελόν μου ... πρὸ προσώπου μου); this messenger is subsequently, in

---

27. This use of Zech. 14.8 may well go back to the end of the first century CE: in *m. Sheqal.* 6.3, *m. Mid.* 2.6 and *t. Sukkah* 3.3, the interpretation of the libation by means of Ezek. 47.1-2 is ascribed to R. Eliezer b. Jacob, a first-generation Tanna.

Mal. 3.23, identified as Elijah. In the synoptic tradition John the Baptist, the returned Elijah, is this messenger, as is shown by marked quotations from Mal. 3.1 (combined with the analogous verse Exod. 23.20) in Mk 1.2; Mt. 11.10 par. In Jn 3.28, the same tradition has been used.

The strange thing is that in the Fourth Gospel, John the Baptist explicitly denies that he is Elijah (1.21), but implicitly seems to admit it (3.28). Identification of John the Baptist with Elijah would make him into the precursor of Jesus, whereas the evangelist sees John the Baptist as a witness contemporaneous with Jesus (see esp. 1.29-37; 3.23-30). At the same time, the evangelist has to acknowledge the historical priority of John the Baptist, whose ministry began earlier than that of Jesus; in 3.28, he does so in terms derived from Mal. 3.1. However, whenever the evangelist acknowledges the historical priority of the Baptist, he emphasizes in the same context his meta-historical inferiority over against Jesus (see 1.15, 27, 30; 3.28, 31–32).[28]

Zeph. 3.13 in Jn 1.47

In Jn 1.47, Jesus characterizes Nathanael as 'truly an Israelite in whom there is no deceit (δόλος)'. That in a pious person there is no deceit is said more than once in the Old Testament, especially in Psalms (see Ps. 15.3; 17.1; 32.2; 34.14; 120.2; Isa. 53.9; Zeph. 3.13). In all these instances, the LXX has δόλος or a derivative of it. What makes Zeph. 3.13 unique among them is that here the theme of 'no deceit' is combined with the name 'Israel': 'the remnant of Israel ... nor shall a deceitful tongue be found in their mouths'. The presence of the same combination in Jn 1.47 makes it legitimate to see here an allusion to Zeph. 3.13. Nathanael represents 'the remnant of Israel'; more generally, Jesus' disciples constitute the nucleus of the eschatological Israel, of which Jesus is king (see 1.31, 47; 12.13).

Zech. 14.21 in Jn 2.16[29]

According to Jn 2.14-16, Jesus drives traders and their merchandise out of the temple, and says on that occasion: 'Take these things out of here! Stop making my Father's house a market-place!' (2.16). The incident in itself, and certainly Jesus' words, make one think of the end of the Book of Zechariah. It is said there, in the context of the description of the eschatological Festival of Tabernacles (see above, on Jn 7.38): 'And there

---

28. See further Menken, *OT Quotations*, pp. 28–35.
29. See A. T. Hanson, *The Prophetic Gospel: A Study of John and the Old Testament* (Edinburgh: T&T Clark, 1991), pp. 44–5.

shall no longer be traders in the house of the Lord of hosts on that day' (Zech. 14.21). By declaring, in both word and deed, temple and trade incompatible, the Johannine Jesus fulfils Deutero-Zechariah's prophecy, and implicitly qualifies his own ministry as the arrival of the eschaton. The allusion is not based on the LXX, which translates כנעני, 'trader', as Χαναναῖος, 'Canaanite'. The connection between the cleansing of the temple and Zech. 14.8 did not originate with John but must have been made earlier, because it is also found, albeit less pronounced, in the Synoptic Gospels (Mk 11.15-17 par.).

Mic. 5.1 (ET 5.2) in Jn 7.42

Mic. 5.1 (ET 5.2) is the only Old Testament passage that can be read as announcing that the Messiah will be born in Bethlehem: 'But you, O Bethlehem of Ephrathah, ... from you shall come forth for me one who is to rule in Israel'. When people in Jerusalem refer to the scripture 'that the Messiah ... comes from Bethlehem', as an argument against the Messianic claims of the Galilean Jesus (Jn 7.42), they therefore point to Mic. 5.1. The same prophecy is found in Matthew's birth narrative (2.5-6), implicitly also in Luke's (2.4, 11). So John once again makes use of an early Christian interpretation of a text from the Twelve Prophets, this time in a misunderstanding on the part of Jesus' opponents. It is not quite clear what John wishes to suggest: do they not know that Jesus was in reality born in Bethlehem, or that in reality he comes from God? The second possibility fits in best with Johannine misunderstandings in which spiritual realities are understood as physical ones (see, e.g., 3.4; 4.11-12).

Mal. 2.10 in Jn 8.41

In the course of a vehement discussion (Jn 8.31-59), Jesus reproves 'the Jews' for not 'doing what Abraham did'; by consequence, they cannot be children of Abraham, but must have another father (vv. 39–41). The opponents answer: 'We are not illegitimate children; we have one father, God himself' (v. 41).The second half of their answer (ἕνα πατέρα ἔχομεν τὸν θεόν) constitutes an allusion to Mal. 2.10: 'Have we not all one father? Has not one God created us?' (LXX, with inversion of clauses: οὐχὶ θεὸς εἷς ἔκτισεν ἡμᾶς; οὐχὶ πατὴρ εἷς πάντων ὑμῶν;). The combination 'one father' is unique in the Old Testament; in John, it occurs together with 'God', who is mentioned in Malachi in the parallel clause. So the allusion is fairly certain. It creates a subtle irony: the Johannine Jews take pride in a statement about their relation with God that in Malachi functions as the beginning of a passage in which the prophet indicts the faithlessness of God's people (Mal. 2.10-16).

Zech. 1.5 in Jn 8.52-53

In a later phase of the discussion of Jn 8.31-59, 'the Jews' contest Jesus' assertion that whoever keeps his word will not die (v. 50). They refer to things that anyone can know: 'Abraham died, and so did the prophets (οἱ προφῆται)... Are you greater than our father (τοῦ πατρὸς ἡμῶν) Abraham, who died? The prophets also died' (8.52-53). We have here an evident allusion to Zech. 1.5: 'Your fathers[30] (LXX: οἱ πατέρες ὑμῶν), where are they? And the prophets (LXX: οἱ προφῆται), do they live for ever?' This is the only Old Testament passage where 'fathers' (in the sense of ancestors) and 'prophets' are collocated in a parallelism in the context of the death of both. In John, we meet the same words, the same collocation, and the same context.

Jonah 1.12-15 in Jn 11.50

When the Jewish authorities are considering what to do with Jesus, Caiaphas says: 'You do not understand that it is better for you to have one man die for the people than to have the whole nation destroyed' (Jn 11.50). There are a few Old Testament episodes in which one person 'dies for the people';[31] of these, Jonah 1.12-15 is probably closest to Jn 11.50. Both Jonah and Jesus are qualified as 'man' (ἄνθρωπος Jonah 1.14 LXX; Jn 11.50), and in both cases, the 'destruction' of the larger group should be prevented (μὴ ἀπολώμεθα Jonah 1.14 LXX; μὴ ἀπόληται Jn 11.50). Both the Johannine Jesus and Jonah offer themselves to be killed (Jonah 1.12; Jn 10.17-18; 15.13; 18.4-11); both are innocent (Jonah 1.14; Jn 18.38; 19.4, 6); and both are restored to life after three days (Jonah 2.1 [ET 1.17]; Jn 2.19). The parallel between Jesus and Jonah was known in early Christianity (see Mk 4.35-41 par.; Mt. 12.39-41 par.; 16.4), and John draws on it here as well.

---

30.   The NRSV has 'ancestors'; I have changed to facilitate comparison.
31.   Hübner, *Vetus Testamentum in Novo 1,2*, pp. 424–9, lists Josh. 7.10-26, 2 Sam. 2.20-22 and Jonah 1.7-15.

Zech. 13.7 in Jn 16.32[32]

At the end of his farewell discourse, the Johannine Jesus says to his disciples: 'The hour is coming, indeed it has come, when you will be scattered (σκορπισθῆτε), each one to his home, and you will leave me alone' (Jn 16.32). Jesus alludes to Zech. 13.7: 'Strike the shepherd, that the sheep may be scattered'. The allusion is not very close to the biblical text (in any case closer to the Hebrew than to the LXX, where 'to be scattered' is missing), but it is close to the marked quotation from Zech. 13.7 in Mk 14.27 par. There we find διασκορπισθήσονται, 'they [the sheep] will be scattered', the quotation occurs at approximately the same point in the gospel narrative, and quotation and allusion have the same function: with it, Jesus announces the near defection of the disciples. Mark and John draw here from a tradition in which an obscure prophecy from Deutero-Zechariah served to show that events surrounding Jesus' death had been foreseen in Scripture, and to interpret Jesus' death as an anticipation of the eschaton. By means of the words 'the hour is coming, indeed it has come', John makes clear that in his view, the death of Jesus is the eschaton. That – as Mark suggests – God strikes Jesus, is absent from John; his Jesus says, on the contrary: 'Yet I am not alone because the Father is with me' (16.32).

Conclusion

The quotation from Zech. 9.9 in Jn 12.15 probably comes from the LXX; for the one from Zech. 12.10 in Jn 19.37 the evangelist used a current early Christian translation of the clause into Greek. The instances of secondary influence of a Minor Prophets passage on a quotation and the allusions to the Minor Prophets hardly allow conclusions on textual form because they are mostly brief and/or free. Besides, we should make a distinction between allusions that are due to the evangelist as editor and allusions that he derived from already existing Christian tradition. For the former category, provenance from the LXX is possible and, taking into account John's dependence on the LXX for the large majority of his quotations, even plausible. For the latter category, John is not directly dependent on Scripture. On the whole, it is striking to see how often John makes use, in both quotations and allusions, of Minor Prophets passages that are also found elsewhere in early Christian writings. He is obviously part of an early Christian tradition of explanation of Scripture.

In 5.39, the evangelist makes Jesus phrase a hermeneutical principle: '... and it is they [the Scriptures] that testify on my behalf' (see also

---

32. See Hanson, *Prophetic Gospel*, pp. 196–7. Zech. 13.7 is also quoted in CD XIX 7–9, as an announcement of the coming judgement.

1.45). He is convinced that Scripture has a hidden meaning that is revealed in the application of the text to Jesus as God's eschatological envoy. Interpretation of Scripture based on this conviction has affinities to the Qumran *pesher* exegesis (see, e.g., 1QpHab): the scriptural text concerns in a veiled way the events of the last days, which are occurring in the experiences of the interpreter and his community. The liberty with which John sometimes handles the scriptural text (see above, especially his treatment of Zech 9.9 in 12.15) is based on the same conviction; it should be noted, however, that this liberty is not unlimited but bound to ancient exegetical rules. John reads the Minor Prophets mainly as witnesses to Jesus: they testify to him, and their words find their realization in Jesus and in what he has done and is still doing for and in his followers.

Chapter 6

THE MINOR PROPHETS IN PAUL

Steve Moyise

Introduction

According to NA[27], there are eight quotations from the Minor Prophets in Paul's undisputed letters. Undoubtedly the most significant is the use of Hab. 2.4b in Rom. 1.17 and Gal. 3.11, both occupying pivotal places in Paul's argument. There are three quotations from the Minor Prophets in Romans 9 (Mal. 1.2-3; Hos. 2.1, 25 [ET 1.10; 2.23]) and two in Romans 10 (Joel 3.5 [ET 2.32]; Nah. 2.1 [ET 1.15]), though UBS[4] is probably correct in classifying Nah. 2.1 as an allusion rather than a quotation. 1 Cor. 15.54-55 introduces words drawn from Isa. 25.8 and Hos. 13.14 with an introductory formula ('then the saying that is written will be fulfilled'), which effectively treats Hos. 13.14 as a quotation, albeit as an extension of Isa. 25.8. In addition, NA[27] lists a further 18 allusions from the undisputed letters, concentrated in Romans (6) and Corinthians (11) but due to limitations of space, only those that have a bearing on the quotations will be discussed here. We will conclude with a short excursus on the quotation of Zech. 8.16 in Eph. 4.25.

Quotations

Hab. 2.4b in Rom. 1.17 and Gal. 3.11

Whereas Paul's interest in Deuteronomy, Isaiah and the Psalms is easily demonstrated by the frequency with which he quotes them,[1] his interest in Habakkuk appears to be confined to the short poignant statement: ὁ δίκαιος ἐκ πίστεως ζήσεται ('the righteous will live by faith' or perhaps 'the righteous by faith will live'). NA[27] lists two further

---

1. See the companion volumes in the series 'The New Testament and the Scriptures of Israel': *The Psalms in the New Testament*; *Isaiah in the New Testament*; *Deuteronomy in the New Testament* (London and New York: T&T Clark, 2004/5/7).

allusions to Habakkuk, both in 1 Corinthians, but neither appears to draw attention to the book. In 1 Cor. 1.24, the first half of the acclamation that Christ is 'the power of God (Χριστὸν θεοῦ δύναμιν) and the wisdom of God' has some similarity with Hab. 3.19, where the prophet says: 'The Lord, God, is my strength' (κύριος ὁ θεὸς δύναμίς μου). Since Paul regards Christ as the Lord (κύριος), one can imagine a scenario where Paul might have interpreted this text as a reference to Christ. However, since Paul does not use κύριος here and the emphasis is on Christ being both the 'power' and 'wisdom' of God, it is difficult to imagine any of his Corinthian readers being directed to Hab. 3.19. In 1 Cor. 12.2, Paul's description of the Corinthians' former life as being 'enticed and led astray to idols that could not speak' (ἄφωνος) has a thematic parallel with Hab. 2.18, where idols are ridiculed because they cannot speak. However, since Paul does not follow the LXX's adjective for 'cannot speak' (κωφός) and the idea is present in other passages (e.g. Ps. 115.5; 3 Macc. 4.16), it is unlikely that Paul is particularly directing his readers to this text. We conclude then that, unlike Psalms, Isaiah and Deuteronomy, Paul's interest in the book of Habakkuk is not widespread but focuses on the particular statement that ὁ δίκαιος ἐκ πίστεως ζήσεται.

This does not necessarily imply that the text is secondary, as if Paul first formulated his understanding of the gospel and only later discovered a succinct summary of it in Hab. 2.4b. It could be that the text was important to Paul prior to his Damascus road experience. Thus Watson suggests that the commentary genre has misled scholars into assuming that Rom. 1.16-17a ('For I am not ashamed of the gospel; it is the power of God for salvation to everyone who has faith, to the Jew first and also to the Greek. For in it the righteousness of God is revealed through faith for faith') is Paul's formulation of the gospel, and 1.17b (ὁ δὲ δίκαιος ἐκ πίστεως ζήσεται) is the supporting proof-text. But the close lexical parallels between formulation and text, especially the unusual genitive construction ἐκ πίστεως ('of faith' or 'from faith') which is only found in Hab. 2.4b (in the LXX), may suggest that it has had a formative role in Paul's thinking. Thus according to Watson, Rom. 1.17a is virtually a paraphrase of Hab. 2.4b: *'The one who is righteous* (that is, with a *righteousness* of God, revealed in the gospel) *by faith* (since this righteousness is received *by faith* and is intended for faith) *will*

2.   F. Watson, *Paul and the Hermeneutics of Faith* (London and New York: T&T Clark, 2004), p. 48, his emphasis. He says that when Paul normally quotes texts, there is close semantic correspondence between assertion and quotation but not a close lexical correspondence. For example, Rom. 3.9-10 asserts that 'we have already charged that all, both Jews and Greeks, are under the power of sin' and is supported by the text ('as it is written'), 'There is no one who is righteous, not even one'. Conceptually, the cited text is in close agreement with the assertion but there is virtually no lexical correspondence, which would be repetitious. It is evident, he says, that Rom. 1.16-17 is different.

live.[2] Furthermore, it also offers an explanation for Paul's unusual characterization of his opponents as ἐξ ἔργων νόμου ('of works of law'), an expression coined on analogy with those who live ἐκ πίστεως.[3]

One factor that could help decide between these alternatives is that Paul has almost certainly modified the source of his quotation. The Hebrew text has a pronominal suffix on the word 'faith' (אמונתו) and hence its meaning is, 'the righteous person shall live by *his* faith'. The Greek tradition has a first-person pronoun, either following the word 'faith' (א B Q V W*vid) or following the word 'righteous' (A). The first would mean 'the righteous person will live by *my* faith', presumably referring to God's faithfulness. The second would probably mean, '*my* righteous person will live by faith', though word order is not decisive in such matters. Either way, Paul's quotation differs from all of these traditions by omitting any pronoun, producing the succinct but ambiguous, ὁ δίκαιος ἐκ πίστεως ζήσεται.[4]

It is more difficult to determine whether Paul has changed the meaning of the Habakkuk quotation. Habakkuk's initial complaint that he is surrounded by destruction and violence (1.1-4) receives the baffling response that God is responsible for 'rousing the Chaldeans, that fierce and impetuous nation, who march through the breadth of the earth to seize dwellings not their own' (1.6). This causes Habakkuk to sharpen his complaint: 'why do you look on the treacherous, and are silent when the wicked swallow those more righteous than they?' (1.13). God responds by telling Habakkuk that there is a vision concerning the end which might appear to be delayed but will surely come. Hab. 2.4 then appears to characterize two responses to this. The first concerns those who are 'puffed up', though the Hebrew is obscure.[5] The second concerns the righteous person, who will live by his faith or faithfulness. In the light of Reformation debates, these two terms have sometimes been seen as quite different; faith focuses on the God who is faithful, whereas faithfulness is a personal quality. But in Habakkuk's context of patiently waiting

---

3.   This explanation for Paul's Greek phrase is perhaps more convincing than the occurrence of the Hebrew phrase in 4QMMT, though one does not necessarily exclude the other. See J. D. G. Dunn, '4QMMT and Galatians', *NTS* 43 (1997), 147–53.

4.   There are a few LXX mss that read this (W^c 17 763* 130 311) but they almost certainly derive from the Pauline tradition. For more details on the textual evidence, see the chapter on Hebrews in this volume by Radu Gheorghita.

5.   הנה עפלה לא ישרה נפשו בו. The last four words mean something like 'his soul is not straight' and the first word is the common 'behold!'. The second word is rare and perhaps corrupt. Read as a pual ('to swell') it perhaps means 'puffed up' or 'arrogant'. The difficulty is how to combine the words syntactically. The NRSV ('Look at the proud! Their spirit is not right in them') has removed the idea of 'failure' from the earlier RSV ('Behold, he whose soul is not upright in him shall fail'). The LXX has taken 'my soul' as a reference to God ('my soul is not pleased in it') but has 'If it draws back' instead of 'Behold, it is puffed up', either because it found the Hebrew too obscure or is dependent on a different Hebrew text.

for the vision, they probably amount to the same thing. Living by faith in God over a period of (unknown) time constitutes faithfulness. The addition of the first-person pronoun in the Greek tradition ('will live by *my* faithfulness') changes the emphasis but amounts to the same thing. Living by God's faithfulness means having faith in God's promises and his faithfulness to keep them.

A further question is the meaning of the verb יחיה/ζήσεται. Is it simply a description of 'being alive' or does it carry a salvific meaning ('life in the world to come')? Watson says that both the Qumran pesherist (1QpHab) and Paul think that it is 'speaking of the divinely ordained way to salvation with a clarity and brevity virtually unparalleled in the rest of scripture'.[6] Since Lev. 18.5 promises life (same verb) by doing the law, Watson thinks that Paul has discovered a fundamental antithesis in Scripture. Hab. 2.4 links with the unconditional promise to Abraham in Gen. 15.6 (LXX: 'Abram believed God and it was reckoned to him as righteousness'). Lev. 18.5 joins countless other legal texts in making life or blessing conditional on obedience to the law. Thus Paul's use of Hab. 2.4b in Gal. 3.11 is part of an antithetical argument that pits 'law' against 'faith' (promise):

> Now it is evident that no one is justified before God by the law; for 'The one who is righteous will live (ζήσεται) by faith'. But the law does not rest on faith; on the contrary, 'Whoever does the works of the law will live (ζήσεται) by them'. (Gal. 3.11-12)

On the other hand, Jewish interpreters like the Qumran pesherist did not see any contradiction between Habakkuk's call for faithfulness and the law's call for obedience. It was obvious to him that the 'righteous' in Hab. 2.4b are those who 'observe the law in the house of Judah', albeit with a sectarian understanding of who exactly was doing this. If this represents the most likely meaning of Hab. 2.4b in its context (faithfulness = obedience), then there are two major alternatives to Watson's interpretation. Either Paul has given the text a salvific interpretation that it did not previously have or Paul is not giving it a salvific interpretation. For the former, Fitzmyer thinks that Paul's idea of 'faith in Christ' is significantly different from the 'faithfulness' proposed by Habakkuk. Commenting on Rom. 1.17, Fitzmyer says that Paul has read the text in the light of his Christian beliefs and has taken '*pistis* in his own sense of "faith," and "life" not as deliverance from invasion and death, but as a share in the risen life of Christ... In this way Paul cites the prophet Habakkuk to support the theme of his letter'.[7] The fact that no other Jewish writer took Hab. 2.4b as antithetical to obedience suggests

---

6.   Watson, *Paul and the Hermeneutics of Faith*, p. 124.
7.   J. A. Fitzmyer, *Romans: A New Translation with Introduction and Commentary* (AB, 33; New York: Doubleday, 1992), p. 265.

that the decisive factor in Paul's interpretation is not its succinct wording but his own Christian beliefs.

The second view is taken by Wakefield, who argues that the verb 'will live' (ζήσεται) in Lev. 18.5 and Hab. 2.4 refers to ordinary life (that is, life within the covenant) and not eternal life, and that is also how Paul understands it. Contrary to the so-called 'Lutheran' view that Paul's opponents were advocating salvation by works, Wakefield thinks the debate in Galatians is about the role of the law in Christian living. Paul's opponents believe that it has an ongoing role in nurturing righteousness; Paul believes that it belongs to the old age and has been set aside. His argument concerning the failure of the law is not that it promised salvation and failed but that it offered a guide to righteousness and failed. If it did not keep Israel from coming under the curse of exile, how can it be the means for developing Christian righteousness?[8]

Fitzmyer would undoubtedly be correct if the reason that Paul omitted the pronouns was because he intended ὁ δίκαιος ἐκ πίστεως ζήσεται to mean 'he who through faith is righteous shall live' (RSV). This would be a deliberate textual manipulation to force Hab. 2.4b to bear witness to his particular understanding of the gospel. However, it is by no means certain that readers of Romans would have interpreted Paul's words thus and it seems more likely that Paul wishes to play on the ambiguity. As Hays says:

> The ambiguity thus created allows the echoed oracle to serve simultaneously as a warrant for two different claims that Paul has made in his keynote formulation of the gospel: in the gospel *God's own righteousness* is revealed; and the gospel is the power of God for salvation *to everyone who believes*. Around these foci Paul plots the ellipse of his argument.[9]

One further point to note is that despite Paul's evident focus on the six-word quotation of Hab. 2.4b, a number of Habakkuk's themes, especially the question of God's faithfulness to Israel, are in fact prominent in Romans. Thus Hays suggests that Paul is not citing Hab. 2.4b to bolster his doctrine of 'justification by faith' but to introduce the theme of theodicy. Of course, there is a considerable difference between the context of Habakkuk and the context of Paul's argument in Romans. Habakkuk is concerned about the 'military domination of the Chaldeans ... over an impotent Israel', whereas Paul's concern is the 'apparent usurpation of Israel's favored covenant status by congregations of uncircumcised Gentile Christians'.[10] In that sense, the echo is 'off-centre'

---

8.   A. H. Wakefield, *Where to Live. The Hermeneutical Significance of Paul's Citations from Scripture in Galations 3.1-14* (Atlanta: SBL, 2003).

9.   R. B. Hays, *Echoes of Scripture in the Letters of Paul* (New Haven: Yale University Press, 1989), pp. 40–1, his emphasis.

10.   Hays, *Echoes of Scripture*, p. 40.

and thus metaphorical (a trope). But there is sufficient similarity to deny that Paul is 'circumventing the text's original referential sense'. Instead, Hays maintains that Paul 'draws on that sense – indeed, on at least two different traditional readings of it – as a source of symbolic resonance for his affirmation of the justice of God's ways in the present time'.[11]

Watts goes further. He thinks that the one who is 'puffed up' in Hab. 2.4a, and is shown to be a thief and idolater in Hab. 2.5, offers a close parallel to Paul's description of those who boast in the law and yet steal and rob temples in Rom. 2.17-24. He then proceeds to find other parallels between Habakkuk and Romans. Thus Hab. 1.4 ('So the law becomes slack and justice never prevails') offers a parallel to Paul's criticisms of the law. Habakkuk's strategy of pronouncing judgement on Judah first and then the Chaldeans (Hab. 1.12; 2.5-20) coheres with Rom. 2.9 ('anguish and distress for everyone who does evil, the Jew first and also the Greek'). And Habakkuk's call for perseverance (Hab. 3.16-17) and concluding song of praise (Hab. 3.2-15) is matched by Paul's many calls for perseverance (Rom. 4.18-21; 5.1-5; 8.18-27) and songs of praise (Rom. 5.6-11; 8.28-39; 11.33-36).[12]

Such parallels are interesting but it has to be said that Paul's critique of the law is considerably different from Hab. 1.4. Texts such as Jer. 7.9-11 offer a closer parallel to Rom. 2.17-24,[13] and the presence of both exhortation and praise is a fairly common feature of biblical writings. It is difficult to see how Paul's readers in Rome would have been particularly directed to their presence in the book of Habakkuk, and Watson's judgement that Paul is strictly focused on the six-word quotation appears to be correct. However, given contemporary understandings of Hab. 2.4, I would suggest that Watson underplays the influence of Paul's Christian beliefs in his interpretation of the text.

Mal. 1.2-3 in Rom. 9.13

After Paul's declaration of anguish for Israel in Rom. 9.1-5, he embarks on an argument to show that despite the current unbelief of many Jews, God's word, namely, his promises, has not failed (ἐκπέπτωκεν). He does this by showing that 'not all of Abraham's children are his true descendants' (Rom. 9.7) and defends it by referring to God's choice of Isaac rather than Ishmael (citing Gen. 21.12) and Jacob rather than Esau (citing Gen.

---

11.   Hays, *Echoes of Scripture*, p. 41. See further S. Moyise, *Evoking Scripture: Seeing the Old Testament in the New* (London and New York: T&T Clark, 2008), pp. 49–77.

12.   R. E. Watts, '"For I am not Ashamed of the Gospel": Romans 1:16-17 and Habakkuk 2:4', in S. K. Soderlund and N. T. Wright (eds), *Romans and the People of God* (Grand Rapids: Eerdmans, 1999), pp. 3–25.

13.   See T. W. Berkley, *From a Broken Covenant to Circumcision of the Heart: Pauline Intertextual Exegesis in Romans 2.17-29* (SBLDS, 175; Atlanta: SBL, 2000).

25.23). The latter ('The elder shall serve the younger') is further supported by the starker declaration of Mal. 1.2-3: 'I have loved Jacob, but I have hated Esau'. Paul follows the LXX's aorists (καὶ ἠγάπησα τὸν Ἰακὼβ τὸν δὲ Ἡσαῦ ἐμίσησα) but has a different word order for the first clause (τὸν Ἰακὼβ ἠγάπησα) and the initial καί is omitted. The result is a 'sharper antithesis through the creation of exact antithetic parallelism'[14] and most scholars think that Paul is responsible for this rather than being dependent on a different textual tradition.

It is unclear whether this is simply a convenient proof-text for Paul or whether the context of Malachi is significant for him. Many scholars consider this section of Romans to be a midrash whereby the key terms of Gen. 21.12 are explained and extended by reference to other texts. If this is the case, it could be that Paul was drawn to Mal. 1.2-3 as one of the few texts outside of Genesis where Jacob and Esau are mentioned together.[15] On the other hand, it is clear that Mal. 1.2b ('Is not Esau Jacob's brother?') is a reflection on the Genesis story and this might have prompted Paul to develop the theme.[16] The case would be strengthened if 1 Cor. 10.21 ('You cannot partake of the table of the Lord and the table of demons') is an allusion to Mal. 1.7 ('offering polluted food on my altar ... thinking that the Lord's table may be despised') but this is far from certain. Paul shows no interest in the two passages that interested other New Testament authors (Mal. 3.1; 3.23 [ET 4.5]) and it may be that he simply wished to close this section with a quotation which sharpens 'to an excruciating degree the focus on the selectivity of God's word'.[17]

Hos. 2.1, 25 (ET 1.10, 2.23) in Rom. 9.25-27

The disturbing idea that God's purposes involve loving some (Jacob) and hating others (Esau) is softened by the quotation from Exod. 33.19 (Rom. 9.15), that such purposes are governed by mercy and compassion ('I will have mercy on whom I have mercy, and I will have compassion on whom I have compassion'). However, the negative aspect returns

---

14. R. Jewett, *Romans* (Hermeneia; Minneapolis: Fortress Press, 2007), p. 580.

15. Josh. 4.4; Obad. 1.18; 4 Esdras 3.15, 16; 6.8, 9.

16. So J. R. Wagner, *Heralds of the Good News: Isaiah and Paul 'in Concert' in the Letter to the Romans* (NovTSup, 101; Leiden: Brill, 2002), p. 51, who claims that 'the wider context of this citation in Malachi suggests that the logic of Paul's argument is deeply rooted in the native soil of Israel's scriptures'.

17. Jewett, *Romans*, p. 580, who thinks that '[w]hile the original text in Malachi referred to the nations of Israel and Edom, Paul's interest in this context is strictly related to the selective quality of God's purpose' (ibid.). NA[27] also suggests that Paul's idea that 'the Day' will disclose the quality of one's work for Christ because 'it will be revealed by fire' is an allusion to Mal. 3.19 (ET 4.1: 'See the day is coming, burning like an oven').

in Rom. 9.18 ('So then he has mercy on whomever he chooses, and he hardens the heart of whomever he chooses'), which becomes explicit in Rom. 9.22 ('What if God, desiring to show his wrath and to make known his power, has endured with much patience the objects of wrath that are made for destruction...'). The sentence is not completed and is perhaps rhetorical ('even if God had destined some to destruction, it would not be grounds for your criticism'). Be that as it may, Paul's focus is primarily positive, stating that God has acted 'in order to make known the riches of his glory for the objects of his mercy', a group composed of Jews and Gentiles (Rom. 9.23-24).

There then follows a series of quotations drawn from Hos. 2.25 (ET 2.23), Hos. 2.1 (ET 1.10), Isa. 10.22-23 and Isa. 1.9, which appears to treat his statement ('not from the Jews only but also from the Gentiles') in reverse order. Hosea provides the support for the inclusion of Gentiles ('Those who were not my people I will call "my people"') and Isaiah provides the support for Jews ('Though the number of the children of Israel were like the sand of the sea, only a remnant of them will be saved').[18] In fact, it is probably more complicated than this for although Paul is here applying Hosea to the Gentiles (or perhaps the new community of Jews and Gentiles), Hosea is actually referring to the restoration of disobedient Israel, a theme that Paul will take up in Romans 11. However, the main interpretative issue at this point is how Paul can imagine that Hos. 2.1, 25 supports his argument for the inclusion of Gentiles into the people of God.

Taken out of context, the form in which Paul quotes Hos. 2.25 ('Those who were not my people I will call "my people", and her who was not beloved I will call "beloved"') looks like a good supporting text. If the Jews are God's people (Rom. 9.4-5) and Jacob/Israel is the one loved (Rom. 9.13), then the Gentiles can aptly be described as 'not my people' and 'not beloved'. The quotation implies a reversal of fortunes, that those who were not God's people have become God's people, precisely what Paul wishes to claim for his Gentile mission. However, the quotation from Hos. 2.1 ('And in the very place where it was said to them, "You are not my people," there they shall be called children of the living God') appears to undermine this, for the specificity of 'in the very place' (ἐν τῷ τόπῳ) is a reminder that the original text was not referring to Gentiles but to Jews of the northern kingdom. Before we can attempt to unravel this, there are a number of textual difficulties that require our attention.

18.   The use of the word 'only' in the NRSV is prejudicial. It does not correspond to anything in the Greek and implies that Paul thought that *only* a few of his kinfolk would be saved. It is evident from Romans 11 that Paul did not think that. See Hays, *Echoes of Scripture*, p. 68.

Compared to the text of Rahlfs and Göttingen, Paul has made three significant changes to Hos. 2.25 LXX. Firstly, he has changed the verb from 'I will say' (ἐρῶ) to 'I will call' (καλέσω), probably to reverberate with the language of election in Romans 9. This has necessitated a change from the dative to the accusative, and from direct speech ('You are my people') to indirect speech ('I will call "my people"'). Second, Paul reverses the order of the clauses so that 'not my people' directly follows 'I will call'. Since 1 Pet. 2.10 does the same ('Once you were not a people, but now you are God's people; once you had not received mercy, but now you have received mercy'), Paul may have been influenced by early Christian tradition, but the third change makes it unlikely that Paul and 1 Peter are using a common text. Instead of 'not mercy' and 'mercy', Paul has 'not beloved' and 'beloved'.[19] This might be to coincide with the earlier quotation of Mal. 1.2-3 ('I have *loved* Jacob, but I have hated Esau'), in which case Paul's point might be that those like Esau (= Gentiles) are no longer hated but loved. Or, as Dunn and others have suggested, it might simply be that Paul 'wanted to retain ἐλεέω in a consistently positive sense throughout these chapters'.[20]

As for Paul's quotation of Hos. 2.1 LXX, the texts printed by Rahlfs and NA[27] are identical. However, the Göttingen edition considers the phrase 'there they shall be called' (ἐκεῖ κληθήσονται) to be an assimilation to Romans, and the text of BQC (κληθήσονται καὶ αὐτοί) to be original. If this is the case, then Paul is responsible for adding ἐκεῖ, which further emphasizes the specificity of 'place' in the Hosea quotation. Since this makes the application to Gentiles more difficult,[21] it could be argued that Rahlfs is more likely to represent the original in this instance. Alternatively, a number of explanations have been offered for why this should not be taken as a reference to 'place'. For example, Cranfield notes that the Hebrew (בִּמְקוֹם) could be translated 'instead of' rather

19. This is assuming with Rahlfs and Göttingen that the reading of B V 407 (καὶ ἀγαπήσω τὴν οὐκ ἠγαπήμενην) is not original but is due to assimilation to Romans.

20. J. D. G. Dunn, *Romans 9–16* (WBC, 38B; Dallas: Word Books, 1988), p. 571. Seifrid disagrees that Paul has reversed the clauses. He thinks that Paul omitted the first clause, 'perhaps because it is connected with the promise of being re-"sown" in the land' (M. A. Seifrid, 'Romans', in G. K. Beale and D. A. Carson [eds], *Commentary on the New Testament Use of the Old Testament* [Grand Rapids: Baker, 2007], pp. 607–94 [647]), and adds the reference to 'beloved' as a summary of what follows, 'in which Hosea is called to embody the redeeming love of the Lord in again taking to himself his adulterous wife' (ibid.). See also pp. 647–50.

21. Unless one agrees with Munck that Paul is thinking of the eschatological pilgrimage of the Gentiles to Zion, as seen in such passages as Isa. 2.2-4; Mic. 4.2; Zeph. 3.9; Zech. 2.11. See J. Munck, *Paul and the Salvation of Mankind* (London: SCM Press, 1959), pp. 306–7.

than 'in the place', a view supported by BDB (s.v. מקום) and Wolff.[22] It is more difficult to argue that Paul's Greek (ἐν τῷ τόπῳ) means this, though Cranfield cites an example from the third-century (CE) historian Herodian.[23] Wagner, on the other hand, thinks the reading found in p[46]FG (ἐὰν κληθήσονται) is original and represents Paul's modification of the LXX's ἐρρέθη αὐτοῖς ('it was said to them'). The effect is to change the emphasis from a specific place to, '*Wherever* people are estranged from God, there God is now actively calling out a people for himself'.[24]

We return to the question of how Paul can apply these texts from Hosea to the inclusion of the Gentiles, about which Wagner says: 'The shocking nature of this interpretive move should not be minimized'.[25] There are three main explanations: (1) Paul saw in Hosea a principle of reversal that he could apply to the Gentiles; (2) Paul interpreted Hosea in the light of contemporary interpretation; and (3) Paul interpreted Hosea in the light of Christian revelation and/or a specific hermeneutical strategy. For the first, Dunn notes that it 'is hardly likely that Paul means to imply that the Gentiles who have responded to God's call have shown themselves thereby to be the lost and dispersed ten northern tribes. It is simply that scripture proves that those who were not God's people can by God's gracious act become his people'.[26] This is not necessarily a case of Paul arbitrarily substituting Gentiles for Jews. It is clear from Romans 11 that Paul thinks the 'hardened Israel' of his own day will be restored and that this is in accord with Scripture. Thus Paul agrees with the thought of Hosea but additionally applies it (by analogy) to the Gentiles.

Second, Goodwin believes that the use of the 'living God' tradition in such texts as Dan. 5.23/6.27 LXX, Bel 5 Theod and *Sib. Or.* 3.762-3, along with *Jos. Asen.* 19, shows that Paul was not alone in seeing a reference to Gentiles in Hosea. He notes that the 'living God' tradition occurs in 'stylized formulations of idol polemic' and as an 'epithet in its missionary language and in texts portraying Gentiles acknowledging the power of Israel's God'. He boldly concludes:

> The Jewish and early Christian evidence thus suggests that 'sons of the living God' was a text already linked to Gentiles and Gentile conversion ... Paul, then, in Rom

---

22. H. W. Wolff, *Hosea* (Hermeneia; Philadelphia: Fortress, 1974), p. 27, who says: במקום אשר (literally, "in the place where") need not denote a location, which would be meaningless in this context. Here, where the passive construction places all the emphasis on the changing of the name, the expression means "instead of," especially since the relative clause is also in the imperfect' (ibid.).

23. C. E. B. Cranfield, *A Critical and Exegetical Commentary on the Epistle to the Romans. Vol II: Commentary on Romans IX–XVI* (ICC; Edinburgh: T. & T. Clark, 1979), p. 501.

24. Wagner, *Heralds*, p. 85.

25. Ibid., p. 82.

26. Dunn, *Romans 9–16*, p. 575.

9:26 can apply Hos 2:1 LXX to Gentile converts with no explanation or clarification because the application was already familiar. Paul operates with a precedent that links Hos 2:1 LXX with Gentile converts and can thus assume his reader's familiarity with this association.[27]

This is, however, an overstatement. It is one thing to show that Gentiles could sometimes be associated with the 'living God' tradition; quite another to claim that 'Paul operates with a precedent that links Hos 2:1 LXX with Gentile converts'. There is no such precedent and Paul's exegesis must have looked 'shocking' to anyone familiar with the book of Hosea, even if it might be understandable given his missionary theology.

Third, Hays considers the application to Gentiles as more direct than an analogy would suggest. Paul with 'casual audacity' performs a 'hermeneutical coup' with his 'revisionary interpretation' and 'scandalous inversions' of the text: 'It is as though the light of the gospel shining through the text has illuminated a latent sense so brilliant that the opaque original sense has vanished altogether'.[28] However, it would be incorrect to say that Paul has simply read the text in the light of the gospel, for Romans 11 shows that he also believes in its message of a restoration for Israel. Wagner builds on this, noting that in Romans, Paul consistently seizes on negative appellations in Scripture in order to find references to Gentiles. Thus Paul identifies Gentiles as the reference to the 'nation without understanding' in Deut. 32.21 (Rom. 10.19), those 'not seeking God' in Isa. 65.1 (Rom. 10.20) and 'those who have not heard' in Isa. 52.15 (Rom. 15.21). Paul thus offers a 'radical rereading of texts foundational to Israel's understanding of election', and in particular, 'Hosea's moving depiction of God's passionate commitment to his people Israel is refracted and refocused into a prophecy of the "riches of God's glory" now showered upon *Gentile* "vessels of mercy."'[29]

Joel 3.5 (ET 2.32) in Rom. 10.13

The universal sounding promise that 'everyone who calls on the name of the Lord shall be saved' (Joel 3.5/2.32) is quoted in Acts 2.21 and Rom. 10.13, and alluded to in Acts 2.39 and 1 Cor. 1.2 (see below). In

27. M. J. Goodwin, *Paul, Apostle of the Living God: Kerygma and Conversion in 2 Corinthians* (Harrisburg: Trinity Press, 2001), p. 153.

28. Hays, *Echoes of Scripture*, p. 66.

29. Wagner, *Heralds*, p. 83. Seifrid ('Romans', pp. 647–8) also considers the reference to be direct rather than analogous, arguing that when Israel became 'not my people', they effectively became a Gentile nation ('fallen and condemned human beings') which God will once again call 'my people'. He also suggests that Paul's change from 'saying' to 'calling' points back to the original reference to Gomer and the naming of her daughter (Hos. 1.6).

Romans 10, Paul has spoken of the 'righteousness that comes from law' and the 'righteousness that comes from faith' (Rom. 10.5-8), leading to the proposition that 'if you confess with your lips that Jesus is Lord and believe in your heart that God raised him from the dead, you will be saved' (Rom. 10.9). This is then identified with the promise of Isa. 28.16 ('No one who believes in him will be put to shame'), quoted earlier in Rom. 9.33 but now with an additional πᾶς ('every').[30] Paul's aim is to show that this applies equally to Jew or Greek for 'the same Lord is Lord of all and is generous to all who call on him' (Rom. 10.12), crowning the argument with the quotation from Joel: 'Everyone who calls on the name of the Lord shall be saved'. The new element is that 'confessing Jesus as Lord', 'believing in him' or 'calling on him' is now identified with calling on the *name* of the Lord. This raises two questions: (1) Does Paul wish to evoke any of the context of Joel 3.5 to fill out his meaning? And (2) Does Paul wish to evoke any other texts or practices that speak of invoking God's name?

At first glance, the answer to the first question appears to be negative, for if we read on from Joel 3.5 (ET 2.28), we find that its message is not quite as universal as Paul suggests. Those who invoke the name are from Judah and Jerusalem (Joel 4.1 [ET 3.1]), and the gathering of the Gentiles mentioned in the following verses is for judgement, not salvation. The passage even reverses Isaiah's famous imperative by advising them: 'Beat your plowshares into swords, and your pruning hooks into spears' (Joel 4.10 [ET 3.10]). Knowledge of this would hardly support Paul's statement that there is no distinction between Jew and Gentile in order to provide a basis for the Gentile mission.

On the other hand, it has been suggested that Joel 2.27 ('And my people shall never again be put to shame') provides the link to the already quoted Isa. 28.16 ('No one who believes in him will be put to shame'), while Paul's exposition in Rom. 10.14-15 ('But how are they to call...? And how are they to believe...? And how are they to hear...? And how are they to proclaim...?') is *facilitated* by the LXX wording of Joel 3.5b. Paul ends this series of rhetorical questions by quoting Isa. 52.7 in the form, 'How beautiful are the feet of those who bring good news (εὐαγγελιζομένων [τὰ] ἀγαθά)'. Neither the Hebrew or LXX of Isa. 52.7 speak of a plurality of heralds but Joel 3.5b LXX reads, 'in Mount Zion and in Jerusalem there shall be one who is saved, as the Lord said, and heralds (εὐαγγελιζόμενοι), whom the Lord called'. According to Strazicich, Paul deliberately modifies the text of Isa. 52.7

---

30.   According to Wagner (*Heralds*, p. 169), this is a 'crystal-clear example of a deliberate modification' of a text by Paul for: (1) It is easy to discern the motive, namely, that Christ is the *telos* of the law to *all* who believe; (2) the only support for it in the LXX tradition comes from a single ninth-century manuscript; and (3) it brings it into line with Joel 3.5 ('everyone who calls...').

because he needs a plurality of heralds to take the message beyond Zion and it is Joel 3.5b LXX that 'provides the necessary linguistic catalyst for activating the switch for the universalization of the message and the apostolic mission'.[31]

As for the second question, there are strong grounds for thinking that Joel 3.5 [ET 2.32] is a conscious allusion to Ps. 116.4, and perhaps also Zeph. 3.9. Psalm 116 repeatedly speaks of calling on the name of the Lord (vv. 4, 13, 17) but in v. 4, direct speech is added: 'O Lord, I pray, save my life!' The verb for 'save' here is the less common מלט, as in Joel 3.5. Zeph. 3.9 does not include a verb for 'save' but the context is the 'Day of the Lord' and the invocation is for 'all of them' (כלם). It is unlikely that Paul intends his readers to see through his quotation of Joel 3.5 to these texts but he may be making the general claim that what Israel knew as invoking God's name, Christians now know as invoking the name of Jesus.

This would appear to be confirmed by 1 Cor. 1.2, where Paul expands the reference to the church in Corinth with the words, 'together with all those who in every place call on the name of our Lord Jesus Christ, both their Lord and ours'. Since Paul follows this with mention of enriched speech (v. 5), spiritual gifts (v. 6) and the 'day of our Lord' (v. 8), the allusion to Joel 3 is unmistakable.[32] However, as with Rom. 10.13, the more one stresses Paul's dependence on Joel 3, the more one highlights the dissonance between them. Not only is Paul transferring the invocation of God's name to the invocation of Jesus' name and the Day of the Lord to the Day of Christ, his addition, 'in every place', can only be a deliberate modification of Joel's message. Though Strazicich's suggestion that the LXX of Joel 3.5b was responsible for Paul's modified quotation of Isa. 52.7 (Rom. 10.13) is speculative, he is surely correct in speaking of Paul's use of Joel 3.5 LXX as an example of interpretative 'transformation'.[33]

---

31. J. Strazicich, *Joel's Use of Scripture and the Scripture's Use of Joel: Appropriation and Resignification in Second Temple Judaism and Early Christianity* (BIS, 82; Leiden: Brill, 2007), p. 323. Wagner (*Heralds*, p. 174 n. 165) says: 'We see here yet another strand of the thick intertextual fabric Paul has woven in this section of Romans'. The LXX translator appears to have read ומבשרים ('heralds') instead of ובשרידים ('survivors'), either because he was using a different *Vorlage*, misread the consonants or, as Strazicich believes, as an *'al tiqrê* interpretation.

32. Strazicich, *Joel's Use of Scripture*, pp. 325–6; A. C. Thiselton, *The First Epistle to the Corinthians* (NIGTC; Grand Rapids: Eerdmans, 2000), pp. 78–9.

33. 'Paul has transformed Joel's Jewish particularism for a Hellenistic–Jewish Christian interpretation' (Strazicich, *Joel's Use of Scripture*, p. 325).

Nah. 2.1 (ET 1.15) in Rom. 10.15

We have already noted that Paul appears to have changed 'herald' to 'heralds' in his quotation of Isa. 52.7 in Rom. 10.15, perhaps influenced by Joel 3.5b LXX. In fact, the relationship between Rom. 10.15 and Isa. 52.7 is extremely complex. Paul's initial 'How beautiful are the feet' could be an abbreviation of the Hebrew ('How beautiful upon the mountains are the feet') but the LXX is quite different: πάρειμι ὡς ὥρα ἐπὶ τῶν ὀρέων ὡς πόδες ('I am here, as the springtime on the mountains, as feet'). Second, against both Hebrew and LXX, Paul omits the clause about 'proclaiming a message of peace'[34] and so joins ἀγαθά ('good things') directly to εὐαγγελιζομένων ('heralds') as the content of what is to be proclaimed. The LXX has this clause as a further comparison ('as one proclaiming good things'). As a result, a number of scholars have argued that Paul is using a revised LXX text, similar to the Lucianic manuscripts that have come down to us.[35] However, although the book of Nahum plays a minimal role in the New Testament,[36] it is worth asking whether Nah. 2.1 LXX has played a role in Paul's formulation here.

Isa. 52.7 LXX	Nah. 2.1 LXX	Rom. 10.15
πάρειμι ὡς ὥρα	ἰδοὺ	ὡς ὡραῖοι
ἐπὶ τῶν ὀρέων	ἐπὶ τὰ ὄρη	
ὡς πόδες	οἱ πόδες	οἱ πόδες
εὐαγγελιζομένου	εὐαγγελιζομένου καὶ	τῶν εὐαγγελιζομένων
ἀκοὴν εἰρήνης ὡς	ἀπαγγέλλοντος εἰρήνην	
εὐαγγελιζόμενος ἀγαθά		[τὰ] ἀγαθά

If Paul only knew this LXX text of Isa. 52.7, then knowledge of Nah. 2.1 LXX might explain why he omits the comparison (ὡς) before 'feet' (πόδες) but there is little else to suggest any influence. Scholars usually explain why New Testament quotations differ from the texts that have come down to us by reference to creative changes on the part of the author or the use of variant texts. In the case of Paul's use of Isa. 52.7, it appears that both are true and Nah. 2.1 LXX is at best an accompanying allusion.

---

34. According to p[46] ℵ* A B C 81 630 1506 1739 1881 *pc* ar co; Cl.

35. C. D. Stanley, *Paul and the Language of Scripture: Citation Technique in the Pauline Epistles and Contemporary Literature* (SNTSMS, 74; Cambridge: Cambridge University Press, 1992), pp. 134–41.

36. NA[27] lists only Nah. 1.6 (Rev. 13.41), 3.4 (Rev. 9.21; 17.2; 18.23) and 3.10 (Lk. 19.44).

Hos. 13.14b in 1 Cor. 15.55

In 1 Cor. 15.54-55, Paul brings his discussion of resurrection to a close with a quotation ('then the saying that is written will be fulfilled') which brings together words from Isa. 25.8 ('he will swallow up death forever') and Hos. 13.14b ('O Death, where are your plagues? O Sheol, where is your destruction?'). Paul's 'quotation', however, differs from both of these texts in significant ways. First, he has used a passive construction ('Death has been swallowed up') and speaks of 'in victory' (εἰς νῖκος) instead of Isaiah's 'forever' (לנצח). The LXX has κατέπιεν ὁ θάνατος ἰσχύσας ('Death has swallowed up and prevailed'), the opposite of Paul's meaning and unlikely to be the source of his quotation. Second, instead of Hosea's 'O Death'/'O Sheol', Paul uses 'O Death' in both clauses. This might be stylistic, resulting in a three-fold repetition of 'Death', or as Barrett suggests, because the Greek 'Hades' had connotations of heathen gods.[37] Third, for Hosea's 'plagues' and 'destruction', which the LXX rendered 'penalty' (δίκη) and 'sting' (κέντρον), Paul has 'victory' (νῖκος) and 'sting' (κέντρον).[38] And fourth, he brings forward the pronoun (σου) and vocative (θάνατε):

Isa. 25.8/Hos. 13.14b LXX	1 Cor. 15.54b-55 NA²⁷	1 Cor. 15.54b-55 NRSV
κατέπιεν ὁ θάνατος ἰσχύσας...	κατεπόθη ὁ θάνατος εἰς νῖκος.	Death has been swallowed up in victory.
ποῦ ἡ δίκη σου, θάνατε;	ποῦ σου, θάνατε, τὸ νῖκος;	Where, O death, is your victory?
ποῦ τὸ κέντρον σου, ᾅδη;	ποῦ σου, θάνατε, τὸ κέντρον;	Where, O death, is your sting?

The resulting saying is undoubtedly elegant in its repetition of 'death' (x3) and 'victory' (x2) and Paul picks up the key words 'death, 'victory' and 'sting' in the exposition that follows: 'The *sting* of *death* is sin, and the power of sin is the law. But thanks be to God, who gives us the *victory* through our Lord Jesus Christ' (1 Cor. 15.56-57). However, if these LXX texts are the source of Paul's 'quotation', then he himself has inserted the idea of 'victory' (νῖκος) into both texts and reversed the meaning of Isa. 25.8, hardly a convincing proof-text. Most explanations for this depend on two points: (1) Paul is drawing on other textual traditions; and (2) The introductory formula refers primarily to Isa. 25.8, which is

---

37. C. K. Barrett, *The First Epistle to the Corinthians* (BNTC; London: A. & C. Black, 1971), p. 383.

38. Κέντρον ('sting') is a possible rendering of קטב, which more generally means 'destruction' (Deut. 32.24; Ps. 91.6; Isa. 28.2). However, δίκη ('penalty', 'punishment') is a mistranslation of דבר ('plague').

then expanded with an 'allusion' to Hos. 13.14b. Thus Hays suggests that Paul is following the Hebrew text of Isa. 25.8, which 'does envision God's ultimate destruction of the power of death, and the reader who follows the allusion to its source will find a richly evocative portrayal of God's universal salvation for "all peoples"'.[39] This is then expanded by a somewhat loose allusion to the LXX of Hos. 13.14b, which is now read in the light of Isa. 25.8. Other scholars find it unlikely that Paul would have moved from a Hebrew text to a Greek text (and made his point dependent on it) and suggest that he had access to a revised LXX text for these verses. We know that the later Greek versions offer a variety of alternatives, Theodotion agreeing exactly with Paul's rendering of Isa. 25.8 (κατεπόθη ὁ θάνατος εἰς νῖκος).[40] Since it is unlikely that Theodotion derived this reading from Paul, it is entirely possible that it bears witness to an earlier tradition of revision that could have been known by Paul.[41]

The context of Hos. 13.14b suggests that its original meaning was negative, either as a summoning of Death and Hades to do their worst[42] or, as Macintosh suggests, what Ephraim *would* say if God were to ransom him from Sheol/Death.[43] The following verses (13.15-16) make it clear that God is not going to do this ('they shall fall by the sword, there little ones shall be dashed in pieces, and their pregnant women ripped open') and 13.14c (נחם יסתר מעיני) is almost certainly negative.[44] Ancient commentators read 13.14a as a series of statements but still took 13.14b in an adversative sense, with the idea of 'in the past I redeemed them but now' (Rashi).[45] To derive a positive sense, it is necessary to take the rare form נחם in 13.14c to mean something like 'vengeance' and hence 'vengeance is hidden from my eyes' but most scholars reject this possibility and it contradicts what follows in 13.15-16. In any case, Paul would have known the LXX rendering παράκλησις κέκρυπται ἀπὸ ὀφθαλμῶν μου ('comfort is hidden from my eyes'; Vulgate: *consolatio*). Thus contrary to the original meaning, 'Paul transforms the words

---

39.   R. B. Hays, *First Corinthians* (Interpretation; Louisville: John Knox Press, 1997), p. 275.

40.   According to the margin of Codex Marchalianus (Q), though it appears with the active verb (κατέπιεν) in the Syrohexapla.

41.   So Stanley, *Paul and the Language of Scripture*, p. 211; J. P. Heil, *The Rhetorical Role of Scripture in 1 Corinthians* (Leiden: Brill, 2005), p. 249. However, G. D. Fee (*The First Epistle to the Corinthians* [NICNT; Grand Rapids: Eerdmans, 1987], p. 803) thinks that εἰς νῖκος is a common enough idiom so that there is no need to suggest dependence on a pre-Theodotion text.

42.   J. L. Mays, *Hosea* (OTL; London: SCM, 1969), p. 182; Wolff, *Hosea*, p. 182.

43.   A. A. Macintosh, *Hosea* (ICC; Edinburgh: T. & T. Clark, 1997), p. 546.

44.   The noun only occurs here but most likely derives from נחם with the meaning 'compassion is hidden from my eyes' or perhaps 'repentance is hidden from my eyes'.

45.   So Macintosh, *Hosea*, p. 546.

into a taunt of Death personified, now rendered powerless by Christ's resurrection'.[46]

Conclusion

Though there is sometimes doubt about the form of the LXX known to Paul (and the text of Paul's epistles), it is interesting that he appears to have made modifications to all but one of his quotations from the Minor Prophets. This varies from changes of word order (bringing 'Jacob' forward in Mal. 1.2), stylistic changes ('Death/Death' for 'Death/Hades' in Hos. 13.14b), omission of the pronoun in Hab. 2.4b ('his' or 'my') and the reformulation of Hos. 2.25 (ET 2.23) ('call' and 'beloved' for 'say' and 'shown mercy'). There are also significant changes in meaning. In particular, the use of Hos. 2.1, 23 (ET 1.10, 2.23) to support the inclusion of the Gentiles is particularly 'shocking' (Wagner) and 'audacious' (Hays), and, although Paul has quoted Joel 3.5 LXX verbatim, the verses that follow show that Joel was not envisaging the inclusion of the Gentiles. Furthermore, despite the textual difficulties surrounding Hos. 13.14, it would seem that Paul has changed a negative statement about Death and Hades into a positive statement that 'Death' has been 'rendered powerless by Christ's resurrection' (Hays). Such changes should not necessarily be regarded as arbitrary, for Hos. 13.14 is coupled with Isa. 25.8 (which does envisage the conquest of death), and Hosea's message that God can change the status of those who were formerly excluded (οὐκ ἠλεημένη, οὐ λαός) has obvious relevance for the inclusion of the Gentiles. It is often possible to suggest a rationale for Paul's interpretative moves but this should not disguise the fact that to his Jewish contemporaries, Paul's interpretations of the Minor Prophets are radical. He is clearly a serious exegete and his methods can be paralleled in contemporary Judaism, but his conclusions are strongly influenced (some would say governed) by his Christian convictions.

Excursus: Zech. 8.16 in Eph. 4.25

The exhortation to no longer 'live as the Gentiles live' (Eph. 4.17) but rather to 'clothe yourselves with the new self' (Eph. 4.24) is then illustrated by a series of admonitions: speak the truth (v. 25); do not show anger (v. 26); do not steal (v. 28); do not speak evil (v. 29); do not grieve the Holy Spirit (v. 30). There is nothing to suggest that any of these admonitions are scriptural quotations except that ὀργίζεσθε

---

46. Hays, *First Corinthians*, p. 276, though he adds that Paul might have been influenced by other passages in Hosea (e.g. 14.5ff) where ultimate salvation is promised.

καὶ μὴ ἁμαρτάνετε ('be angry but do not sin') agrees exactly with the LXX of Ps. 4.4 and λαλεῖτε ἀλήθειαν ἕκαστος μετὰ τοῦ πλησίον αὐτοῦ (Lit. 'Let each speak the truth to his neighbour') is almost identical to the LXX of Zech. 8.16 (λαλεῖτε ἀλήθειαν ἕκαστος πρὸς τὸν πλησίον αὐτοῦ). Sampley[46] attempts to show that the context of Zechariah 8 has had an influence on this pericope but few have found this convincing. Muddiman regards it as an allusion, 'probably to Zech. 8.16 (LXX)... which in turn echoes the commandment, "You shall not bear false witness against your neighbour (Exod. 20.16)"'.[47] He suggests that the effect of the biblical allusion is to narrow the scope of the reference to God's people. The text of Zech. 8.16 is also found in *T. Dan.* 5.2 (exactly as LXX) and in a variant form, *T. Benj.* 10.3 exhorts the readers to 'do the truth' to one's neighbour, using the same genitive construction (μετὰ τοῦ πλησίον) as Eph. 4.25. Lincoln is therefore probably correct when he concludes that the author is not intending to cite Scripture here but is drawing on well-known ethical tradition.[48]

46.   J. P. Sampley, 'Scripture and Tradition in the Community as seen in Eph 4:25ff.', *ST* 26 (1972), 101–9.

47.   J. Muddiman, *The Epistle to the Ephesians* (BNTC; London and New York: Continuum, 2001), pp. 224–5.

48.   A. T. Lincoln, *Ephesians* (WBC, 42; Dallas: Word Books, 1990), p. 300.

Chapter 7

THE MINOR PROPHETS IN HEBREWS

Radu Gheorghita

Introduction

Πολυμερῶς καὶ πολυτρόπως, 'in many and various ways', the alliterative collocation describing God's communication in times past (Heb. 1.1) suitably characterizes the author of Hebrews' use of the Scriptures. The epistle exhibits an impressive scriptural repository of quotations; extensive use of its language and ideas; references to its important cultic institutions, events and persons; a variety of summaries, parallels, allusions; and echoes of scriptural texts. Paul Ellingworth's appraisal, 'the language and thought of the epistle are steeped in the Old Testament',[1] echoes the indisputable consensus on the importance of the Scriptures for the epistle's theological argument. The author's indebtedness to and command of the Scriptures are second to none among the New Testament writers.[2]

Alongside the dominant role played by the Scriptures, the epistle unveils another quintessential characteristic of the author's thought, namely, a theology that is thoroughly eschatological. The extent of the epistle's eschatological interest is captured by Williamson's assertion, 'from start to finish, Hebrews is an *eschatological* "exhortation"'.[3] In particular, the

---

1. P. Ellingworth, 'The Old Testament in Hebrews: Exegesis, Method and Hermeneutics' (PhD dissertation, University of Aberdeen, 1978), p. 307.
2. The indispensible monographs on the topic include K. J. Thomas, 'The Use of the Septuagint in the Epistle to the Hebrews' (PhD dissertation, University of Manchester, 1959); F. Schröger, *Der Verfasser des Hebräerbriefes als Schriftausleger* (Regensburg: Pustet, 1968); J. C. McCullough, 'Hebrews and the Old Testament' (PhD dissertation, Queen's University, 1971) and Ellingworth, 'Old Testament'. For the *status quaestionis* and an insightful commentary on the use of the Old Testament in Hebrews, see G. H. Guthrie, 'Hebrews' Use of the Old Testament: Recent Trends in Research', *CBR* 1 (2003), 271–94, and G. H. Guthrie, 'Hebrews', in G. K. Beale and D. A. Carson (eds), *Commentary on the New Testament Use of the Old Testament* (Grand Rapids: Baker Academic, 2007), pp. 919–95.
3. R. Williamson, *Philo and the Epistle to the Hebrews* (Leiden: Brill, 1970), p. 145, italics mine.

epistle addresses a wide range of eschatological issues, understood in the technical sense as the subject matter dealing specifically with future- and end-times. No major eschatological topic was overlooked by the author, as he, explicitly or implicitly, referred to the events associated with the end-times: the death and the resurrection of believers (11.35), the eschatological judgement (9.27) with its reward of life for the righteous and destruction for the apostates (10.37-38), the heavenly gathering of those made righteous (12.22-23), the severe punishment reserved for the apostates (10.26-31), the *parousia* (9.28; 10.25, 37, 38), and the final cataclysmic act of God, by which his unshakeable kingdom will be established once and for all (12.25-29).

The epistle's perspective on the last two of these events emanates from the author's engagement with the prophetic books of Habakkuk and Haggai, the only two writings of the Minor Prophets quoted in the epistle. Resonating with the New Testament perspective, the author frames his eschatology within the transition from 'these days' to 'the days to come'. For him, 'the last days' have commenced with God's speaking in the Son (1.2) and the transition from one age to the other is markedly gradual (8.13).[4] The full manifestation of this new eschatological reality, however, is still awaited, and the author appeals to the prophecies of Habakkuk and Haggai to chart out the definitive theological map of the closing events of 'this age'.

The author develops his eschatological blueprint as he reflects on the life and ministry of Jesus in light of these two passages. He reads them in a Greek textual tradition, a text replete with useful theological nuances which he masterfully investigates. Then, with pastoral responsibility, he explores their meaning in the closing stages of his exhortation written to a group of fellow believers, whose identity is as unknown to us as that of the author himself. Both prophetic passages are quoted in the part of the epistle in which the focus of the argument shifts to eschatology.[5] More importantly, both quotations from a Minor Prophets book respectively seal the argument for the last two warning passages in the epistle, Heb. 10.19-31 and Heb. 12.1-25.[6]

---

4.   See especially K. L. Schenck, *Cosmology and Eschatology in Hebrews* (SNTSMS, 143; Cambridge: Cambridge University Press, 2007), pp. 78ff.

5.   So A. Vanhoye, *Structure and Message of the Epistle to the Hebrews* (SB, 12; Rome: Pontificio Institutio Biblico, 1989), a perspective contested by others; see J. Swetnam, 'Form and Content in Heb. 7–13', *Bib* 55 (1974), 333–48.

6.   A more precise delimitation of their role to the overall structure would be desirable, but the consensus on the epistle's structure remains as elusive as ever; see G. H. Guthrie, *The Structure of Hebrews* (NovTSup, 73; Leiden: Brill, 1994); L. L. Neeley, 'A Discourse Analysis of Hebrews', *OPTAT* 3–4 (1987), 1–147; C. L. Westfall, *A Discourse Analysis of the Letter to the Hebrews* (LNTS, 297; London: T & T Clark International, 2005).

Quotations

Hab. 2.3-4 in Heb. 10.37-38

Textual considerations
The original Hebrew text of Habakkuk underwent various changes before it reached its particular form in Hebrews. The Hebraic textual tradition is represented primarily by the Masoretic text[7] and has received considerable support from the Qumran evidence.[8] For the purpose of this study, however, it has only indirect importance as it sets the backdrop for the more important Greek textual traditions.

Hab. 2.3-4 [NRSV, slightly modified]	Hab. 2.3-4 [NETS] [9]
For there is still a vision for the appointed time;	For there is still a vision for an appointed time,
it speaks of the end, and does not lie.	and it will rise up at the end and not in vain.
If it seems to tarry, wait for it;	If it should tarry, wait for it,
it will surely come, it will not delay.	for when it comes it will come and not delay.
Look at the proud!	If it draws back,
His spirit is not right in him,	my soul is not pleased in it.
but the righteous shall live by his faith.	But the just shall live by my faith.

There are several divergences between the two textual traditions, the most important of which deserve close attention. The translator rendered the masculine pronoun in 'wait for it' (חֲכֵּה־לוֹ) by the accusative masculine pronoun 'wait for him' (ὑπόμεινον αὐτόν). The antecedent of

7.   The present study, while acknowledging the difficulties posed by MT Hab. 2.3-4, does not advocate any emendation of the text. For a survey of the proposed solutions, see R. Gheorghita, *The Role of the Septuagint in Hebrews* (WUNT, 2/160; Tübingen: Mohr-Siebeck, 2003); also F. F. Bruce, 'Habakkuk', in T. E. McComiskey (ed.), *The Minor Prophets: Volume 2* (Grand Rapids: Baker, 1993), pp. 831–96; F. I. Andersen, *Habakkuk* (AB; Garden City: Doubleday, 2001); R. L. Smith, *Micah–Malachi* (WBC; Waco: Word, 1984).

8.   Among the sectarian documents, at times quite fragmentary, the Pesher on Habakkuk (1QpHab) gives considerable support to the MT Hab. 2.3-4. While minor deviations are to be expected, the scroll usually confirms the roots preserved in the MT; see W. H. Brownlee, *The Midrash Pesher of Habakkuk* (SBLMS, 24; Missoula: Scholars Press, 1979).

9.   A. Pietersma and B. G. Wright (eds), *A New English Translation of the Septuagint* (Oxford: Oxford University Press, 2007).

the pronominal element in the Greek text is no longer the feminine noun 'vision' (ὅρασις), to correspond with the Hebrew text. This translation option, whether intentional or not, triggered a series of momentous divergences between the two texts. Notable is a sustained gender discrepancy between the Greek and Hebrew texts, most evident in the translation of the idiomatic 'it will surely come', ὅτι ἐρχόμενος ἥει for כי־בא יבא. Thus, the masculine participle 'coming' (ἐρχόμενος), while matching its Hebrew counterpart, no longer maintains as its antecedent the feminine noun 'vision' (ὅρασις) in the Hebrew text.

Several peculiar lexical equivalences also set apart the two text traditions. The conditional 'if' (ἐάν), most likely due to a different *Vorlage*, stands for the interjection 'behold!' (הנה), a possible, yet rare equivalent.[10] While it is possible that the translator attributed the unique equivalent ὑποστείληται to the difficult lexeme עפלה it seems more reasonable to suggest either that the translator had a *Vorlage* reading derived from the root עלף or that he misread his text as such.[11] Similarly, since εὐδοκεῖν never translates ישר, most commentators suggest the root רצה in the *Vorlage*.

Given the graphic similarities between the pronominal suffixes, it is not difficult to explain the divergent pronouns in the two texts, 'my soul' (ἡ ψυχή μου) corresponding to 'his soul' (נפשׁו) and 'my faith/faithfulness' (ἐκ πίστεώς μου) for 'his faith/faithfulness' (באמונתו). Regardless of the causes, however, the divergences have significant implications for the overall meaning of each textual tradition.[12]

The quotation from Hab. 2.4 is used three times in the New Testament, twice by Paul (Rom. 1.17 and Gal. 3.11) and once by the author of Hebrews (Heb. 10.37-38). In the Nestle-Aland edition the two texts are almost identical, ὁ δὲ δίκαιος ἐκ πίστεως ζήσεται (δέ is missing in Gal. 3.11). The text reflects LXX Hab. 2.4, even though in general the apostle gives no evidence of being bound to a particular text, Greek or Hebrew, in his quotations.[13] The notable departure from the Septuagintal

10.   BDB, *ad loc.*

11.   P. Humbert, *Problemes du Livre d'Habacuc* (Neuchâtel: University of Neuchâtel, 1944), p. 148.

12.   The reception of the Septuagint (or more correctly, the Old Greek translation) among various Jewish communities was neither unanimous nor uniform; see G. Veltri, *Eine Tora für den König Talmai* (Tübingen: Mohr-Siebeck, 1994); N. Fernández Marcos, *The Septuagint in Context* (Leiden: Brill, 2000); A. Wasserstein, *The Legend of the Septuagint* (Cambridge: Cambridge University Press, 2006). The desire to bring the Greek text into closer conformity to the Hebrew text generated in the following centuries several revisions and recensions of the Old Greek translation. See E. Tov (ed.), *The Greek Minor Prophets Scroll from Naḥal Ḥever* (DJD, 8; Oxford: Clarendon Press, 1990); D. Barthélemy, *Les Devanciers d'Aquila* (VTSup, 10; Leiden: Brill, 1963); J. A. Fitzmyer, 'Habakkuk 2.3-4 and the New Testament', in J. Doré, P. Grelot and M. Carrez (eds), *De la Torah au Messie* (Paris: Descleé, 1981), pp. 447–57.

13.   C. D. Stanley, *Paul and the Language of Scripture* (SNTSMS, 74; Cambridge: Cambridge University Press, 1992), p. 67.

text comes in Paul's decision to drop altogether the possessive pronoun, a textual detail found in all other surviving traditions. Such uniform representation suggests that Paul consciously adapted the Habakkuk text to give better support to his theological argument.[14] In doing so, however, he generated a distinct Greek textual tradition of Hab. 2.4 void of its key pronominal element, which very likely influenced other textual traditions.

The text of the Habakkuk quotation in Hebrews is longer than the Pauline text and differs from its original form more than the Pauline text. Besides many similarities between the source and target texts of the quotation, there are significant differences, involving several difficult textual issues. Foremost among them stands the line ὁ δὲ δίκαιός μου ἐκ πίστεως ζήσεται ('my righteous one will live by faith'), which has been preserved by both LXX Hab. 2.3-4 and Heb. 10.37-38 in two other variants: ὁ δὲ δίκαιος ἐκ πίστεώς μου ζήσεται and ὁ δὲ δίκαιος ἐκ πίστεως ζήσεται.[15]

The difficulty of this text-critical problem resides in the relatively even manuscript support for each variant, and in the complexity of their cross-influence during the transmission history of both texts. The probability of the New Testament text influencing the LXX text was just as real as the reverse. The *crux interpretum* revolves around the pronominal element 'my' (μου) in LXX Hab. 2.4, whether it belongs to the original text or not, and whether it qualified the noun 'faith' or the adjective 'righteous'.

In LXX Hab. 2.4, the variant δίκαιος ἐκ πίστεώς μου stands as the most probable original text. With regard to the pronoun's position, this variant follows the Hebrew text most closely even though the pronominal elements do not match. Internal evidence alone is insufficient to dismiss as not original either one of the other readings, δίκαιος ἐκ πίστεως or δίκαιός μου ἐκ πίστεως. These two variants, however, are most likely the result of scribal activity. The former dropped the pronoun altogether while the latter resulted from aligning the Septuagint to the Hebrews' textual tradition.[16]

As far as Heb. 10.37-38 is concerned, δίκαιος ἐκ πίστεως is the least likely original reading, in light of the established Pauline non-pronominal usage.[17] In fact, it is remarkable that a first-century theologian was bold

14. Contra M. A. Seifrid, 'Paul's Use of Habakkuk 2:4 in Romans 1:17: Reflections on Israel's Exile in Romans', in S.-W. Son (ed.), *History and Exegesis* (New York: T&T Clark, 2006), p. 139.

15. For the textual data, see Gheorghita, *Role*, p. 172.

16. The possibility of cross-influence in the transmission history of the Septuagint and the New Testament texts has long been recognized; see especially A. H. Cadwallader, 'The Correction of the Text of Hebrews towards the LXX', *NovT* 34.3 (1992), 257–92. For a fuller analysis see Gheorghita, *Role*, pp. 171ff., and D.-A. Koch, 'Der Text von Hab 2.4b in der Septuaginta und im Neuen Testament', *ZNW* 76.1-2 (1985), 82–3.

17. Koch, 'Text', pp. 82–3; Stanley, *Paul and the Language of Scripture*, p. 83.

enough not to allow himself to be influenced by the emerging Pauline textual tradition.[18] Between the other two pronominal variants, a stronger case can be made for δίκαιός μου ἐκ πίστεως as the original reading on both external and internal evidence. It is not only the variant with a slightly superior textual support, but also the one most unlikely to have been generated by the alternative variants.

The text of Hab. 2.3-4, in its Hebraic forms as well as in its ensuing translations, has occasioned a number of distinct interpretative traditions. Given the importance of this prophetic oracle, it is warranted to assert that these traditions have influenced the subsequent usage of the prophetic oracle. The effect of such influence can be discerned in the author's use of LXX Hab. 2.3-4. While the text quoted in Heb. 10.37-38 differs from both the MT and LXX Hab. 2.3-4, the essential textual components of LXX Hab. 2.3-4 are duplicated in the epistle's quotation, with several distinctly Septuagintal readings essential to the author's argument.

Contextual considerations
The contextual considerations focus on two types of parallels connecting the Books of Habakkuk and Hebrews. The first is an essentially literary set of parallels surfacing within the matrix of intertextuality between Habakkuk and other books adjacently quoted in Hebrews. The second one, with only indirect literary support, finds common ground in the particular *Sitz im Leben* of the original addressees of both Habakkuk and Hebrews, as discerned from various relevant passages in the books.

The intertextual links between the Book of Habakkuk and other Old Testament passages quoted in the same section illustrate the author's predilection not only for reading biblical texts in their larger contexts but also for weaving their ideas throughout the argument. All four other Old Testament passages quoted in this section alongside Habakkuk, Deuteronomy 32–33, Isaiah 26, Haggai 2 and Proverbs 3 show remarkable verbal and thematic parallels with the Book of Habakkuk.

Isaiah 26, the source for the barely observable opening quotation in Heb. 10.37a, and Habakkuk 2 allude in similar ways to God's eschatological visitation. The larger contexts of both chapters emphasize the imminence of God's appearance in a manifestation of his judgement (Hab. 3.2, 8 and Isa. 26.20, 21).[19]

Similar thematic cohesiveness is discernable between the Books of Habakkuk and Deuteronomy, especially Habakkuk 3 and Deuteronomy

18.   Manson goes so far as to commend the author for not succumbing to the pressure of the Pauline tradition when using the Habakkuk quotation. T. W. Manson, 'The Argument from Prophecy', *JTS* 46 (1945), 135.

19.   The theme of the eschatological day of God's wrath is discernible also in the context of several other major quotations in the epistle: Ps. 109.5 [110 MT], 94.11 [95 MT], and Ps. 2.12.

32–33, chapters that focus on the motif of God's visitation of his people.[20] The thematic and verbal parallels between these two texts most likely contributed to bringing them together in support of the judgement theme in the paraenesis of Hebrews 10.[21] The stern warning in Heb. 10.19-31 concludes with a quotation from Deut. 32.36, followed by a short paragraph (10.32-34) describing the readers' situation, and culminating in the exhortation (10.35-39) built on the quotation from Hab. 2.3-4.

Grouping the quotation from Proverbs and Habakkuk is most likely the result of a distinct meaning of LXX Hab. 1.12b where the Greek text 'he has formed me to expose his chastisement' stands for 'and you, O Rock, have established them for judgement'. The specific reference to God's 'correction' (παιδείαν) administered to his people forms a key thematic link with the author's development of the same theme in Hebrews 12 as he quotes from Prov. 3.11-12, 'my child, do not despise the Lord's discipline or be weary of his reproof'.

In Hebrews' final warning passage, reference to the eschatological climax prophesied by Haggai brings to a close the theological discourse and offers another example of a common motif between two Old Testament passages used by the author in relative proximity. The parallels between the two passages include the similar manifestations of God's visitation (compare LXX Hab. 3.6 with LXX Hag. 2.6, 21) as well as their effect on the crop and livestock (compare LXX Hab. 3.17 with LXX Hag. 2.19).

Alongside this multilayered intertextuality stands a second set of parallels between Habakkuk and Hebrews, emerging from the similarities between the historical situations of Habakkuk's and the author's original addressees. It is not by chance that the quotation from Habakkuk is introduced immediately following the description of the persecution endured by this particular Christian assembly.[22]

---

20.   See the discussion on the use of the Habakkuk canticle as part of the Haphtarot for the Feast of Pentecost in H. St. J. Thackeray, *The Septuagint and Jewish Worship* (London: Milford, 1921), p. 47; for a more recent evaluation, see G. Gelardini, 'Hebrews, an Ancient Synagogue Homily for *Tisha Be-Av*: Its Function, its Basis, its Theological Interpretation', in G. Gelardini (ed.), *Hebrews: Contemporary Methods – New Insights* (BIS, 75; Leiden: Brill, 2005), pp. 107–27.

21.   Horbury makes a convincing case in favour of the messianic link between the Song of Moses and Hab. 2.3-4; see W. Horbury, 'Messianism in the Old Testament Apocrypha and Pseudepigrapha', in J. Day (ed.), *King and Messiah in Israel and the Ancient Near East* (JSOTSup, 270; Sheffield: Sheffield Academic Press, 1998), p. 81.

22.   Along the same lines, an insightful analysis on the use of Hab. 2.4 in Paul's argument in Romans 1–3 has been drawn by R. E. Watts, ' "For I Am Not Ashamed of the Gospel": Romans 1:16-17 and Habakkuk 2:4', in S. Sonderlund and N. T. Wright (eds), *Romans and the People of God* (Grand Rapids: Eerdmans, 1999), pp. 3–25. See also Seifrid, 'Paul's Use'.

In spite of no consensus on the exact identity of the community addressed by the author, there is sufficient information for drawing a profile of the addressees, identified in the epistle as recipients of the apostolic kerygmatic activity (2.1-4; 13.17). The faith that developed solid roots in some members of the congregation (6.1-6) failed to produce in others the maturity expected by the author (5.11-14). Most of them endured various forms of persecution (10.32-34) as a result of their new allegiance to Christ. The persecution, construed by the author as a character-forming privilege, was expected to intensify (12.3-4). The challenges facing this congregation, both the anticipation of an intensified persecution and the danger of stagnant faith or even apostasy, are addressed by the author with a battery of warning passages.

For such a community, the profile of the 'righteous one' drawn in the prophetic Book of Habakkuk serves as a suitable example to emulate. Habakkuk's prophetic message originated during a turbulent period in Judah's history. Hab. 1.2-4 depicts a society in complete social, political, economic and religious chaos. In addition to the deplorable internal situation, the prospect of Chaldean invasion loomed large on the horizon (Hab. 1.5). Faced with these problems, the prophet utters two scathing laments accusing God of aloofness and indifference (Hab. 1.2-3) and, worse still, of injustice (Hab. 1.13). The prophet's complaints are answered by God in the revelation of a permanent and viable truth, which forms the theological centre of the book, 'the just shall live by faith' (Hab. 2.4).

The Book of Habakkuk concludes with a prayer that leads the prophet to one of the most memorable expressions of faith in the Scriptures. In the midst of uncertainties about the future and the prospect of complete devastation, the prophet resolves to cling to the Lord as his only source of salvation and joy (Hab. 3.18). The prophet's example of trust in the face of imminent adversity is an inspiring and imitable example of faith to the very end, one that the author of Hebrews was eager to present to his readers in the hope of eliciting the proper response from them.[23]

In depicting the addressees' situation, the author uses terms reminiscent of Habakkuk. In referring to their confiscated possessions, τῶν ὑπάρχονων (Heb. 10.34), he used a cognate of the verb that describes in Habakkuk the total devastation of crop and flock, καὶ οὐχ ὑπάρχουσιν (LXX Hab. 3.17). Similarly, the joy displayed by the Christians facing the first wave of persecution, μετὰ χαρᾶς προσεδέξασθε (Heb. 10.34), echoes the joy expressed by the prophet in his determination to trust, χαρήσομαι ἐπὶ τῷ θεῷ τῷ σωτῆρί μου (LXX Hab. 3.18).

---

23.   The author's understanding of 'faith' as the interpretative key to the lives of the Old Testament heroes and implicitly to the scriptural texts to which he alludes in Hebrews 11 was most likely influenced by LXX Hab. 2.3-4. The prevalence of catch-words between Heb. 10.36-39 and Hebrews 11, such as 'faith', 'righteous', 'life/live', 'inheritance' and 'promise' provides sufficient proof of that influence.

Theological considerations

Of all the quotations in Hebrews, LXX Hab. 2.3-4 underwent the most extensive textual adjustment. The ensuing examination of the theological dimension will probe the author's rationale for using this quotation, for modifying it, and for its contribution to the overall argument.[24] Foremost, it will focus on the degree of coherence between the changes made by the author and the overall theology of LXX Habakkuk, the original theological milieu of the quotation.[25]

Behind Heb. 10.37-39 stand the form and content of LXX Hab. 2.3-4, a text in its own right, whose meaning has to be determined in light of its larger literary and theological contexts in LXX Habakkuk.

Hab. 2.3-4 [NETS]	Heb. 10. 37-38 [NRSV]
For there is still a vision for an appointed time,	
and it will rise up at the end and not in vain.	
If it should tarry, wait for it,	For yet [in a very little while,]
for when it comes it will come and not delay.	the one who is coming will come and will not delay;
If it draws back,	but my righteous one will live by faith.
my soul is not pleased in it.	My soul takes no pleasure,
But the just shall live by my faith.	in anyone who shrinks back.

The text of LXX Hab. 2.3-4 underwent various modifications in Hebrews. First, there is a shift in the relative position of several components that resulted in a new overall structure. The possessive pronoun 'my' (μου) no longer qualifies the noun 'faith' (πίστεως) but the adjective 'righteous' (δίκαιος). Similarly, the main clause 'but my righteous one will live by faith' (ὁ δὲ δίκαιός μου ἐκ πίστεως ζήσεται) precedes and not follows the conditional clause 'if he shrinks back' (ἐὰν ὑποστείληται). Second,

24. There are other explanations for the modifications in the text, such as imprecision due to quotation from memory; see M. Karrer, 'The Epistle to the Hebrews and the Septuagint', in W. Kraus and R. G. Wooden (eds), *Septuagint Research: Issues and Challenges in the Study of the Greek Jewish Scriptures* (SBLSCS, 53; Leiden: Brill, 2006), p. 343.

25. The preliminary stages of this type of investigation include a thorough analysis of the translation technique in LXX Habakkuk, which in turn enables the sketching of a theological profile for both textual traditions, articulated primarily around the significant differences between the two texts. See Gheorghita, *Role*, pp. 180ff., and D. Cleaver-Bartholomew, 'An Analysis of the Old Greek Version of Habakkuk' (PhD dissertation, Claremont Graduate University, 1998).

there are notable additions to or deletions from the quoted text. The most significant instance is the insertion of the masculine nominative article 'the [one]' (ὁ) before the participle 'coming' (ἐρχόμενος). Third, there are changes in the morphological characteristics of several words, none of which are significant for the present argument. All these modifications most likely originated with the author.

Whatever the nature of these modifications, behind them lies a theological intention which led to this particular alteration of the quoted text. Moreover, a modified quotation elicits in its new literary context important theological consequences for the message of Hebrews, not least for its Christology and eschatology.[26] First, the article ὁ appended to the participle 'coming' (ἐρχόμενος) exploits the messianic potential of LXX Habakkuk, transforming it into a clear messianic reference to Christ's *parousia*. Second, the change of the relative position of the pronoun 'my' (μου) shifts the emphasis from God's faithfulness to the faith(fulness) of the New Covenant believer, the sole responsibility of those whom God gave the status of 'righteous one' (ὁ δίκαιος). The inversion of the sentences attenuates the ambiguity of Hab. 2.3-4 LXX, a solution that not only maintains the contrast between ὁ δίκαιος and the one who draws back (ὑποστείληται), but also prevents a reading construing ὁ ἐρχόμενος as the subject of ἐὰν ὑποστείληται.

The author's changes to LXX Hab. 2.3-4 concur with the reading of LXX Habakkuk as a text in its own right. In particular, LXX Hab. 2.1-4 is a passage marked not only by several divergences from the Masoretic tradition, but also by a series of syntactical and logical incongruences. Anyone attempting to use this text would have to sort out its inner difficulties in order to convey a coherent message. The present study contends that the author followed the same route: he modified the quotation to underscore one way of reading LXX Hab. 2.3-4 in a coherent manner, rather than one of the other legitimate alternatives. In doing so, he abandoned the concern to maintain referential consistency in favour of logical and syntactical consistency throughout the passage.[27] Thus, 'the vision' is limited to LXX Hab. 2.2, while a masculine entity is assumed as the subject for the two conditional statements. The identity of the 'anonymous "he"',[28] while determined in part through grammatical means by tracing the antecedents within the text, must be clarified not

26. See especially A. Strobel, *Untersuchungen zum eschatologischen Verzögerungsproblem auf Grund der spätjüdisch-urchristlichen Geschichte von Habakuk 2,2 ff* (NovTSup, 2; Leiden: Brill, 1961); J. A. Sanders, 'Habakkuk in Qumran, Paul and the New Testament', in C. A. Evans and J. A. Sanders (eds), *Paul and the Scriptures of Israel* (JSNTSup, 83; Sheffield: Sheffield Academic Press, 1993), pp. 98–118; Fitzmyer, 'Habakkuk'.

27. While not identical, the solutions of Fitzmyer, 'Habakkuk', p. 450, and of Cleaver-Bartholomew, 'Habakkuk', p. 165, support this position.

28. Manson, 'Argument', p. 133.

only by the logic of the text itself, but also by the broader literary and theological contexts of LXX Habakkuk.

The solution proposed here does not solve all the conundrums of LXX Hab. 2.3-4, but offers a reasonable explanation for the changes introduced by the author. First of all, the addition of the article before the participle with the resultant text 'the coming one' (ὁ ἐρχόμενος) is justified on the grounds of the Septuagint's referent for the participle 'coming' (ἐρχόμενος), who, according to the LXX Habakkuk, is 'the Lord' (ὁ κύριος, LXX Hab. 3.8), or 'God' (ὁ θεός, LXX Hab. 3.2). Furthermore, the purpose for his coming, according to the LXX Habakkuk, is the salvation of his elect, 'to save your anointed ones' (τοῦ σῶσαι τοὺς χριστούς σου, LXX Hab. 3.13). The phraseology suggests the reason behind the epistle's change from 'the righteous one' (ὁ δίκαιος) to 'my righteous one' (ὁ δίκαιός μου). Lastly, in anticipation of the One coming (ὁ ἐρχόμενος) and considering a possible delay, the righteous one in Hebrews must avoid becoming like 'the ungodly' (ὁ ἀσεβής) in LXX Hab. 1.4 and must not draw back (ἐὰν ὑποστείληται, LXX Hab. 2.3). Alternatively, 'the righteous one' (ὁ δίκαιος) in Hebrews is to imitate the example of the faith and trust of the righteous one in Habakkuk, the one who will find life, typified in LXX Habakkuk by none other than the prophet himself (LXX Hab. 3.18-19).

The changes to the Habakkuk quotation introduced by the author are just as indicative of his efforts to make sense of the text he found in LXX Habakkuk as of his method used to apply that text to a new situation. They represent a legitimate rearrangement of the text intended to untangle the meaning of LXX Hab. 2.3-4, while informed by the details of the overall message of the LXX Habakkuk.

Hag. 2.6, 21 in Heb. 12.26

Textual considerations

The text of the quotation from Haggai in Hebrews, while neither as long nor as altered as the quotation from Habakkuk, raises several text-critical issues. First of all, the source of the quotation needs to be established since two passages, LXX Hag. 2.6 and 2.21, are in contention as possible candidates. Once the source has been identified, the textual variants have to be assessed in order to trace the textual changes in subsequent usages. The Hebrew text tradition of Haggai is limited primarily to the Masoretic text, which does not benefit from the same measure of support from the Dead Sea Scrolls as Habakkuk.[29]

29. There is no surviving Pesher on Haggai, but texts from Haggai have been identified in several Scrolls; see D. L. Washburn, *A Catalogue of Biblical Passages in the Dead Sea Scrolls* (TCS, 2; Atlanta: SBL, 2002), pp. 152-3. In the fragmentary instances of potential Haggai texts, the Scrolls confirm the Masoretic text.

Hag. 2.6 [NRSV]	Hag. 2.6 [NETS]
For thus says the LORD of hosts:	For this is what the Lord Almighty says,
Once again, in a little while,	Once again I will shake
I will shake the heavens and the earth	the sky and the earth
and the sea and the dry land.	and the sea and the dry land,

Hag. 2.21 [NRSV]	Hag. 2.21 [NETS]
Speak to Zerubbabel	Say to Zerobabel, the son of Salathiel,
governor of Judah, saying,	from the tribe of Ioudas, saying,
I am about to shake the heavens and the earth.	I am shaking the sky and the earth
	and the sea and the dry land.

There are no striking divergences between the Hebrew text and its Greek rendition of Hag. 2.6 or 2.21. Among the routine cases, two translation choices show opposite tendencies. First, notice should be made of the shorter Greek text in 2.6b, which preserves only the adverbial, a-temporal qualifier 'once again' (ἔτι ἅπαξ) to translate the rather obscure phrase in the MT 'yet once more, in a little while' (עוֹד אַחַת מְעַט הִיא).[30] The other qualifier in the Hebrew text, 'in a little while' (עוֹד מְעַט), was dropped by the translator altogether. With this omission, the resultant Greek text no longer communicates the immanence conveyed by the use of a temporal qualifier in the Hebrew text. Second, LXX Hag. 2.21 exhibits a textual amplification[31] which gave Haggai the reputation for having 'by far the greatest number of textual additions in the LXX in proportion to the size of the book'.[32] The harmonization tendency at work here can be documented in several other Haggai passages.[33]

In addition to these cases of variation in length displayed by the Greek text, another translation option has affected the overall meaning of LXX Haggai, namely, the inconsistent translation of the participial phrase אֲנִי מַרְעִישׁ, once as a future tense ἐγὼ σείσω in LXX Hag. 2.6 and then as a present tense ἐγὼ σείω in LXX Hag. 2.21. While this difference

30.   Smith, *Micah–Malachi*, p. 156.
31.   Cf. LXX Hag. 2.6 with B.A. Jones, *The Formation of the Book of the Twelve* (SBLDS, 149; Atlanta: Scholars Press, 1995), p. 100.
32.   Ibid., p. 98.
33.   See, for example, the harmonization of the reference to the governor in LXX Hag. 1.12 aligned with LXX Hag. 1.1, 14; 2.2, 21; or the addition of the prophet's name in LXX Hag. 2.20 following LXX Hag. 1.1, 12; 2.1, 10, and several others; ibid., p. 98.

between the two texts is not monumental, it does play a critical role in deciding in favour of LXX Hag. 2.6 as the source text for the quotation in Hebrews.

Not surprisingly, there is extensive cross-influence in the manuscript witnesses, not only between LXX Hag. 2.6 and 2.21, but also between the LXX and Hebrews. However, the majority of witnesses favour the future tense in v. 6 and the present tense in v. 21. Consequently, the alternative reading of a present tense in v. 6 and a future tense in v. 21 can be explained as the result of either cross-influence among Haggai manuscripts, or, more likely, as the influence exerted by the quotation form in the Hebrews manuscripts on Haggai. Similarly, the longer variant of LXX Hag. 2.21, with the inserted qualifier ἔτι ἅπαξ lacking from the correspondent Hebrew text, can be explained as the result of the influence exerted either by the parallel LXX Hag. 2.6 or by Hebrews. When both internal and external factors are considered, the reconstructed text of Ziegler seems to be the most probable form of the original text.[34]

The author of Hebrews is unique among New Testament writers in quoting from the Book of Haggai. The quotation displays a similar degree of cross-influence between the New Testament and LXX manuscripts as Habakkuk, albeit with fewer and less complicated variants and possible permutations. Before the more important of these are considered, the exact source of quotation in Hebrews must be resolved. The majority of commentators favour LXX Hag. 2.6 to Hag. 2.21 on the basis of closer textual affinities, especially the use of the adverbial ἔτι ἅπαξ in LXX Hag. 2.6 and its absence from 2.21, and this is adopted in this study.[35]

As far as the form of the quotation is concerned, the Hebrews text is very similar, yet not identical, to LXX Hag. 2.6. The text of the quotation underwent three minor modifications: first, there is an interchange of positions τὸν οὐρανὸν καὶ τὴν γῆν to read τὴν γῆν...καὶ τὸν οὐρανόν; second, a standard rhetorical phrase οὐ μόνον...ἀλλά is inserted within the text of the quotation; and third, the text of Haggai is shortened, retaining only the first pair of cardinal realms τὴν γῆν and τὸν οὐρανόν, and leaving aside the other pair, τὴν θάλασσαν and τὴν ξηράν. All three textual changes can reasonably be explained as alterations introduced by the author, for reasons that will be explored later. All, however, are situated well within the author's regular pattern of quoting from Scripture. With regard to the tense of the main verb 'to shake' (σείν), both the LXX Hag. 2.6 and Heb. 12.26 have preserved similar textual variants, using either the present tense 'I am [about] to shake' (σείω), or

34. Unlike Hab. 2.3-4, there is no surviving evidence of Hag. 2.6, 21 in the subsequent revisions and recensions of the Septuagint.

35. Without any variants in Hebrews devoid of the adverbial qualifier, LXX Hag. 2.6 emerges as the more probable choice.

the future tense 'I will shake' (σείσω). The weight of mss. evidence in Hebrews as well as in Haggai supports the future tense.

It is safe to conclude that for both LXX Hag. 2.6 and Heb. 12.26 the texts with the strongest manuscript support are also the ones that most correctly represent the original text in the author's Greek Vorlage and in his epistle. They constitute the basis for the following contextual and theological analyses.

Contextual considerations

The complex intertextuality between Haggai and the other Scriptural passages employed by the author, as well as the similarities between the *Sitz im Leben* of the epistles' addressees and that of the original hearers of Haggai's oracle, will be considered next to uncover the author's interest and purpose in using this particular passage.

First, at the level of intertextuality, the thematic overlap between the two Minor Prophets' books has been explored earlier. The theme of God's eschatological activity, whether his visitation of the people in judgement (Habakkuk) or his apocalyptic 'shaking' of kings, thrones, nations (Haggai) features prominently in both books. Similarly, this activity of God will bring about comparable results in the lives of the people addressed by the prophets, not least a devastation in the life-sustaining essentials, mentioned in close verbal parallels both in LXX Hab. 3.17 and LXX Hag. 2.19. Moreover, both books summon the people to give the proper response to this imminent reality, either faith for the righteous in order to live (LXX Hab. 2.4) or confidence in God's being present among his people (LXX Hag. 1.13; 2.4).

A similar thematic correlation is noticeable between Haggai and other books featured in the author's quotations. The short catena in Hebrews 13 comprises two brief quotations from LXX Deut. 31.6 and LXX Ps. 117.6 [118 MT], both alluding to God's presence among his people, which is also a *Leitmotiv* in Haggai. The God who 'will not fail you or forsake you' (LXX Deut. 31.6) is a God always present, as Haggai repeatedly reminded his contemporaries of the promise, 'I am with you' (LXX Hag. 1.13; 2.4, 5). Consequently, the exhortation to have no fear with God as helper, 'with the LORD on my side I do not fear. What can mortals do to me?' (LXX Ps. 117.6-7), echoes the summon to courage in LXX Hag. 2.5, 'my Spirit remains in your midst; be courageous!'. Notably, the last verb in LXX Hag. 2.5 θαρσεῖν (be courageous) is synonymous and homophonic with the verb θαρρεῖν (be confident, be courageous) that introduces the catena quotation in Heb. 13.6.[36]

Second, the similarity between the historical context of the Judeans who witnessed the prophetic activity of Haggai and that of the Hebrews addressees could well have contributed to the author's examination of

36.   Ellingworth, 'Old Testament', p. 284.

this prophetic book. Haggai records his intense prophetic activity at a crucial time in the post-exilic Jewish history.[37] In a cascade of prophetic pronouncements delivered in a relatively short period of time, Haggai summons all the people of Judah to rebuild the house of God (Hag. 1.8). The modicum of religious and cultic activity in Jerusalem was about to be increased through the restoration of God's Temple. While this house of God fell short of the splendour and glory of its predecessor (Hag. 2.3), its intended function remained valid and in the future it would come to know a reversal of its fortunes (Hag. 2.9). God's responsibility was to bring about an even greater glory than in former days (Hag. 2.9), and to restore the Davidic lineage (Hag. 2.23). Accordingly, the people's responsibility was to prioritize the restoration of God's house above their own interests (Hag. 2.9-10). They were summoned to manifest that change of priorities by getting involved in work for the house of God (Hag. 1.8).

By the time the author quotes from Haggai, the theme of the 'house of God' has already surfaced several times in the earlier parts of the epistle, with one significant caveat. In light of Christ's work and as a consequence of the inaugurated New Covenant, the whole concept of 'house of God' had to be redefined. That is the purport of the author's argument in Hebrews 3, who defined 'the house of God' not in terms of a man-made structure, but rather as a community of likeminded believers, holding to the end the testimony of faith and their confidence (Heb. 3.6). Even though redefined, the rising up of this 'house of God', assembling the people of the New Covenant, is to be done by 'work' as well: work done not with wood, stone or mortar, but rather with fellowship, love and good deeds (Heb. 10.24-25). While there is a significant discontinuity between the two covenants regarding the nature of God's house, there is great continuity as to what is expected from God's people in erecting and fortifying the edifice.

Theological considerations

The quotation from Haggai provides the scriptural foundation for the final warning in the epistle (Heb. 12.25-29). Following the pattern of earlier warnings, the author's last admonition not only brings into focus the contrast between the two covenants, but also echoes, in an inclusion-type fashion, the very first warning in the epistle (Heb. 2.1-4). Both the opening and closing warnings are expressed in *a fortiori* terms. In 2.1-4 the greater responsibility emanated from the different nature of the intermediaries: the angels in charge of delivering the first covenant (2.2) were inferior to the Lord himself (2.3). Likewise, in 12.25-29, the

---

37. See C. L. Meyers and E. M. Meyers, *Haggai, Zechariah 1–8* (AB; Garden City: Doubleday, 1992); J. A. Motyer, 'Haggai', in T. E. McComiskey (ed.), *The Minor Prophets. Volume 3* (Grand Rapids: Baker, 1998), pp. 963–1002; Smith, *Micah–Malachi*.

weight of responsibility parallels the message's place of origin: to refuse the one speaking from earth, as the Israelites did, had considerably fewer consequences than rejecting the one speaking from heaven. The reference to God's speaking is linked contextually not only to the blood of Abel speaking (12.24), but also to the overarching theme in the epistle that God is a speaking God, one who addressed his people in the past and continues to do so as part of his eschatological speaking in the Son.[38] Even more importantly, this last reference to God's address confirms more vigorously than any of the earlier references that, under the auspices of the New Covenant, God's address is essentially a speech-act. God's eschatological message in the Son cannot be reduced to a simple verbal communication: it is also a salvific act.

It is at this juncture that the author quoted LXX Hag. 2.6, revealing his understanding of the final eschatological event, and thus gaining leverage in exhorting the New Covenant believers to understand their greater responsibility. That responsibility is intrinsically linked with the final event in salvation history, the ultimate eschatological shaking of heaven and earth. The form and context of LXX Hag. 2.6 stand behind the quotation in Heb. 12.26 as the author lays out scriptural support for the future event. The changes he introduced exhibit his understanding of the prophetic oracle and its role in the author's argument.

Hag. 2.6 [NETS]	Heb. 12.26 [NRSV]
For this is what the Lord Almighty says,	but now he has promised,
Once again I will shake	'Yet once more I will shake
the sky and the earth	not only the earth but also the heaven'.
and the sea and the dry land,	

The source and target texts of the quotation differ in significant ways. First, there is the addition of the adverbial qualifier 'not only ... but also' (οὐ μόνον ... ἀλλά), a rhetorical ornamentation which marks the author's intention to augment the importance, magnitude and all-encompassing scope of the very last eschatological event. The rhetorical effect thus introduced is unmistakeable, leaving no doubt that the earlier 'shaking' of the earth (associated with the first covenant) is no match for the final 'shaking' of all creation. The special emphasis on the locus of the eschatological quaking, not only the earth but also, rather unexpectedly, the heavens, is confirmed by a double alteration of the quotation. The author reversed the relative position of 'earth' and 'heaven' in the text.

---

38. R. P. Gordon, *Hebrews*, ed. J. Jarick (NBC; Sheffield: Sheffield Academic Press, 2000), p. 159.

The LXX pair 'heaven–earth' (οὐρανόν–γῆν) becomes 'earth–heaven' (γῆν–οὐρανόν), with the latter occupying the emphatic slot at the end of the sentence. The duality 'earth'/'heaven', often paired before in the epistle (chs 1, 2, 8), has never been framed in a sharper contrast. The culmination of God's eschatological address, commencing with his speaking ἐν υἱῷ (1.2), will be an event no longer limited to the earthly domain, but will affect the heavenly one, as well.

Another modification of the quotation text is the replacement of the quadruple merism in the original text (heaven, earth, sea and dry land) with a dual one (heaven and earth). Since these two spheres have been consistently explored in relationship to each other, it is reasonable to assume that the author chose to trim down the text to avoid an unnecessarily complicated theatre of the final eschatological event.

The author himself emphasized the results of these changes in the concluding remarks that follow the quotation. First, he singles out the expression ἔτι ἅπαξ, the Septuagintal reading of Haggai, to highlight that the final act in the eschatological timetable has not yet taken place. The Septuagintal form carries not so much the imminency of the prophecy's fulfilment, as the Hebraic text does, but rather its ultimate, definitive character. As Gordon correctly asserts, 'once again' should be understood as the equivalent of an emphatic 'only one more time'.[39]

Furthermore, the author surprisingly construed the prophetic oracle as a promise addressed to the author's contemporaries, 'now he has promised' (νῦν δὲ ἐπήγγελται, Heb. 12.26), not only to Haggai's original audience. The Book of Haggai does end with a decree of God, who will make Zerubbabel like a signet ring in order to uphold the Davidic royal lineage. The hermeneutics of this type of Scripture reading has been evident throughout the epistle. While Caird did not include Hag. 2.6 in his analysis, the passage fits very well within his assertion that the author repeatedly explores the 'self confessed inadequacy'[40] of the first order: 'the Old Testament is not only an incomplete book but an avowedly incomplete book'.[41] Just as 'the rest' given by Joshua, already by the time of David, proved to be an avowedly incomplete rest before the time of Christ (Heb. 4.7-9), so also the 'shaking' of primarily (though not exclusively) earthly realities associated with the first covenant (Jud. 5.4, LXX Ps. 67.9 [MT 68.8]) is avowedly incomplete and indeterminate until the final, eschatological one. The final state to be established by this cataclysmic act of God is a kingdom marked by uncontested permanency.

39. Gordon, *Hebrews*, p. 160.
40. G. B. Caird, 'The Exegetical Method of the Epistle to the Hebrews', *Canadian Journal of Theology* 5 (1959), p. 47.
41. Ibid., p. 49.

Allusions

Old Testament usage in the epistle includes many allusions and verbal parallels that form a substantial part of the epistle's overall argument. This is true also for the Minor Prophets, albeit to a lesser extent than the other Tanakh corpora. Several verbal parallels, not unanimously acknowledged as such by commentators, deserve to be mentioned. All of them, with one exception, are found in the latter part of the epistle, within relative proximity to the quotations from the Minor Prophets.

The epistle's prologue, highlighting God's speaking through the prophets in past times (ὁ θεὸς λαλήσας ... ἐν τοῖς προφήταις), echoes LXX Hos. 12.11 (ET 12.10) (λαλήσω πρὸς προφήτας), itself a later variation of this theme of Num. 12.6 (ἐὰν γένηται προφήτης ὑμῶν ... λαλήσω αὐτῷ). From the same prophetic book, 'we will offer the fruit of our lips' (ἀνταποδώσομεν καρπὸν χειλέων ἡμῶν) in LXX Hos. 14.3 (ET 14.2) stands as the closest verbal parallel in the Jewish canon to Heb. 13.15 'offer a sacrifice of praise ... that is, the fruit of lips'(ἀναφέρωμεν θυσίαν αἰνέσεως ... τοῦτ' ἔστιν καρπὸν χειλέων). Both semantically and contextually, however, *Ps. Sol.* 15.3 seems to be a preferred alternative.[42]

The Book of Zechariah is echoed twice in the epistle. The reference to the great priest (ὁ ἱερεὺς ὁ μέγας) is limited to the historical sections of the Apocrypha, with the exception of Zech. 6.11,[43] in which Joshua, the high priest ('Ἰησοῦ...τοῦ ἱερέως τοῦ μεγάλου), is commissioned to rebuild the house of the Lord. The same appellative is used for Jesus in Heb. 10.21 (ἱερέα μέγαν), in an epistle with a keen interest in the house of the Lord (3.5; 10.25). The 'blood of the covenant' (ἐν αἵματι διαθήκης) in Zech. 9.11, with eschatological tones and the image of God's people as a flock in its context,[44] can serve as backdrop for the doxology's reference (ἐν αἵματι διαθήκης αἰωνίου) in Heb. 13.20.

Finally, the reference in Zeph. 1.8 to the all-consuming fire (ἐν πυρὶ ζήλους αὐτοῦ καταναλωθήσεται πᾶσα ἡ γῆ) parallels the equally stern prospect of judgement in Heb. 10.27 (φοβερὰ δέ τις ἐκδοχὴ ... πυρὸς ζῆλος), although the author could have had in mind even closer parallels, such as LXX Isa. 26.11.[45]

42.   Ellingworth, 'Old Testament', p. 303.
43.   Ibid., p. 207.
44.   Ibid., p. 304.
45.   H. Attridge, *Hebrews* (Hermeneia; Philadelphia: Fortress, 1989), p. 293 n. 20.

Conclusion

The quotations in Hebrews from the Minor Prophets, while neither as numerous nor as dominant as those from the other corpora, have nevertheless etched an indelible mark on the eschatology of the epistle. Of all the scriptural alternatives available, the author turned to Habakkuk and Haggai in order to chart the events awaiting the plenary manifestation of the Eschaton. The *parousia* of Jesus as well as the arrival of the unshakeable kingdom will climactically end the present reality, as it was known by the author and his readers, whether contemporary or subsequent. There remain, of course, many questions left unanswered about the author's view of the Eschaton and the best way to harmonize it with other New Testament perspectives. In his epistle, however, the author left sufficient data to trace and understand an important stage in the development of Christian eschatology during the first century.

With the coming of Christ and the inauguration of the New Covenant, the Eschaton has dawned and many promises made to the patriarchs have finally become reality. Between the stages of promise made and promise fulfilled, both important for the author, faith proved to be the essential ingredient ensuring that a promise would follow its course from utterance to reality (11.1). God's eschatological promises made to the forefathers under the Old Covenant were appropriated and anticipated by faith, but not experienced as reality: 'all of these died in faith without having received the promises but from a distance they saw and greeted them' (11.13).

New Covenant believers also have promises that point to a reality now perceivable 'but from a distance'. The author reminded them that their faith, just as that of the heroes in the great cloud of witnesses (12.1), has a future dimension, because the full Eschaton reality has not yet arrived. Faith, in order to qualify as faith and be rewarded as such, requires an eschatological dimension. The author understood very well this quintessential nature of faith, and by reading the prophetic oracles of Habakkuk and Haggai in light of Christ he found scriptural support for the pair of events heralding the full manifestation of the Eschaton. In anticipation of their fulfilment, he summoned his readers to a life of faith, that *sine qua non* quality not only for pleasing God (11.6), but also for participating in the fullness of the Eschaton.

Chapter 8

THE MINOR PROPHETS IN JAMES, 1 & 2 PETER AND JUDE

Karen H. Jobes

Introduction

The New Testament letters of James, Peter and Jude are steeped in the Scripture and traditions of Second Temple Judaism. James, Peter and Jude each presents himself as standing in the prophetic line of this tradition by referring to himself, sometimes along with other descriptors, as a 'servant of Jesus Christ' (δοῦλος Ἰησοῦ Χριστοῦ; Jas 1.1, 2 Pet. 1.1, Jude 1.1).[1] This designation would no doubt have been understood by the original readers of these letters as a reference to those who enforced God's covenant as found in the prophetic texts of the Jewish Scriptures where, beginning with Moses as founding mediator of Israel's covenant with Yahweh, the prophets who enforced this covenant were referred to as 'servants of God/the LORD' (e.g. Amos 3.7; Zech. 1.6; Mal. 3.24 [ET 4.4]; possibly Jonah 1.9). Therefore the continuation of this designation in New Testament epistles may be a convention that would have invoked the prophetic tradition as a contextual background for construing the author's message.

Of the many ways James, Peter and Jude could have introduced themselves in these epistles, it is significant that after identifying themselves as a 'servant of Jesus Christ' they then include language, themes, motifs and images from the Old Testament prophets as they instruct, rebuke and warn their *Christian* readers about life under the new covenant established by Jesus Christ. The letters of James, 2 Peter and Jude ring with the prophetic voices of Yahweh's previous servants who brought words of both judgement and hope to God's people. In contrast to James, 2 Peter and Jude, the author of 1 Peter introduces himself not as a servant of Jesus Christ but as an 'apostle' of Jesus Christ

---

1.   The question of pseudepigraphal authorship lies beyond the scope of this essay. Suffice it to say that as these letters stand they are written from James, Peter and Jude and were therefore intended to be read in light of the knowledge of those historical figures. For that reason these authors will be referred to by their traditional names throughout this work.

(1 Pet. 1.1) and the letter lacks the prophetic tone, language and images of judgement that characterize James, 2 Peter and Jude, while instead offering apostolic encouragement and instruction for its readers as they live in a society hostile to the Christian message and values. In other words, James, 2 Peter and Jude are concerned with confronting issues *within* the Christian community as if they were a reconstituted Israel; 1 Peter is concerned with the issue of how Christ's covenant community relates to society.

A Brief Word on Methodology

It is clear that James, Peter and Jude appropriate themes, motifs, images and language that are found in the prophetic genres of the Old Testament in general and the Minor Prophets in particular. Although the Book of the Twelve existed in both its Hebrew and Greek forms at the time these epistles were written, it is difficult to conclude with any certainty that the authors of these epistles used the *text* of the Twelve, even where an allusion seems obvious, such as the reference to 'my people' in 1 Pet. 2.10 (see discussion below).

The use of the *text* of the Old Testament in the New (as opposed to the use of its concepts, themes, theology, etc.) involves discerning *distinctive verbal* parallels defined as 'the occurrence of two or more passages of distinctive content, ranging in length from a few significant words to several sentences, which display identical or minimally divergent wording'.[2] In James, 1 & 2 Peter and Jude there are no verbal parallels with the text of the Minor Prophets that are long enough to warrant the designation of quotation, though other books of the Old Testament, such as Isaiah and Psalms, are clearly quoted. The parallels of James, 1 & 2 Peter and Jude with the text of the Twelve are such that in a similar study Helmut Utzschneider recently concluded 'that most (if not all) short citations are aphorisms that have their roots beyond their respective literary references, in the oral tradition and in the general knowledge of the time, and are not bound to the written tradition'.[3] Even those parallels that may seem rather striking at first glance may not be a deliberate parallel to the *text* of the Minor Prophets for there are several ways of explaining such brief parallels.[4]

---

2.   R. Schultz, *The Search for Quotation: Verbal Parallels in the Prophets* (JSOTSup, 180; Sheffield: Sheffield Academic Press, 1999), p. 19. See also the significant methodological work of R. B. Hays in *Echoes of Scripture in the Letters of Paul* (New Haven and London: Yale University Press, 1989), esp. pp. 29–32.

3.   H. Utzschneider, 'Flourishing Bones: The Minor Prophets in the New Testament', in W. Kraus and R. G. Wooden (eds), *Septuagint Research: Issues and Challenges in the Study of the Greek Jewish Scriptures* (SBLSCS, 53; Atlanta: SBL, 2006), p. 282.

4.   Schultz, *Search*, p. 58.

Nevertheless, if it can be shown on other grounds that a New Testament writer is using the Greek version of the Old Testament and if a number of distinctive Greek words are found together in near proximity in the same or similar contexts in both a New Testament passage and the Greek version of a passage in the Old Testament, then the probability of a deliberate allusion increases. If the New Testament writer is clearly citing from the Hebrew Scriptures, then the New Testament use of the Old must take into consideration a more complex study of the lexical equivalents between the Hebrew and the conventions and traditions of Greek translation of the Scripture.

The Minor Prophets in James

Introduction

Of the Twelve, Amos is often recognized as having the greatest influence on James, who has even been called 'the Amos of the new covenant'.[5] Although all the prophetic books bring a message of judgement, hope, and a call for repentance, the Twelve speak primarily a message that God's people are covenant violators who have become morally and spiritually as bad as the surrounding pagan nations. The Twelve announce that the chosen status of Judah and Israel will not protect them from God's judgement when they presume upon their relationship with God and violate the covenant. Analogously, James wants his Christian readers to recognize that their faith in Jesus Christ does not give licence to live like pagans, but that the moral and spiritual demands represented in God's covenant with ancient Israel are still his standard for faithful Christian living.

Textual Affinity

As D. A. Carson observes, almost all quotations and allusions to the Old Testament in James align with the LXX.[6] For instance, Jas 2.23 quotes the text of Gen. 15.6 LXX almost exactly, with only small syntactical and morphological differences (a postpositive δέ instead of καί and ἀβρααμ instead of ἀβραμ). In comparison, the Hebrew text does not include the proper name and the verb translated 'reckoned' is in active

---

5.   J. B. Adamson, *The Epistle of James* (NICNT; Grand Rapids: Eerdmans, 1976), p. 20.

6.   D. A. Carson, 'James', in G. K. Beale and D. A. Carson (eds), *Commentary on the New Testament Use of the Old Testament* (Grand Rapids: Baker Academic, 2007), p. 997.

voice. James's quotation of Prov. 3.34 in 4.6 also clearly follows the LXX text, 'The Lord resists the arrogant, but he gives grace to the humble' (NETS), which is very different from the MT's reading, 'He mocks proud mockers but shows favor to the humble and oppressed'.

To these two clear examples could also be added Lev. 19.18 in Jas 2.8, the order of the commandments mentioned in Jas 2.11, and the allusion to Jer. 12.3 in Jas 5.5 which also indicate use of the Greek Old Testament. If the traditional ascription of authorship is taken seriously, this pervasive use of the *Greek* Jewish Scriptures in an epistle written by the leader of the church *in Jerusalem* to Jewish Christians adds further evidence to the extent the Greek language in the Roman period was used in Palestine, even beyond the Galilee.

Quotations from the Twelve

The question asked in Jas 3.13, 'Who is wise [σοφός] and understanding [ἐπιστήμων] among you?' is the closest James comes to quoting the Twelve, echoing the final verse of Hos. 14.10 (ET 14.9), which in summary of the prophet's entire message asks, 'Who is wise [τίς σοφός] and will understand [συνίημι] these things, or prudent [συνετός] and will comprehend [ἐπιγινώσκω] them?' [NETS].[7] As a covenant enforcer, Hosea indicts both Judah and Israel for being unfaithful to their covenant with the Lord. With this question Hosea challenges his audience to return to covenant obedience of the Lord's statutes and rules, an obedience which in Deut. 4.6 LXX would earn Israel the description as a wise [σοφός] and understanding [ἐπιστήμων] nation.

James may be alluding to Deut. 4.6 directly, because the language of 'a wise and understanding [σοφός καὶ ἐπιστήμων] people' matches exactly the predicate adjectives of Jas 3.13. On the other hand, James phrases the challenge to his audience as a rhetorical question, matching the form of Hos. 14.10. Furthermore, an important allusion to Hosea tilts toward the conclusion that if James has Deut. 4.6 in mind, he is thinking of it as mediated through the message of Hosea.

Allusions to the Twelve

Following upon the echo of Hosea in Jas 3.13, James uses a word so striking that it should be considered an allusion to Hosea, even though one word is usually insufficient to constitute an allusion. In Jas 4.4,

---

7.   Ps. 107.43 (LXX 106.43) also ends with the phrase τίς σοφός but there the context is a call to remember the Lord's gracious acts of deliverance. The context of Hosea's question better fits James's message.

introducing the most invective part of the letter, James exclaims using a *feminine* plural vocative, 'Adulteresses! [μοιχαλίδες] Do you not know that friendship with the world is enmity with God? Therefore whoever wishes to be a friend of the world becomes an enemy of God' (modified NRSV). [8] James has already mentioned in 2.21-23 the friendship of Abraham 'our father' with God. Conversely, James accuses those who are friends with the world to be enemies of God and 'adulteresses'.

The textual variant in Jas 4.4 that adds the masculine form, 'adulterers and [μοιχοὶ καί] adulteresses' is certainly not original, for as Metzger explains, scribes were likely puzzled why James mentions only women in a moral failing that by definition involved both sexes and 'considered it right to add a reference to men as well'.[9] Moreover, the shorter reading of the feminine plural alone is strongly attested by both Alexandrian and Western witnesses.

Perhaps for the same reason, virtually every major English translation except the NASB and ASV obscures this significant allusion to Hosea by translating it either as a generic masculine, 'Adulterers!' (NRSV, NLT) or as, 'You adulterous people' (TNIV, NIV, ESV). The KJV and NKJV join some of the ancient scribes who further confuse the allusion by adding the masculine form to the feminine, 'Adulterers and adulteresses!' Such a translation leads the reader's mind in too literal a direction, for although marital unfaithfulness is one expression of spiritual unfaithfulness, this feminine vocative invokes the distinctive metaphor that describes the covenant relationship between God and his people. When viewed in light of the Greek version of Hosea, its use in James becomes powerfully clear.

Second only to Jonah in the belly of the whale, Hosea is probably the best known of the Twelve because of his scandalous marriage to Gomer, who in Hos. 3.1 LXX, is referred to with the feminine noun μοιχαλίς ('adulteress'). The substantive μοιχαλίς or its cognate verb (μοιχεύω) appear several other times in the Greek Hosea (2.4; 4.2, 13, 14; 7.4) along with occurrences of synonymous or closely related words to communicate by analogy the violation of the covenant with God. Furthermore, the divided person (δίψυχος; Jas 1.8; 4.8) who wants to be both a friend of the world and of God echoes Hos. 10.2 LXX, which speaks of the heart divided by the good things in the land, sadly fulfilling the prediction of covenant breaking in Deut. 8.11-20.

Though the form μοιχαλίς appears several times in the Greek Old Testament (Prov. 18.22; 30.20; Hos. 3.1; Mal. 3.5; Ezek. 16.38; 23.45 [2x]), only in Hos. 3.1, Mal. 3.5 and Ezek. 23.45 is it used as a label for God's people who have broken the covenant. Distinctive to the Twelve, in

---

8. The NRSV will be used throughout unless otherwise noted.

9. B. M. Metzger, *A Textual Commentary on the Greek New Testament* (Stuttgart: Deutsche Bibelgesellschaft, 1994), p. 612.

Mal. 3.5 LXX the *feminine* plural accusative 'adulteresses' (μοιχαλίδας) occurs where the Hebrew text has a *masculine* plural participle מנאפים ('adulterers'):

> And *I will draw near to you* in judgement; I will be a swift witness against the sorceresses and against the *adulteresses* and against those who *swear* by my name falsely and against those who *defraud the hired worker of his wages and those who oppress the widow and those who buffet orphans* and those who turn aside justice from the guest and those who do not fear me, says the Lord of hosts. (Mal. 3.5; emphasis added, slightly modified NETS)

Clearly the Greek translator of Malachi, the last book of the Twelve, is interpreting 3.5 in the light of Hosea's use of the adulteress imagery to introduce the theme of covenant unfaithfulness, forming a type of inclusio. Hosea always stands first in the corpus of the Twelve and Malachi last, even though the sequence of the intervening books varies among ancient witnesses.[10] This interpretive unity of the Greek Minor Prophets is picked up in the New Testament.

By echoing Hosea's closing verse (Hos. 14.10) in his rhetorical question in Jas 3.13, James brings Hosea's call to covenant obedience into view for his *Christian* readers. By referring to world-friendly Christians as 'adulteresses', James accuses them of the same kind of unfaithfulness to the new covenant in Christ as condemned by the Twelve.[11] But because James is using the *Greek* Scriptures, this striking vocative also brings into view Mal. 3.5 LXX which includes not only the reference to adulteresses but also to some of the same ethical issues and even the language found also in James, as highlighted in italics above. Echoing Mal. 3.5 LXX, James twice mentions the Lord drawing near (4.8; 5.8) with a call to strengthen and purify hearts. Jas 5.12 prohibits swearing (ὀμνεύω) lest it bring condemnation as in Mal. 3.5. The defrauded wages of hired workers (ἀποστερέω) mentioned in Mal. 3.5 cry out in Jas 5.4. For James, religion that God calls pure and undefiled is to care for the widow and orphan, a failure condemned in Mal. 3.5. Furthermore, the thought in the very next verse, Mal. 3.6, about God's unchanging nature is also found in Jas 1.17. The concern for the poor that James shares with Amos

---

10. See R. Fuller, 'The Form and Formation of the Book of the Twelve: The Evidence from the Judean Desert', in J. W. Watts and P. R. House (eds), *Forming Prophetic Literature: Essays on Isaiah and the Twelve in Honor of John D. W. Watts* (JSOTSup, 235; Sheffield: Sheffield Academic Press, 1996), pp. 86–101; P. R. House, *The Unity of the Twelve* (Sheffield: Almond Press, 1990); B. A. Jones, *The Formation of the Book of the Twelve: A Study in Text and Canon* (Atlanta: Scholars Press, 1995).

11. This striking allusion to the Twelve should therefore inform exegesis of the much-debated Jas 4.5, and its Old Testament background should be considered from the Greek, not the Hebrew, where the verb translated 'yearn jealously' (ἐπιποθέω) is found with God as the subject in Deut. 32.11 and Jer. 13.14.

has apparently caused some interpreters to overlook James's allusions to the 'bookends' of the Twelve: Hosea and Malachi.

Furthermore, a comparison of twenty-six distinctive words from the epistle of James also found in the Twelve in the same or similar context shows that James shares language with every book of the Greek Minor Prophets except Nahum.[12] The distinctive vocabulary of James clusters most frequently with Hosea, followed, interestingly, by Zechariah, with Amos ranking third. Hosea and Amos also share much of the same language, though with distinctive differences in their purposes. Writing about the redactions made to Hosea and Amos when they were brought together into one corpus, Jeremias observes, 'The influence of the book of Hosea can be observed in nearly every chapter [of Amos]'.[13] Therefore, it may be Hosea behind the language of James where the influence of Amos has previously been seen. Niehaus, for instance, associates Jas 3.18 ('a harvest of righteousness is sown in peace for those who make peace') with Amos 6.12, presumably because both include the words 'fruit of righteousness' (καρπὸς δικαιοσύνης).[14] However, the command in Hos. 10.12, 'Sow for yourselves unto righteousness [σπείρατε ἑαυτοῖς εἰς δικαιοσύνην]; 'reap unto the fruit of life' (NETS) better fits the reference in James.

Conclusion

The teaching of James is strongly influenced by the message of the Twelve, especially by Hosea, Amos and Malachi. The first book of the Twelve, Hosea, challenges God's people to return to covenant faithfulness by asking, 'who is wise and will understand these things, or prudent and will comprehend them? For the ways of the Lord are upright, and the just will walk in them, but the impious will be weak in them' (Hos. 14.10 NETS; ET 14.9). Jas 3.13 asks the same question, 'who is wise and understanding among you? Show by your good life that your works are done with gentleness born of wisdom'. This may suggest that the well-recognized wisdom motif in James is mediated more through the prophetic message of the Greek Old Testament than through the wisdom literature of Second Temple Judaism. God's wisdom (Jas 3.13) makes peacemakers (Jas 3.17) in a community where fighting and quarrelling (Jas 4.1) come from those who want more than they have (Jas 4.2) and

12. Unfortunately, space constraints here prevent a complete listing of these words and citations.

13. J. Jeremias, 'The Interrelationship between Amos and Hosea', in J. W. Watts and P. R. House (eds), *Forming Prophetic Literature: Essays on Isaiah and the Twelve in Honor of John D. W. Watts* (JSOTSup, 235; Sheffield: Sheffield Academic Press, 1996), p. 177.

14. J. Niehaus, 'Amos', in T. E. McComiskey (ed.), *The Minor Prophets: An Exegetical and Expository Commentary* (Grand Rapids: Baker Academic, 1998), I, p. 446.

are drawn to spiritual adultery by becoming friends with the world to get it (Jas 4.4). Some will even forget God in their quest for the wealth that comes from being friends with the world (Jas 4.13-17; cf. Hos. 13.6) and be driven even to the dishonest gain of exploiting and oppressing others, bringing themselves to a miserable end under God's judgement (Jas 5.1-6).

James views the moral and ethical demands of God's covenant as transposed by Jesus Christ. It is well recognized that James echoes much of Jesus' teaching from the synoptic tradition,[15] especially the Sermon on the Mount, a teaching that does not abolish the Law of the Sinai covenant but underscores its extent and demand for internal transformation. Jesus was not being innovative with respect to the moral and ethical demands of God's standard; he was revealing the true nature of the requirements of the covenant and the innate inability of human beings to meet them. In this, Jesus took up Israel's prophetic tradition, transposing it into a higher key and atoning for its violation. Just as in Galatians where the apostle Paul explains the continuity (and discontinuity) of the covenant in Christ with the Torah, James presents similar instruction to underscore that the Christian life of faith is nevertheless comprised of the moral and ethical obligations that God has always expected of his people.

The Minor Prophets in 1 Peter

Introduction

Peter states a hermeneutical principle in 1.10-12 that it was the 'Spirit of Christ' who inspired the prophets of old. He then immediately applies this principle of continuity between the Jewish Scriptures and the Christian gospel by applying several of the designations for ancient Israel to his Christian readers, many of whom were Gentiles. He applies the distinctive phrases from Hosea, 'not my people'/'not received mercy', to show that the restoration promised by Hosea has been fulfilled in those whose faith is in Jesus Christ.

Textual Affinities

Although 1 Peter does not quote the Minor Prophets, the use of the Greek Jewish Scriptures in 1 Peter has been well established on the basis of the substantial quotations from Isaiah and Psalms in the book (e.g. Isa. 40.6-8 LXX in 1 Pet. 1.24-25 and Ps. 34.13-17 LXX [ET 34.12-16]

---

15.   P. J. Hartin, *James and the Q Sayings of Jesus* (JSOTSup, 47; Sheffield: Sheffield Academic Press, 1991), esp. pp. 140–72.

in 1 Pet. 3.10-12).[16] Because of Peter's use of the Greek Old Testament in quotation, any allusions to the Twelve would probably also be to the Greek version.

Allusions

The distinctive phrase in 1 Pet. 2.9, εἰς περιποίησιν ('God's own people'), is an allusion to Mal. 3.17 LXX where the same phrase is found as a reference to those faithful who do not lose heart and give up, those whom God will claim to be a people of his own:

> Those who fear the Lord spoke against these things, each to his neighbor. And the Lord took note and listened ... And they shall be mine, says the Lord Almighty, in the day *when I make them my acquisition* [εἰς περιποίησιν], ... And you shall turn and discern ... between the one who is subject to God and the one who is not subject. (Mal. 3.16-18 NETS; italics added)

Although περιποίησις occurs two other times in the Greek Old Testament (2 Chron. 14.12; Hag. 2.9), the context of its occurrence in Mal. 3.17 LXX best fits Peter's message to not lose heart and give up when struggling with social opposition because of faith in Christ, for it will make a difference in the end.

The phrases 'not a people' and 'not received mercy' in 1 Pet. 2.10 echo those same phrases in Hos. 1.6, 9; 2.25 LXX (ET 2.23). It is possible, however, that Hosea is not directly behind the thought in 1 Pet. 2.10 since there is evidence that, following Jewish precedent, the 'my people' motif was closely associated with the so-called 'stone' passages (Ps. 118.22; Isa. 8.14; 28.16) in early Christianity. The 'stone' passages of 1 Pet. 2.6, 7, 8 are in close proximity to the 'my people' reference in 2.10, as also occurs in Rom. 9.25, 26 ('my people') and 9.33 (a conflation of the stone passages from Isa. 8.14 and 28.16); see also *Barn.* 6.2-4.[17]

The allusion to Hosea, the book which always stands first of the Twelve regardless of the subsequent sequence, points to the people's inability to be faithful to God, making them 'not my people'. The allusion to Malachi, always standing as the last of the Minor Prophets, points to the promise of restoration of a people who would be God's distinctive possession. Even if mediated through the Jewish tradition as reflected in the Greek version, Peter's application of these phrases to his Christian readers indicates his understanding that in Christ the promised

16. See K. H. Jobes, 'The Septuagint Textual Tradition in 1 Peter', in W. Kraus and R. G. Wooden (eds), *Septuagint Research: Issues and Challenges in the Study of the Greek Jewish Scriptures* (SBLSCS, 53; Atlanta: Scholars Press, 2006), pp. 311–33.

17. R. J. Bauckham, *Jude and the Relatives of Jesus in the Early Church* (Edinburgh: T&T Clark, 1990), p. 224.

restoration has come and that the people to whom he wrote represented a fulfilment of the prophetic promises of Hosea and Malachi. Moreover and perhaps most astonishing, even Gentiles who had never previously been God's people are now deemed God's people because of their faith in Jesus Christ.

Kelly Liebengood suggests that the Book of Zechariah might be more important to 1 Peter than has been previously recognized. He argues that 1 Pet. 2.24-25, by 'employing the Jewish exegetical technique *gezerah shavah*, links LXX Isa 53.5-6 with LXX Zech 10.2 via the catchwords ὡς πρόβατα ['as sheep'] and ἰάθημεν / ἴασις ['we might be healed'/'healing'], so that the two texts and their wider text plots mutually interpret each other'.[18] Liebengood points out the significant role of Zechariah's prophecy in the passion narratives of the Gospels and argues that because 1 Pet. 2.21-25 functions as a passion midrash on the theme 'Christ suffered on your behalf' (1 Pet. 2.21), the sheep/shepherd theme in 2.25 alludes not to Isaiah but to Zech. 10.2, bringing the wider themes from Zechariah 9–14 into view. Liebengood points out that Zech. 10.2 is a fitting text to link with Isa. 53.5 because (1) God's people are in need of restoration because they lack healing; (2) a major theme of Zechariah 9–14 is that YHWH will return his sheep (Zech. 10.10) through the affliction of the shepherd-king (Zech. 13.7-9); and (3) 'sheep' and 'healing' are found together only in Isa. 53.5-7 and Zech. 10.2. Although it is difficult to decide if Peter is citing one or the other of these texts, it may not be necessary to do so. The invocation of both Isaiah and Zechariah would create an intertextual space where concepts from the shepherd theme in both prophets could mutually play upon and amplify each other.[19]

This present study shows further that indeed there is a high clustering of distinctive words shared between 1 Peter and Zechariah, considerably more so than with any other of the Twelve. Of a list of nineteen distinctive words in 1 Peter, many more by far are shared *in the same context* – that is, in the same theme, motif or image – with Zechariah than with any other of the Minor Prophets.[20] On the other hand, virtually all of these words and the themes, motifs or images they represent are also found in the major prophets, especially in Isaiah. It is indeed quite difficult to differentiate a *distinctive* background for 1 Peter in Zechariah as opposed to Isaiah or the prophetic tradition in general.

That said, it is nevertheless interesting that Zech. 13.9 shares three elements with 1 Peter: (1) the theme of testing (δοκιμάζω) expressed (2)

---

18.   K. Liebengood, '1 Peter and Zechariah's Shepherd-King' (paper presented at the annual meeting of the Society of Biblical Literature, San Diego, CA, 17 November 2007), p. 4.

19.   See Hays, *Echoes of Scripture*, pp. 105–21.

20.   And so, for instance, the adjective ἐκλεκτός occurring in Amos to refer to 'choice gifts' would not be counted because Peter uses the adjective to refer to people (cf. the use of the adjective in Zech. 11.16, 'the flesh of the chosen [people]').

by the metaphor of gold being refined in fire (1 Pet. 1.7) along with (3) the Lord's pronouncement that those so tested are 'my people'. Only Peter's further designation in 1 Pet. 2.10 that these formerly 'had not received mercy, but now you have received mercy' precludes Zech. 13.9 as alone sufficient and brings Hosea into view. And since the theme of testing by fire is not found in Hosea, it appears that Peter is conflating Hosea's promise to 'not-received mercy' with the testing by fire imagery from Zechariah. This type of conflation may be evidence that Peter viewed the Twelve as one prophetic voice.

The greatest clustering of distinctive words in 1 Peter with the Greek Zechariah falls within chapters 9–12, where the prophet uses the imagery of the shepherd and sheep to describe the evil of the leaders who became rich while not tending to those under their care (especially Zech. 11.5). This resonates with the admonition in 1 Pet. 5.1-4 (especially v. 2) to 'tend the flock of God that is in your charge, ... as God would have you do it – not for sordid gain but eagerly'. Zech. 10.3 and 11.16 both use the verb ἐπισκέπτομαι ('to care for') to describe God's concern for his sheep and the evil shepherd's lack thereof, respectively. If Zech. 10.3 and 11.6 are indeed the background for 1 Pet. 5.1-5, then the originality of the cognate verb ἐπισκοπέω in 1 Pet. 5.2 is further grounded.[21]

More importantly for the message of 1 Peter, it is Jesus who is both the shepherd and the guardian (ἐπίσκοπος) to whom Peter's readers, like straying sheep, have returned (2.25). First Peter 2.25 then becomes an almost direct fulfilment of Zech. 9.16, 'And on that day the Lord will save them, his people like sheep...' (NETS). Furthermore, this verse in Zechariah follows closely after 9.9, which is the prophecy that Mt. 21.4, 5 points to as having been fulfilled when Jesus entered Jerusalem for the last time, 'Rejoice greatly, O daughter Zion! ... Lo, your king comes to you; ... humble and riding on a donkey, on a colt, the foal of a donkey'.

Despite these striking similarities between 1 Peter and Zechariah, the shepherd/sheep motif is ubiquitous in the prophetic tradition of ancient Israel. Elsewhere in the Twelve it is also found in Hos. 13.5 and Mic. 2.12; 5.4, though not as fully developed as in Zechariah. It is also a major theme in Isaiah, Jeremiah and Ezekiel (e.g. the Greek versions of Isa. 40.11; Jer. 3.15; 10.21; 12.10; 13.17; 20; 23.1-4; 27.6; 38.10; Ezek. 34.2-12, 23, 31; 37.24). Although it is difficult to prove that Peter draws from a specific text rather than the broader prophetic tradition, Liebengood's point 'that the two texts [1 Peter and Zechariah] and their wider text plots mutually interpret each other' deserves further consideration.[22]

---

21. See Metzger, *A Textual Commentary*, p. 625 for a discussion of this textual problem.

22. Liebengood, 'Zechariah's Shepherd-King'.

Conclusion

Using the Greek Scriptures, Peter makes clear allusions to the theme of the restoration of God's people as promised in Hos. 2.25 LXX (ET 2.23) and Mal. 3.17, the 'bookends' of the Minor Prophets. Even if mediated through Christian interpretive tradition, 1 Pet. 2.10 clearly alludes to Hosea's prophecy when addressing Christian believers of northern Asia Minor: 'Once you were not a people, but now you are God's people; once you had not received mercy, but now you have received mercy'. Using Malachi, Peter reminds his readers that despite their society's hostility to the Christian gospel, there is a distinction between the righteous and the wicked, between the one who serves God and the one who does not (Mal. 3.16-18).

In addition to these distinctive phrases from the Twelve, he uses others from Exodus and Isaiah to describe his Christian readers, applying his stated hermeneutical belief that it was the 'Spirit of Christ' who inspired the prophets of ancient Israel, prophets which Peter claims no longer belong uniquely to Jewish tradition but who serve those to whom the gospel of Jesus Christ has been preached, even Gentile converts (1 Pet. 2.10-12). Among those Christ-inspired prophets is Zechariah, which may have played a greater role in 1 Peter than has previously been recognized.

The Minor Prophets in 2 Peter

Introduction

It is both generally well known and obvious to any reader that 2 Peter, especially chapter 2, and the epistle of Jude appear to have a close relationship best explained as literary borrowing. The consensus of current New Testament scholarship is that the author of 2 Peter follows the sequence of thought and borrows the language of Jude. Even though discussed in traditional canonical order here, we anticipate the discussion of Jude below by noting that the language Jude shares with Amos and Zechariah is not found in 2 Peter.

Textual Affinities

According to Richard Bauckham, '2 Peter's allusions are habitually to the LXX'.[23] He observes that the author of 2 Peter replaces two of Jude's rather unusual phrases with equivalent phrases that occur frequently in

23.   R. J. Bauckham, *Jude, 2 Peter* (WBC, 50; Waco: Word Books, 1983), p. 138.

the LXX. When discussing those who indulge depraved tendencies, 2 Pet. 2.10 employs a form of the verb πορεύεσθαι and the preposition ὀπίσω ('to go after') which occurs eighty-six times in the Greek Old Testament, three of which are in Hosea (2.15; 5.11; 13.4). In comparison, Jude 7 uses ἀπελθοῦσαι ὀπίσω ('to go after'), which occurs in only one other place in the New Testament (Mk 1.20) and not at all in the LXX. In 2 Pet. 3.3 the frequently occurring phrase ἐπ' ἐσχάτων τῶν ἡμερῶν ('in the last days') is found where Jude 18 reads ἐπ' ἐσχάτου [τοῦ] χρόνου ('in the last of time'), a phrase that appears only elsewhere in 1 Pet. 1.20 and not at all in the LXX. This indicates only that the author of 2 Peter was familiar with certain expressions in the Greek Old Testament that were most likely living idioms in Jewish Greek usage. (And that Jude was most likely not using the Greek Jewish Scriptures; see discussion below.)

Allusions

Not surprisingly, 2 Peter shares language and themes with the Minor Prophets. Sodom as the proverbial symbol of wickedness and judgement (2 Pet. 2.6) is also found in Amos 4.11 and Zeph. 2.9. The phrase 'day of the Lord' (2 Pet. 3.10) also occurs in Joel (5x); Amos 5.18, 20; Obad. 15; Zeph. 1.7, 14; and Mal. 4.5 (Heb. 3.23), but also in Isa. 13.6, 9 and Ezek. 13.5; 30.3. Scoffers who question God's justice in 2 Pet. 3.4 are also found in Mal. 2.17 and 3.18. Judgement by fire in 2 Pet. 3.7, 10–12 is a common prophetic theme also found in Amos 7.4; 9.5; Zeph. 1.17-18; and Mal. 4.1, and calls into question Motyer's belief that '[i]t is from Zephaniah as much as from any other biblical writer that Peter learned that the present cosmic order is reserved for fire in the day of the Lord'.[24]

Conclusion

There is nothing in 2 Peter that can be said to be distinctively from the Book of the Twelve. Peter's reminder that God will be certain to bring the wicked to judgement on a fiery day of the Lord while preserving the righteous is a common prophetic theme in the tradition of ancient Israel and he uses traditional prophetic language to express that message.

---

24.   J. A. Motyer, 'Zephaniah', in T. E. McComiskey (ed.), *The Minor Prophets: An Exegetical and Expository Commentary* (Grand Rapids: Baker Academic, 1998), III, p. 924.

The Minor Prophets in Jude

Introduction

The letter of Jude is a severe warning to Christians about self-deceived believers in the church whose false teaching in word and deed call forth Jude's scathing judgement. Jude perceives a danger that many in the church could be led astray, and therefore the letter's primary exhortation is to contend for the true Christian faith (v. 3), to be built up in the faith (v. 20), and to keep oneself in the love of God (v. 21). 'These people', as Jude often refers to the false Christians, will find their destiny in deepest darkness despite their self-identification as Christians (v. 13).[25] Their sins are as egregious as those of the fallen angels and the cities of Sodom and Gomorrah, both of which serve typologically as examples of certain and irreversible judgement (vv. 6–7). Several Old Testament figures are named, including Moses (v. 9), Cain (v. 11), Balaam (v. 11), Korah (v. 11), Enoch (v. 14), and the archangel Michael (v. 9). Vivid images of judgement from the Old Testament colour Jude's message: wind-driven clouds without rain (Prov. 25.14) and wave-tossed mud (Isa. 57.20).

Textual Affinities

Since the work of Richard Bauckham, most scholars have abandoned the idea that Jude alludes to the Greek Old Testament, for it shares only a few terms with the Greek version.[26] Bauckham argues that 'Jude's use of these terms really only proves his familiarity with Jewish Greek, in which there were common Greek renderings, used both in the Septuagint and in other Jewish Greek literature, for certain Old Testament Hebrew expressions'.[27] He believes Jude to have made his own Greek translation of his allusions to the Hebrew Old Testament. Firstly, the allusion to Prov. 25.14 in Jude 12 is more fitting to Jude's context as it appears in the Hebrew ('Like clouds and wind without rain is one who boasts of a gift never given') than in the Greek ('As winds and clouds and rains are exceedingly apparent, so are they who boast over a false gift'). Secondly, according to Bauckham, the reference in Jude 12 to shepherds who feed only themselves stands closer to the Hebrew of Ezek. 34.2 ('Ah, you shepherds of Israel who have been feeding yourselves!') than the Greek ('Oh, you shepherds of Israel, do shepherds feed themselves?'). The most decisive case in Bauckham's judgement is the allusion to Isa. 57.20 in

---

25.   See J. D. Charles, ' "Those" and "These": The Use of the Old Testament in the Epistle of Jude', *JSNT* 38 (1990), 109–24.

26.   Bauckham, *Jude, 2 Peter*, p. 7.

27.   Bauckham, *Jude and the Relatives*, p. 136.

Jude 13 ('But the wicked are like the tossing sea that cannot keep still; its waters toss up mire and mud') compared to the Greek ('But thus shall the unrighteous be tossed like waves and shall not be able to rest').[28]

Both Davids and Carson find it surprising that Jude does not seem to depend to any substantial degree on the LXX, picking up only some of the expressions found in it that were of the common stock of Jewish Greek idiom.[29] Only a few recent scholars have claimed that Jude uses the Jewish Greek Scriptures. Earl Richard states, but unfortunately does not substantiate, that 'the style and language of [Jude] are those of a Hellenist whose appeal to the Hebrew Scriptures and to Jewish apocryphal works in their Greek form point to a Jewish writer of the Diaspora'.[30] Harm Hollander argues further that the Greek version of Zech. 3.3-4 is the source of Jude's language in vv. 22–23.[31] Jude 22–23 exhorts the readers to 'have mercy on those who doubt; save others by snatching them out of the fire; and have mercy on still others with fear, hating even the clothing stained by flesh' (my translation). While it is true that both the snatching from the fire and the filthy clothing are motifs found in Zech. 3.2-3, the wording in Jude does not match any extant Greek version of these verses and may instead indicate that Jude had in mind the Hebrew text of Zech. 3.2, 3 for reasons discussed below.

Quotations

Despite Jude's heavy dependence on Old Testament themes and images, there are no quotations of the Old Testament in this brief letter. At first glance the reference in Jude 14 to the 'ten thousands of his holy ones' accompanying the Lord may seem to paraphrase Zech. 14.5 that 'the LORD my God will come, and all the holy ones with him'. But Jude 14 is clearly a quotation of 1 Enoch 1.9 (which may have derived from Zech. 14.5), 'He comes with his myriads and with his holy ones, to make judgement against all, and he will destroy all the ungodly, and convict all flesh about all works of their ungodliness which they in an ungodly way committed and the harsh words which they have spoken, and about

---

28.   Bauckham, *Jude and the Relatives*, p. 137.

29.   P. H. Davids, *The Letters of 2 Peter and Jude* (Grand Rapids: Eerdmans, 2006), p. 26; D. A. Carson, 'Jude', in G. K. Beale and D. A. Carson (eds), *Commentary on the New Testament Use of the Old Testament* (Grand Rapids: Baker Academic, 2007), p. 1069.

30.   E. J. Richard, *Reading 1 Peter, Jude, and 2 Peter: A Literary and Theological Commentary* (Macon, GA: Smyth & Helwys, 2000), p. 237.

31.   H. W. Hollander, 'The Attitude towards Christians who are Doubting: Jude 22–3 and the Text of Zechariah 3', in C. Tuckett (ed.),*The Book of Zechariah and its Influence* (Burlington, VT: Ashgate, 2003), pp. 130–1.

all which the ungodly sinners have spoken evil against him'.[32] Edward Mazich argues further that Jude's source was an Aramaic version of 1 Enoch,[33] reinforcing the view that Jude used Semitic, not Greek, sources.

Allusions

Even the several people and events Jude refers to from Genesis and Numbers refer not directly to the text of the Old Testament but to the interpretive tradition of the Hebrew Scripture. Jude 11, which pronounces woe on false Christian teachers who 'go the way of Cain' is a good example of this.[34] What we know of Cain from Genesis 4 is that his offering was inferior to that of his brother Abel, whom he murdered in a jealous anger. It is not clear from Genesis 4 alone in what way the false teachers condemned by Jude are like Cain. But in post-biblical Jewish tradition, Cain was referred to as 'the archetypal sinner and the instructor of others in sin'.[35] Josephus characterizes him by greed, violence and lust (*Ant.* 1.52-66). Philo, Targum Neofiti and *T. Benj.* 7.5 also elaborate on the wickedness of Cain.

Jude 23 exhorts its readers to 'save others by snatching them out of the fire; and have mercy on still others with fear, hating even the tunic defiled by their bodies'. This is likely an allusion to Zech. 3.2, where Joshua the high priest and representative of God's people who had been restored from exile, stands before Satan and the angel of the Lord. The rebuke of Satan in Zech. 3.2 is deferred to the Lord much as Michael the archangel defers in Jude 9. Jewish interpretive tradition (e.g. *The Assumption of Moses*) explains that when Moses died, Satan wanted to claim his body to signal Moses' failure to obey God, just as Satan seems to be making some claim on Joshua in Zech. 3.2. The clear differences between Jude 9 and Zech. 3.2 prohibit a direct allusion, but both texts observe the same dynamic between angels, Satan, and the Lord.

In Zech. 3.2 the Lord asks, 'Is not this man [Joshua] a brand plucked from the fire?'[36] In the context of Zechariah, the fire was an image for

---

32. Translated by C. A. Evans, assisted by D. Zacharias, M. Walsh and S. Kohler, Acadia Divinity College, Wolfville, Nova Scotia, Canada. Accordance 7.4.1; OakTree Software, Inc., 2007.

33. E. Mazich, '"The Lord Will Come with His Holy Myriads": An Investigation of the Linguistic Source of the Citation of 1 Enoch 1, 9 in Jude 14b–15', *ZNW* 94 (2003), 276–81.

34. See T. Wolthuis, 'Jude and Jewish Tradition', *Calvin Theological Journal* 22 (1987), 21–41; also J. D. Charles, 'Jude's Use of Pseudepigraphical Source-Material as Part of a Literary Strategy', *NTS* 37 (1991), 144.

35. Bauckham, *Jude, 2 Peter*, p. 79.

36. The uncommon English word 'brand' refers to a smoldering stick of wood that is about to ignite into flames.

exile, a precarious situation for God's chosen. McComiskey comments, '[B]y snatching them from the flames of exile, [the Lord] revealed that his grace was greater than their guilt'.[37] Jude is probably similarly using the image, which may have become a common one in Jewish tradition, to represent the immediate spiritual danger of the influence of false Christians.

Zech. 3.3 also refers to the filthy clothing that Joshua the high priest was wearing as he stood before the angel of the Lord. The Hebrew word refers specifically to filth from excrement or vomit, a disgusting image that connotes how repulsive is the sin that clung to God's people even after the restoration. Hollander's claim that the cause of the tunic's defilement in Jude 23 (presumably the phrase ἀπὸ τῆς σαρκός) supports 'the assumption that the author quoted the Old Testament (LXX) from memory' is puzzling, for the Greek text of Zech. 3.3 has no such distinction, reading ἱμάτια ῥυπαρά.[38] Because the Hebrew word (צוֹאִים) used in Zech. 3.3 is more specific as to the source and kind of filth than is the corresponding Greek word (ῥυπαρά), one could argue, contra Hollander, that Jude must have had the Hebrew text in mind and needed to add the prepositional phrase (ἀπὸ τῆς σαρκός) to make the allusion to the repulsive image of the Hebrew expression clearer.

Together the images of the firebrand and the removal of filthy clothing indicate that the charges of the Accuser, who is also present in this scene, cannot stand before the Lord's sovereign mercy. In the context of Jude, those on the verge of following the false Christians into sin are to be plucked from the danger; mercy is to be extended but without tolerance for the teaching of the false teachers, which is to be regarded as disgusting as clothing soiled by excrement.

While the images of the firebrand and the filthy clothing together seem to point toward Zechariah as the background of Jude's language, Amos 4.11 also refers to a brand plucked from the fire. Moreover, Amos 4.11 contains a second reference also found in Jude, the destruction of Sodom and Gomorrah, '"I overthrew some of you, as when God overthrew Sodom and Gomorrah, and you were like a brand snatched from the fire; yet you did not return to me," says the LORD'. However, the firebrand and the filthy clothing stand together in Jude 23 as they do in Zech. 3.2-3, which seems the more likely source.

Although the reference to the exodus from Egypt in Jude 5 may suggest the Pentateuch as its source, the point Jude makes is that the Lord did not hesitate to destroy even those he delivered because of their subsequent unbelief. As Carson puts it, '[W]e learn that just because people belong to the right community does not mean that they can

---

37. T. E. McComiskey, 'Zechariah', in T. E. McComiskey (ed.),*The Minor Prophets: An Exegetical and Expository Commentary* (Grand Rapids: Baker Academic, 1998), III, p. 1070.

38. Hollander, 'Jude 22–3 and the Text of Zechariah', pp. 130–1.

escape the judgement of God, any more than could the Israelites after God had delivered them from Egypt and before they had been brought into the promised land'.[39] Therefore Jude may be referring to the exodus motif as mediated by Amos 3.1, 2, which makes a similar, though milder, point: 'Hear this word that the LORD has spoken against you, O people of Israel, against the whole family that I brought up out of the land of Egypt: You only have I known of all the families of the earth; *therefore I will punish you* for all your iniquities' (italics mine).

Conclusion

Among the many images Jude finds in the Old Testament, his concluding exhortation may use metaphors found in Zechariah as he raises a prophetic voice of both judgement and hope. However, the metaphors of the firebrand and the filthy clothing may have become expressions in the idioms of Judaism rather than being a reference to the text of the Twelve. There is no evidence that Jude used the Greek version but there is some evidence that his sources were Semitic.

Summary of Conclusions

The use of the Minor Prophets in this section of the New Testament canon suggests that the Twelve were viewed as one book and one voice. James and 1 Peter clearly draw from the Greek Jewish Scriptures and Jude most likely from the Hebrew, whereas 2 Peter presents only Greek expressions commonly found in the Septuagint and other Greek Jewish literature.

The Twelve exert the greatest influence in the letter of James where the messages of Hosea, Amos and Malachi are used to underscore the moral and ethical demands of the new covenant in Christ. The translator of the Greek Malachi apparently has interpreted 3.5 in light of Hosea. Allusions in James previously thought to be from Amos are likely to have come from Hosea and Malachi.

The letters of 1 and 2 Peter each stand in a different relationship to the Minor Prophets. 1 Peter uses Hosea and Malachi to reinforce his readers' identity as God's people and, following the pattern of the Synoptics, perhaps uses the shepherd theme from Zechariah in his passion midrash in 2.21-25. In stark contrast, 2 Peter contains nothing that can be said to distinctively allude to the Minor Prophets, though it draws language from the Greek prophetic tradition. Its verbal similarities to Jude do not extend to Jude's possible allusion to Zech. 3.1, 2.

39.   Carson, 'Jude', p. 1070.

This study generally supports Utzschneider's conclusion, 'that most (if not all) short citations are aphorisms that have their roots beyond their respective literary references, in the oral tradition and in the general knowledge of the time, and are not bound to the written tradition'.[40] It is clearly true that Isaiah overshadows the Twelve in the New Testament, but the evidence of James, 1 Peter and possibly Jude suggests that his claim that the the book of the Twelve was 'not really of great literary and theological relevance for the New Testament authors' is an overstatement.[41] Utzschneider's conclusion that 'the citations from the Minor Prophets seem mostly to be part of a non-individualized prophetic tradition' is most apt in this section of the New Testament canon only for 2 Peter.

40.   Utzschneider, 'Flourishing Bones', p. 282.
41.   Ibid.

Chapter 9

THE MINOR PROPHETS IN REVELATION

Marko Jauhiainen

Introduction

An analysis of the use of an Old Testament book in Revelation is a particularly challenging exercise. In the absence of formal quotations, the readers are left to their own devices in trying to discern allusions and echoes that John has woven into his rich apocalyptic tapestry. Not only is there the problem of identifying John's possible sources but also many an interpreter does not have a well-defined idea of what constitutes an allusion or echo – or how they function in the text. Even scholars who claim to employ identical criteria for detecting allusions can arrive at very different results. All this points to the fact that a study such as the present one is always – despite occasional claims to the contrary – a rather subjective enterprise.[1]

As for John's sources, I am working with the extant texts, though I recognize the complex nature of Old Testament textual witnesses and that he may have had different texts – provided that he had any sources at all, in the sense that we normally think.[2] Furthermore, I have not made an *a priori* judgement concerning the language of John's preferred source(s) but rather examine each case independently.

My approach to allusions is based on Ziva Ben-Porat's account of how readers actualize an allusion in the text.[3] According to her, it is a

---

1. I have treated the topic of detecting and analysing allusions at some length in my monograph, *The Use of Zechariah in Revelation* (Tübingen: Mohr Siebeck, 2005), esp. pp. 18–36, 133–9.

2. For possibilities, see S. Moyise, *The Old Testament in the New: An Introduction* (London: Continuum, 2001), pp. 16–18. For a more extended discussion of John's sources, see Jauhiainen, *Zechariah*, pp. 9–13, 140–2. Of course, John did not have our MT or critical Greek editions as such, though he may have had access to texts that are reflected in our MT and LXX/OG.

3. Z. Ben-Porat is one of the leading allusion theorists whose insights started to influence biblical – mostly Old Testament – scholarship in the 1990s. She ('The Poetics of Literary Allusion', *PTL: A Journal for Descriptive Poetics and Theory of Literature* 1 [1976], 105–28 [here: 107–8]) defines literary allusion as 'a device for the simultaneous

four-stage process where they first recognize a *marker*, an 'identifiable
... element or pattern [in one text] belonging to another independent
text'.[4] Second, they identify the evoked text that contains the *marked*.[5]
Third, they modify their interpretation of the signal in the alluding text
on the basis of the marked sign.[6] Fourth – and this stage is optional – they
activate the evoked text as a whole in an attempt to form connections
between the two texts that are not necessarily based on the marker or the
marked. This activating of extra elements is 'the particular aim for which
the literary allusion is characteristically employed'.[7]

Ben-Porat uses the term 'literary allusion' to distinguish it from
'allusion in general', by which she means 'a hint to a known fact'.[8] In
Revelation, a suspected allusion frequently turns out to be this kind of
'simple' allusion to an Old Testament image, phrase or motif that may
be familiar to the author from more than one document. In other words,
there is no specific text that is being alluded to (stage two) and thus
neither modified interpretation on the basis of the evoked text (stage
three), nor activation of extra elements between the marker text and the
marked text (stage four).[9]

The Minor Prophets are replete with images and language that John is
using, but in the vast majority of cases it is impossible to identify a single
text whose context he would wish to evoke by means of an allusion. The
present study therefore focuses on 'literary' rather than 'simple' allusions.
The goal, then, is not to offer a full picture of John's indebtedness to
traditions found in the Minor Prophets, but merely to analyse his use of
these documents by means of allusions as perceived by one scholar.

activation of two texts. The activation is achieved through the manipulation of a special
signal: a sign [i.e., a sentence, phrase, motif, pattern, idea, etc., that contains the "marker"
or of which the "marker" is one aspect] ... in a given text characterized by an additional
larger "referent." This referent is always an independent text'. Her definition concludes
with an observation that is especially fitting in the context of Revelation: 'The simultaneous
activation of the two texts thus connected results in the formation of intertextual patterns
whose nature cannot be predetermined'.

4.   Ibid., p. 108.

5.   I.e., the 'marker' as it appears in the evoked text. In most cases, steps 1 and 2
are virtually simultaneous, but sometimes one can recognize the presence of an allusion
without remembering (or even knowing) the text that contains the marked.

6.   In other words, a true allusion usually sheds light on the text, as many interpreters
have intuitively recognized.

7.   Ben-Porat, 'Poetics', p. 111. Thus, although the author plants the allusion in the
text, its discovery and actualization ultimately depend on the competence and perception
of the reader. Ben-Porat's analysis of how an allusion functions also helps to define and
explain marker signs that formally resemble allusions but whose marked signs (if such can be
located) have no bearing on the interpretation of the text (i.e., they never reach stage three).
I call these marker signs 'echoes' (following B. D. Sommer, *A Prophet Reads Scripture:
Allusion in Isaiah 40–66* [Stanford: Stanford University Press, 1998], pp. 15–17).

8.   Ben-Porat, 'Poetics', p. 108.

9.   Of course, these 'known facts' may still influence one's interpretation.

Allusions

Zech. 12.10-13.1 in Rev. 1.7[10]

Immediately after the formal letter opening in Rev. 1.4-6, John switches into prophetic gear: 'He is coming with the clouds; every eye will see him, even those who pierced him; and on his account all the tribes of the earth will wail'. Verse 1.7b-d appears to allude to the Hebrew version of Zech. 12.10-12,[11] yet it has been suggested that John's immediate source is either the Synoptic (Mt. 24.30; cf. Jn 19.37) or some independent tradition.[12] The hypothesis of a written testimonia or logion tradition as an intermediate source is impossible to disprove,[13] yet as I have argued elsewhere,[14] the data could also be explained by John's direct use of the Hebrew text of Zechariah (in addition to possible influence by the Synoptic tradition).[15]

10. Instead of listing individual verses, I am indicating the unit to which the marked sign belongs.

11. Although the idea of piercing is missing in Zech. 12.10 LXX, there is no need to posit a different Hebrew *Vorlage* (M. Menken, *Old Testament Quotations in the Fourth Gospel: Studies in Textual Form* [Kampen: Kok Pharos, 1996], pp. 172–3).

12. For detailed treatments on Rev. 1.7, see D. E. Aune, *Revelation 1–5* (WBC, 52A; Dallas: Word Books, 1997), pp. 53–7; R. Bauckham, *The Climax of Prophecy: Studies on the Book of Revelation* (Edinburgh: T&T Clark, 1993), pp. 318–22; G. K. Beale, *The Book of Revelation: A Commentary on the Greek Text* (NIGTC; Grand Rapids: Eerdmans, 1999), pp. 196–9; and L. Vos, *The Synoptic Traditions in the Apocalypse* (Kampen: J. H. Kok, 1965), pp. 60–71; cf. also Menken (*OT Quotations*, pp. 167–85), who discusses the verse in connection with Jn 19.37.

13. M. C. Albl ('*And Scripture Cannot Be Broken': The Form and Function of the Early Christian* Testimony *Collections* [NovTSup, 96; Leiden: Brill, 1999], p. 286) acknowledges that there is no direct evidence for written *testimonia* in New Testament times, yet argues that their existence is 'probable by analogy with excerpt collections from contemporary Greco-Roman literature... [and] Qumran documents' and 'made virtually certain by the presence of authoritative non-standard quotations' in the New Testament, of which 'close verbal parallels' to Zech. 12.10 (here Albl relies on Menken's analysis), Isa. 6.9-10 and Isa. 28.16 are 'especially persuasive'. From the perspective of this study, the argument is partly circular as the weightiest evidence for written *testimonia* consists in part of the New Testament references to Zech. 12.10.

14. Jauhiainen, *Zechariah*, pp. 102–5.

15. So also R. H. Charles (*A Critical and Exegetical Commentary on the Revelation of St. John* [ICC; 2 vols; Edinburgh: T&T Clark, 1920], I, pp. 17–18), who thinks that John's wording derives directly from Zechariah 12 MT, but that its combination with Dan. 7.13 comes from Matthew. If Matthew was written before Revelation (see, e.g., a recent analysis of Matthew's date in J. Nolland, *The Gospel of Matthew: A Commentary on the Greek Text* [NIGTC; Grand Rapids/Cambridge: Eerdmans, 2005], pp. 14–16), it seems very likely that it would have reached Ephesus, an important Christian centre with which John was associated, fairly quickly (on the circulation of documents in early Christianity, see R. Bauckham [ed.], *The Gospels for All Christians: Rethinking the Gospel Audiences* [Grand Rapids: Eerdmans, 1998]). Yet even if Matthew was not available to John, it is probable that John and his audience were nevertheless aware of the Synoptic traditions in oral format, if they indeed go back to Jesus himself.

However, all scholars agree that 1.7b-d is ultimately derived from the Hebrew version of Zech. 12.10-12, regardless of possible intermediary sources, and it is almost certain that John knew the same text as well.[16]

There are a number of ways readers could benefit from actualizing an allusion to Zechariah 12 in Rev. 1.7. First, the context shows that while Zechariah apparently envisaged the scope of mourning to be the land of Israel/Judah, John has the whole earth; hence the understanding of πᾶσαι αἱ φυλαὶ τῆς γῆς as 'every tribe of the earth' rather than 'every family of the land'. As the first of many instances, this paves the way for John's habit of universalizing his sources. Second, John does not say whether the mourning has a positive or negative sense, but the allusion to Zechariah suggests that it may be a sign of repentance.[17] Third, the fact that Zechariah compares the mourning for the pierced one to the way one mourns for the only child, or for a firstborn, fits well the early Christian emphasis on Jesus as God's 'only son' and the 'firstborn' in more than one sense, thus enhancing the reading experience.[18] Fourth, while Zech. 12.10 is enigmatic in the way it seems to meld Yahweh and his representative, Rev. 1.7 makes the pierced one Christ, thus removing – or heightening, depending on one's theological presuppositions – the ambiguity.

Finally, the placement of the allusion – at the beginning of the letter embedded in John's prophecy – is significant, for in ancient documents the first sentence or first paragraph would often give important information regarding the subject matter of the document.[19] The allusions in 1.7 to Zechariah 12 and to the motif of Christ's coming (Mk 14.62; Mt. 24.30; 26.64; ultimately pointing to Dan. 7.13) offer important interpretive keys, suggesting at least three things. First, the coming of Jesus is a central theme in Revelation – an observation that will be amply confirmed by the rest of the document. Second, if John saw the coming of the pierced one, who in Zechariah 12 is Yahweh, in terms of Jesus' coming, then this

---

16.   The evangelists certainly expected their audiences to recognize the allusion. The piercing in Jn 19.37 and the mourning by all the tribes of the earth in Mt. 24.30 are clearly not stock prophetic expressions but rather attempts by the authors to show how Jesus fulfils the prophecy found in Zechariah 12. While they may have understood the fulfilment differently from John the Seer, all three marker texts still point to the same marked text.

17.   John may also have intentionally left this ambiguous, for while Yahweh's coming in Zechariah initiates renewal and deliverance of the remnant of God's people, it also means judgement for the oppressing nations.

18.   Cf. Jn 1.14; 3.16, 18; Rom. 8.29; Col. 1.15, 18; Heb. 1; 1 Jn 4.9; Rev. 1.5.

19.   Aristotle, *Rhetorica* 1414b; Lucian, *Vera Historia* 53; D. E. Smith, 'Narrative Beginnings in Ancient Literature and Theory', *Semeia* 52 (1990), 1–9. The most important key for locating the central theme(s) of Revelation is obviously the prologue (1.1-3); see further M. Jauhiainen, 'Ἀποκάλυψις Ἰησοῦ Χριστοῦ (Rev. 1:1): The Climax of John's Prophecy?', *TynB* 54.1 (2003), 99–117.

could lead the audience to expect other instances in Revelation where Jesus takes the role that traditionally belongs to Yahweh. This is, of course, precisely what the reader will encounter throughout Revelation.[20] Third, the double allusion activates the eschatological framework of the three primary narratives that were available to the early church regarding the details of the final events: Zechariah's version, Daniel's version and Jesus' version, known to us as the Synoptic Apocalypse.[21] In Mt. 24.3, when Jesus' disciples ask what the '*sign* of your coming and of the close of the age' would be, Jesus first warns them of false *signs* (24.24) and then proceeds to describe the '*sign* of the Son of Man', as he comes on the clouds and all the tribes of the earth will mourn (24.30). The reference to this same sign at the beginning of John's prophetic letter thus helps to orient his audience: the close of the age is at hand – and so are the final tribulation and the subsequent deliverance and restoration of God's people.

Zech. 3.1-4.14 in Rev. 5.6

Before the throne of God, John sees a Lamb that has 'seven eyes, which are the seven spirits of God sent out into all the earth' (5.6). The marked text of the 'seven eyes' is Zechariah 4, where the Interpreting Angel identifies the seven lamps of the golden lampstand as seven eyes of Yahweh that 'range through the whole earth' (4.10).[22] This understanding is supported by three observations: (1) the operating range of the eyes in both verses is worldwide; (2) 'seven eyes' in the Old Testament are only found in Zechariah;[23] and (3) John weaves together other motifs from Zechariah 4 with the seven eyes.[24]

In addition to Zechariah 4, the seven eyes also appear in Zech. 3.9, which is part of the wider marked context of Rev. 5.6. There is no consensus regarding the interpretation of 3.9, yet one's interpretation of the allusion depends on one's reading of Zechariah 3. In my judgement, the seven eyes belong to Yahweh; they are introduced in 3.9, where they are merely focused on the stone; and they are identified several verses later in ch. 4 which provides the extra elements that the reader is intended

20.   See R. Bauckham, *The Theology of the Book of Revelation* (Cambridge: Cambridge University Press, 1993), pp. 54–65.

21.   For a classic treatment of the words and sayings of Jesus in Revelation, see Vos, *Synoptic*.

22.   So the MT; the LXX has eyes that 'are looking at the whole earth'. On the various interpretive issues of Zechariah 4, see Jauhiainen, *Zechariah*, pp. 46–9.

23.   2 Chron. 16.9 mentions the eyes of Yahweh ranging 'throughout the whole earth', but apparently assumes two rather than seven eyes.

24.   See further ibid., pp. 85–92.

to activate.[25] More specifically, John's allusion to the 'seven eyes' makes another contribution to his relatively high Christology: the 'seven eyes of Yahweh' from Zechariah 4 are now the eyes of the Lamb.

Zech. 1.8-17 in Rev. 6.1-8

The four horsemen in Revelation 6 are frequently seen to allude to two visions in Zechariah – the vision of the horses in 1.8-17 and the vision of the four chariots in 6.1-8. However, a closer analysis reveals that there are only two obvious links between the visions of Zechariah and John: (1) all three visions feature a number of *horses*, and (2) they are of *different colours*, even if the only colours they have in common are white and red.[26] There are a number of differences between the visions as well, yet in the larger context of ancient Jewish and Christian writings, these two similarities are enough to suggest that John is alluding to Zechariah 1 and/or Zechariah 6.

However, recognizing the presence of an allusion is not sufficient; we also need to ask whether John intended to allude only to one of the two visions in Zechariah, or to both. While the latter possibility is usually favoured by commentators, there are nevertheless two good reasons for seeing Zechariah 1 as more prominent.[27] First, the use of horsemen rather than chariots in Revelation 6 quite naturally forms a stronger link with Zechariah 1. Second, both passages reflect a situation where the nations have the upper hand over the people of God, and there is the question of when the roles will be reversed. Moreover, in both contexts, the description of the horses is not only followed by the cry, 'How long?', but also by God's comforting answer.

How, then, do aspects of Zech. 1.8-17 enhance the interpretation of Revelation 6, provided that we have identified the marked text correctly? Zech. 1.8-17 follows Zechariah's exhortation to his audience to respond appropriately to Yahweh's gracious initiative. The vision of the horsemen

---

25.   Another stream of interpretation sees the stone as having the eyes, thus claiming that the primary purpose of the allusion is the demonstration of the slain Lamb as the mysterious stone that is set before the high priest Joshua and functions as some kind of a sign of the coming Branch and his work. For Jesus as the fulfilment of various Old Testament 'stone' texts, see, e.g., Acts 4.11; Rom. 9.33; Eph. 2.20-21; 1 Pet. 2.4, 7; and the discussion in B. Lindars, *New Testament Apologetic: The Doctrinal Significance of the Old Testament Quotations* (London: SCM, 1961), pp. 169–86.

26.   Furthermore, though the number of the horses is different, Zechariah 1 LXX, Zechariah 6 and Revelation 6 all have horses in *four* different colours (Zechariah 1 MT has only three colours).

27.   Contra Beale (*Revelation*, p. 372), who sees Zechariah 6 as the 'most obvious' background; similarly H. B. Swete, *The Apocalypse of St. John* (London: Macmillan, 1906), p. 84.

and the accompanying prophetic oracle begin a series of visions concerning the imminent restoration of the fortunes of God's people. Though the nations are currently at peace, they will be punished, Yahweh will come, his dwelling place will be built, Jerusalem will be restored and the people will prosper. The horsemen are thus a preliminary step before Yahweh acts to fulfil various promises of restoration. They also function as messengers or tokens of the fact that God is in control and that the day of reckoning is approaching.

These are some of the elements of Zech. 1.8-17 and its context that enhance the portrayal of the four horsemen in Revelation 6, suggesting similar developments. However, unlike Zechariah's horsemen, John's riders – among whom Death and Hades are counted – are not God's faithful servants.[28] Yet even these evil forces are portrayed as ultimately under God's control as they traverse the earth, seriously undermining the *Pax Romana* ushered in by Caesar Augustus.[29] For those familiar with the traditions reflected in the Synoptic Apocalypse (Matthew 24 par.), these horsemen function as necessary preliminaries of the coming Day of the Lord and the havoc they wreak is merely the beginning of the birth pains. As in Zechariah, the horsemen thus signal the imminent restoration of the people of God, who has once again taken the initiative and is calling the audience to make sure that they respond appropriately.

Zech. 1.8-17 in Rev. 6.9-11

It is not uncommon to understand the martyrs' cry, 'How long, O Lord?' after the opening of the fifth seal as a reference to Zech. 1.12.[30] The cry itself occurs several times in the Old Testament, yet the proximity of the horsemen in both visions and the perceived similarities between their contexts is considered to make a direct allusion to Zechariah likely.

If John intended to allude to the LXX version of Zechariah, then the lack of verbal links between Zech. 1.12-13 and Rev. 6.9-11 becomes a potential problem. The latter, together with the LXX of every other possible background passage, has ἕως πότε as the question, whereas the former

28. Some see the first rider as Christ or some other positive figure; for different interpretations and their merits, see D. Aune, *Revelation 6–16* (WBC, 52B; Nashville: Thomas Nelson, 1998), pp. 393–4; and Beale, *Revelation*, pp. 375–8.

29. As J. M. Court (*Myth and History in the Book of Revelation* [London: SPCK, 1979], p. 58) has observed, '[t]here may well be some irony in the reapplication of Zechariah's "peaceful patrols" and "messengers of promise" to the subject-matter of the Apocalypse'.

30. See, e.g., Beale, *Revelation*, p. 393; A. Farrer, *A Rebirth of Images: The Making of St John's Apocalypse* (Westminster: Dacre, 1949), p. 111; and S. W. Pattemore, *The People of God in the Apocalypse: Discourse, Structure, and Exegesis* (SNTSMS, 128; Cambridge: Cambridge University Press, 2004), p. 84.

has ἕως τίνος.[31] Furthermore, though Yahweh is addressed in a number of ways in these Old Testament passages, only Zechariah uses 'Lord Almighty' (κύριε παντοκράτωρ) and only John uses 'Master' (ὁ δεσπότης). Had John wished to establish a stronger link with Zech. 1.12 LXX, he could have used κύριε παντοκράτωρ instead. However, if John was dependent on Hebrew, then the lack of verbal links is not so striking: עד־מתי ('how long?') can be translated with either ἕως πότε or ἕως τίνος[32] and ὁ δεσπότης is occasionally used to translate 'LORD of hosts' (יהוה צבאות) (Isa. 1.24; 3.1; 10.33), though κύριος παντοκράτωρ is more frequent.

Yet, regardless of the language of John's source(s), it could be argued that since the context of Zech. 1.8-17 has just been opened and accessed, there is no need to employ an exact verbal parallel in order to establish a link between the marker text and the marked text.[33] Both texts not only concern the coming reversal of the roles of the oppressed and the oppressors, but also have the cry for vindication followed by God's comforting answer, missing in other possible background texts. Thus, while the question 'how long?' on its own would not allude specifically to Zechariah, its placement in Rev. 6.1-11 strengthens the possibility that the pericope as a whole is drawing on Zech. 1.8-17, among other texts. The extra elements being activated between the two contexts are largely the same as with the previous allusion, the expectation that God will act decisively on behalf of his people perhaps being the uppermost.

Joel 2.18-3.5 in Rev. 6.12

After the opening of the sixth seal, John describes the arrival of the Day of the Lord by using a collage that draws on various Old Testament passages. Though the imagery may with good reason be described as 'stock-in-trade', many have nevertheless identified Joel 3.4 (ET 2.31) as the marked text of Rev. 6.12.[34] The reason behind this lies primarily in the observation that while the idea of the sun becoming dark or black occurs frequently in the Old Testament, the image of the moon turning to 'blood' or becoming 'like blood' is unique to Joel and Revelation (and

---

31. The following LXX verses all contain 'how long?' addressed to the Lord or God: Ps. 6.4; 12.1-2; 73.10; 78.5; 79.5; 88.47; 89.13; 93.3; Isa. 6.11; Hab. 1.2. The last one has ἕως τίνος; all the others have ἕως πότε.

32. A good example of this is Dan. 8.13, where θ has chosen the former and the OG the latter.

33. See further Pattemore (*Apocalypse*), especially the discussion on the application of Relevance Theory to the intertextuality in Revelation, pp. 36–50.

34. Beale, *Revelation*, pp. 396–7.

Acts 2.20 which cites Joel 3.4). Usually the moon is merely darkened along with the sun, and is not giving its light.[35]

How might John's audience benefit from actualizing this allusion to Joel? There are several possible connections that can be made between John's narrative and Joel's prophecy. First of all, the marked text in Joel is part of an extended description of the Day of the Lord,[36] apparently well known in the early church. Joel's pictorial language signals the nearness of this great event and John's imagery does no less. The readers are therefore encouraged to think in terms of the Day of the Lord as John's vision unfolds.[37] Second, embedded in the oracles regarding the approaching Day in Joel there is a call to return to the Lord. The original admonition in Joel was addressed to believers and, judging by the tone of Revelation 2 and 3, John undoubtedly would have liked many in the seven churches to hear this call as well. Third, also embedded in Joel's prophecy are various important promises: the fortunes of God's people will be reversed and, despite the impending judgement, those who call on the name of the Lord will be saved and will be 'in Mount Zion and in Jerusalem' (3.5 [ET 2.32]). Such turns of event have not yet been explicitly articulated in John's narrative, but if the evoking of Joel 2 creates these expectations in the readers, they do not have to be disappointed. Finally, by alluding to an important text that has already been partly fulfilled (Acts 2.16-21), John reminds his audience of their prophetic vocation – another theme which will be further developed later in the book.

Hos. 10.1-15 in Rev. 6.15-16

John continues his description of the arrival of the Day of the Lord by alluding to the reaction of the earth-dwellers: they 'hid in the caves and among the rocks of the mountains, calling to the mountains and the rocks, "Fall on us and hide us."' The first part of this portrayal draws from Isa. 2.6-22, while the desire to die rather than experience divine wrath appears to allude to Hos. 10.8 and its context.

At first sight, these allusions help to explain why the one seated on the throne and the Lamb are about to unleash their wrath. It is due not only to the developments that the horses symbolize, or to the killing of the servants of the Lord, but also to idolatry, prevalent among earth-dwellers from all walks of life and – to John's horror – making inroads even into the seven churches. In Isaiah 2, the larger context is the judgement of

35. Isa. 13.10; Ezek. 32.7; Joel 2.10; 4.15 (ET 3.15); cf. Mt. 24.29; Mk 13.24; Rev. 8.12.

36. Indeed, as D. Stuart (*Hosea–Jonah* [WBC, 31; Dallas: Word, 1987], p. 231) points out, 'the concept of the Day of Yahweh permeates the book'.

37. See further M. Jauhiainen, 'Recapitulation and Chronological Progression in John's Apocalypse: Towards a New Perspective', *NTS* 49.4 (2003), 543–59.

Judah, though vv. 12–22 especially use language that is appropriate for the judgement of human pride and human trust in wealth and power in general. The context of Hosea 10 is likewise the judgement of Israel, yet the scope of the imagery is narrower, focusing more clearly on the problem of idolatry among God's people.

While John is obviously interested in the future of the nations, it must be kept in mind that his prophetic letter is addressed to churches where some people are involved in idolatry and thus in danger of suffering the fate of idolaters when the Day of the Lord arrives. If an allusion to Hosea 10.8 is intended, the audience would do well to meditate on the significance of the evoked text as a whole to John's narrative. Do they think there is no reason to fear the Lord or his judgement (10.3)? Do they think that their religious leaders are somehow exempt from wrong influences (10.5)? Do they think that it is acceptable to be involved with pagan shrines and practices (10.8)? If so, they are foolish and will be disciplined (10.10). Yet they can still avoid the judgement of the idolaters if they repent and seek the Lord (10.12). Undoubtedly John would like his audience to seriously ponder these issues, lest they be among those who unsuccessfully attempt to hide from the coming wrath.

Joel 1.2–2.17 in Rev. 9.7-9

The blowing of the fifth trumpet in Rev. 9.1 releases a plague of locusts that come to torment those dwelling on the earth and not having the protective seal of God. In describing their appearance, John alludes to two 'invading locust[-like] army' passages in Joel: their teeth were like lions' teeth (1.6) and the sound of their wings is like the sound of chariots (2.5). If John did not intend these allusions to be mere echoes, how might his audience modify their interpretation of Rev. 9.7-9 or activate extra elements between the two texts?

There are various possibilities of how readers familiar with Joel might benefit from actualizing the allusions. First, though the description of the first locust attack in Joel 1 appears to be in the past, the second attack was expected to take place on the Day of the Lord – which is precisely what John has started to narrate after the opening of the seals. Second, the description of the impending attack in Joel 2 begins with a call to blow a trumpet and is repeated later in the pericope after the exhortation to the people to repent. In Revelation, the locusts likewise follow the blowing of a trumpet. No exhortation to repent is narrated and the reader does not know what effect the locusts will have. Perhaps they will be effective in inducing repentance, as was the case in Joel? Another trumpet blows and the question of the reader is answered: those not killed by the plagues 'did not repent' (9.20), suggesting that the locusts were not effective, either. Third, John uses again the semantic range of the word γῆ/אֶרֶץ

('land, earth') to his advantage: in Joel, the Day of the Lord should cause the inhabitants of the land to tremble, but in Revelation this has been universalized – it is the inhabitants of the whole earth that ought to tremble. Finally, Joel 2.2-11 is adamant that nothing escapes the locusts, suggesting that the tormentors in Revelation 9 are equally thorough in their operation. Yet this time – and this should increase the gratefulness of John's readership – there is an exception: those having the seal of the living God are not harmed.

Zech. 4.1-14 in Rev. 11.4

In Rev. 11.3, John introduces two witnesses to his audience and in v. 4 tells them that 'these are the two olive trees and the two lampstands that stand before the Lord of the earth'. From this we may deduce that John expects his audience to recognize these particular olive trees and lampstands. Indeed, his comment would remain rather puzzling without any knowledge of Zechariah 4. However, in Zechariah's vision there is only *one* lampstand, flanked by two olive trees, and nothing in the context suggests the kind of identification of the lampstand(s) with the olive trees that the reader encounters in Rev. 11.4. What is John trying to communicate by transforming the imagery this way?

In order to appreciate John's creative craftsmanship we need to take into account what the reader already knows. In Zechariah, the olive trees are two unidentified 'anointed ones' (literally, 'sons of fresh oil'[38]) who stand by Yahweh and through whom the lamps in the lampstand are kept burning, which symbolizes and guarantees Yahweh's presence in his temple and among his people. In the context of the vision, the lampstand itself functions as a token of the glorious future temple that will be built, by the power of Yahweh's Spirit, regardless of any opposition.[39]

In John's narrative, the olive trees do not appear before chapter 11, but the lampstands have already been introduced to the reader. In fact, Rev. 11.4, usually seen as the only 'lampstand' verse that directly alludes to Zechariah, is actually the last occurrence of the word ($\lambda \upsilon \chi \nu \acute{\iota} \alpha$) in the book, though its interpretation is connected to that of the earlier occurrences.[40] In the opening scene of John's vision, the reader encounters seven lampstands (1.12-13) and is told that they symbolize the seven churches (1.20), which are in the presence of Christ (2.1) but in certain circumstances may forfeit this privilege (2.5). John leaves the obvious

---

38. So the MT; LXX has οἱ δύο υἱοὶ τῆς πιότητος.
39. See further Jauhiainen, *Zechariah*, pp. 46–9.
40. *Pace* Farrer (*The Revelation of St. John the Divine* [Oxford: Clarendon, 1964], p. 65), who claims that John picks up Zech. 4.1-2 LXX already in Rev. 1; and Aune (*Revelation 1–5*, p. 89), who suggests that 1.12 is also at least partly based on Zechariah 4.

unstated: a lampstand is a stand for a lamp or lamps and in order to fulfil its purpose (i.e., give light), a lampstand needs to have one or more burning lamps.[41] However, since he has chosen to portray God's Spirit as a sevenfold Spirit, symbolized by seven burning, fiery lamps (4.5), we may conclude that the lampstand imagery in general speaks of the church as a locus of God's Spirit.

The change from Zechariah's one lampstand to two of Revelation 11 may have been prompted by various concerns. John may have simply wanted to match them with the number of witnesses, two of whom were traditionally required for a testimony to be binding.[42] Another option is that the close identification of two lampstands with two olive trees (rather than equating the two witnesses collectively with one lampstand) intimates that they both ultimately represent the same entity, though from two different angles. A third reason may be that having more than one lampstand suggests that, contrary to the way it was normally perceived in the Old Testament, God's presence is no longer tied to one particular location, but goes into all the earth with his people whom He indwells.

As for the identification of the lampstands with the olive trees, since both are equated with the two witnesses, this becomes ultimately a question of why the witnesses are called lampstands. There seem to be at least two reasons for this. First, the lampstands symbolize churches, as the audience has already been told (1.20). The story of the two prophetic witnesses, then, is a story about the prophetic witness of the church(es).[43] Second, the narrative of the witnesses has both implicit and explicit allusions to the career of Jesus himself, whom the early church identified as Yahweh's servant, with a mission to be a light to the nations (Isa. 42.6; 49.6; cf. Lk. 2.32). After the death and resurrection of Jesus, this mission was understood to be part of the call of the church (Acts 13.47). Equating the two witnessing prophets, servants of the 'Lord of the earth', with lampstands is thus very appropriate.[44] Yet unlike the cultic lampstands of the old era, these are not hidden in the temple or tabernacle but shine their light in the world.

41.   Cf. M. McNamara, *New Testament and the Palestinian Targum to the Pentateuch* (Rome: Pontifical Biblical Institute, 1966), p. 192: 'Each of the branches of [the lampstand in the tabernacle] bore a lamp (λύχνος), and we can presume that the lampstands of the Apocalypse, whether we understand these as separate or merely as the branches of the seven-branched lampstand, did the same'.

42.   Num. 35.30; Deut. 17.6; 19.15; cf. Mt. 18.16; Jn 5.31; 8.17; Acts 5.32; 2 Cor. 13.1; 1 Tim. 5.19; Heb. 10.28.

43.   Bauckham, *Climax*, pp. 273–83.

44.   In Zechariah, the 'Lord' is obviously Yahweh, but John may have Jesus in mind instead (cf. 1.12-2.1). The reference to the 'Lord of the earth' in Zechariah emphasizes the power and universal lordship of Yahweh at the time when the people are struggling to rebuild the nation. In Revelation the emphasis shifts slightly; the witnesses are on the offensive as they are testifying to the universal lordship of their master before the inhabitants of the earth.

The evoking of Zechariah 4 in Rev. 11.4 speaks about the mission of the church(es) in many ways. With his 'X is Y' statement, John identifies his two witnesses as the two mysterious Zecharian olive trees. Just as the olive trees in Zechariah 4 are necessary for the realization and proper functioning of the coming temple, so the witnesses are crucial in the preparation of the eschatological temple, the New Jerusalem. With the same 'X is Y' statement, John also identifies the witnesses as lampstands, which speaks of the churches as the locus of God's Spirit. John's changed theological circumstances thus enable him to both preserve and enlarge the original imagery: the witnesses as olive trees are not merely necessary for the temple; as lampstands they themselves *are* temples.[45] Yet unlike Zechariah, John does not explicitly mention the lamps, though one may assume that the lampstands give their light and are able to fulfil their prophetic vocation only insofar as they have lamps that are burning. This is clearly a challenge to some of the lampstands of Revelation 2–3. Finally, just as in Zechariah, the temple in Revelation is not to be built by [human] might, nor by [military] power, but by God's Spirit (Zech. 4.6); the beast and the Lamb have completely opposite methods of expanding their kingdom and achieving their purposes.[46]

Joel 4.1-21 (ET 3.1-21) in Rev. 14.14-20

There seems to be broad agreement that the description of the harvest(s) of the earth in Rev. 14.14-20 alludes to Joel 4.13 (ET 3.13): 'Put in the sickle, for the harvest is ripe. Go in, tread, for the wine press is full. The vats overflow, for their wickedness is great'. According to this view, the [grain] harvest in 14.14-16 points to 4.13a while the grape harvest in 14.17-20 points to 4.13b-c. All agree that Joel 4.13 and Rev. 14.17-20 are images of judgement, but there is disagreement over the precise nature of the harvest imagery in 14.14-16. Is it another portrayal of judgement or does John have something else in mind?[47]

45. Though John uses Old Testament cultic imagery, he seems to have shared the early Christian understanding of God's faithful people forming a temple insofar as the temple was understood as the locus of God's presence; cf., e.g., Mk 14.58; 1 Cor. 3.16; 1 Pet. 2.4-5; Rev. 3.12.

46. Cf. Bauckham, *Theology*, pp. 110–5.

47. Bauckham (*Climax*, p. 290) maintains that John has seen two different harvests, a grain harvest and a grape harvest, in the Hebrew text of Joel 4.13, and has then transformed the first into a positive image that speaks about the conversion of the nations. Beale (*Revelation*, pp. 770–9), on the other hand, insists that the harvests in Rev. 14.14-20 must both be images of judgement because that is how Joel uses them. Furthermore, he points out that LXX has a plural, 'sickles' (which John has presumably understood as two sickles, one for each image). The problem with the invoking of the LXX is that the *grain* harvest is thereby lost, as the Greek text speaks of 'vintage' (τρύγητος) instead of 'harvest' (θερισμός). G. R. Osborne (*Revelation* [BECNT; Grand Rapids: Baker Academic, 2002], pp. 550–3) straddles the fence, interpreting the first harvest as a judgement of mercy of the redeemed.

In the larger context of John's narrative, it makes most sense to connect the harvest depicted in 14.14-16 to the first fruits mentioned earlier in 14.4. While this in itself does not necessarily require that the later image is also positive, it certainly suggests as much. Likewise, all Gospel traditions refer to the coming redemptive harvest of the kingdom of God.[48] Furthermore, in contrast to the description of the grape harvest, the nature of the grain harvest is not explicitly stated (and thus the debate). The issue therefore has to do with the primary background: would the audience take their clues from the harvest imagery of 14.4 and, in light of the Jesus tradition, infer that the image is positive, or would they recall Joel 4.13 instead? I suggest that the context tips the balance in favour of the former.[49] What we find in 14.14-16 is thus a portrayal of 'one like the Son of Man' first receiving an authorization from an angel coming from the presence of the one seated on the throne and then reaping the harvest that he himself has sown.[50]

While the audience would not necessarily use Joel 4.13 as a hermeneutical key in their interpretation of Rev. 14.14-16, the situation is different when they encounter the grape harvest of 14.17-20. Rather than finding two different harvests in Joel 4.13,[51] the description in 14.17-20 seems to follow the (chrono)logical development of Joel: the harvest is ripe and it is time for the sickle(s) (4.13a / 14.18); once the grapes have been gathered, the winepress is full and needs to be trodden (4.13b / 14.19); and the treading results in the overflowing of 'wine' (4.13c / 14.20).

Yet it is not enough to show that John's description follows the pattern in Joel – we also need to offer an account of the purpose for which he has employed the allusion. It seems that there are at least three extra elements between the marker and marked contexts that the reader may activate. First, the reason for the judgement in Joel is the mistreatment of 'my people' by the nations (4.2-3, 19); Yahweh 'will avenge their blood' (4.21). In Revelation, the judgement depicted in ch. 14 can thus be seen as a partial answer to the martyrs' cry in 6.10. Second, the judgement of the nations is accompanied by the restoration of the fortunes of God's people (4.1, 17–18, 20). Third, the means of judgement in Joel is war (as opposed to other possible calamities). This suggests that the beast and those siding with him will suffer a similar fate in the narrative of Revelation as well, despite their apparent initial success. Of course, such

---

48.   Mt. 9.37-38; Mk 4.26-29; Lk. 10.2; Jn 4.35-38.

49.   Note also the immediately preceding macarism in 14.13: 'Blessed are the dead who from now on die in the Lord'.

50.   Mt. 13.3-23 par.

51.   The theory of two harvests would seem to require that John had no access to the LXX (cf. n. 47 above) and that John understood קָצִיר as a semantically marked noun signifying only grain harvest rather than as an unmarked noun capable of denoting both harvest in general or grain harvest in particular, depending on the context.

an expectation is manifestly vindicated by the approaching climax of John's story.

Zech. 14.1-19 in Rev. 22.3

It is widely recognized[52] that Rev. 22.3a, 'there will no longer be any curse' [NET] (καὶ πᾶν κατάθεμα οὐκ ἔσται ἔτι), is an allusion to Zech. 14.11b, 'there shall be no more anathema' [NET] (καὶ οὐκ ἔσται ἀνάθεμα ἔτι).[53] In addition to the verbal links, the larger context of both texts is the same, namely, the description of the (re)new(ed) Jerusalem. Moreover, there are a number of points of contact with Zechariah 14 and Revelation 21–22.[54] But how does the allusion function in its context?

Rev. 22.3a is not a simple fulfilment of Zech. 14.11. Indeed, καὶ πᾶν κατάθεμα οὐκ ἔσται ἔτι does not refer to the city itself, which has never been destroyed, but to something else. It seems likely that 22.3a is yet another example of John's universalizing tendency. Zechariah's concern is the safety of Jerusalem and he continues his account with a description of the plague that strikes the nations that have come against Jerusalem. In contrast, John emphasizes that there are no longer any curses, including bans of destruction on the nations (cf. Isa. 34.1-2; Jer. 50–51); indeed, the nations will be healed (22.2) rather than devoted to destruction. Moreover, while Zechariah leaves open the possibility that some survivors from the nations will not come and attend the Feast of Tabernacles in Jerusalem annually, John appears to assume that the survivors from the nations have all become God's servants and serve him in the New Jerusalem.[55] Thus,

---

52. See, e.g., D. E. Aune, *Revelation 17–22* (WBC, 52C; Waco: Word Books, 1998), pp. 1178–9; Bauckham, *Climax*, pp. 316–8; Beale, *Revelation*, p. 1112; and Swete, *Apocalypse*, p. 296.

53. MT וחרם לא יהיה־עוד. κατάθεμα is a hapax, but a near synonym for ἀνάθεμα and an acceptable translation of חרם; cf. Mt. 26.74 and its parallel, Mk 14.71. All three words can denote either the thing accursed or devoted to destruction, or the curse or ban of destruction itself (BDB, pp. 355–6; BDAG, pp. 63, 517). In the Old Testament, חרם is most frequently found in military contexts, where the enemy and their property are dedicated to Yahweh and destroyed completely. The immediate context of Zech. 14.11 is the security of Jerusalem, which suggests that חרם/ἀνάθεμα denotes the ban of destruction rather than the thing devoted to destruction; the restored and renewed Jerusalem will never again be destroyed by the attacking nations (C. L. Meyers and E. M. Meyers, *Zechariah 9–14: A New Translation with Introduction and Commentary* [AB, 25C; New York: Doubleday, 1993], p. 448). As for Rev. 22.3, translations and commentators are divided on the meaning of πᾶν κατάθεμα. While some see it as a reference to accursed things or people (e.g. Swete, *Apocalypse*, p. 296), most take it as denoting the ban of destruction itself (e.g. Bauckham, *Climax*, p. 316; and Charles, *Revelation*, II, p. 209). Yet this is a moot point, since the net effect of both views is the same: if there is no ban of destruction, then there will be nothing that is devoted to destruction; and if there will no longer be anything devoted to destruction, then there is no ban of destruction either.

54. See further Jauhiainen, *Zechariah*, pp. 121–3.

just as John's announcement regarding the absence of the temple (21.22) is highlighted when seen against the background of Ezekiel 40–48, so the appreciation of John's statement is increased when considered in light of Zechariah 14.

Conclusion

John's use of the Minor Prophets does not appear much different from his use of other Old Testament prophetic texts. He seems especially attracted to passages that speak of the coming, imminent reversal of fortunes (i.e. when sinners will be judged, the faithful will be delivered, and various other 'eschatological' expectations will be fulfilled). While many of the passages deal with the judgement of the oppressing nations, some also contain a warning to idolaters within God's people: repent or perish with the wicked when the Day comes.

Yet unfulfilled promises of restoration are not the only texts John wishes to evoke in the minds of his audience. Some passages are shamelessly harnessed for the service of his high Christology: Jesus/Lamb now takes the role belonging to Yahweh. Other passages are used to remind Christians of their true vocation as followers of Jesus Christ, the faithful witness. John is also not afraid to clarify perceived ambiguities in the marked text, or to exploit the semantic range of certain words and expressions. Frequently knowing the Old Testament context of John's allusion gives insight into what is presently taking place in his narrative and also prepares the reader for what will follow later.

As for the language of John's preferred sources, everything obviously hinges on the question of how closely our critical editions resemble the texts to which he may have had access. Our limited analysis suggests that had John been using texts known to us, almost all of the perceived allusions would have been actualizable through both languages. In only one case – albeit rather important – the marker sign is found in the Hebrew but not in the Greek text of the Old Testament passage in question.

In terms of individual documents within the Twelve, the Book of Zechariah appears to be by far the most popular marked text. This is undoubtedly due to its length, its subject matter and its style. In relation to its length, Joel is not far behind. It does not contain visions à la Zechariah and Revelation, but its singular focus on the approaching Day of the Lord has certainly made it easier for John to utilize its rich imagery. In our analysis, only one allusion was detected to books other than Joel and Zechariah. However, had there been space to also examine echoes and

---

55. This thus completes the process described in 7.9-17 (cf. 21.3-4), where people from all nations are coming out of the great tribulation and are said to serve God day and night in his temple.

less certain allusions, another five prophets – Amos, Zephaniah, Nahum, Micah and Malachi – would have entered the discussion. There is more to the influence of the Minor Prophets on John's narrative than meets the eye in the present study.

INDEX OF QUOTATIONS AND ALLUSIONS

NEW TESTAMENT ORDER

MINOR PROPHET ORDER

INDEX OF AUTHORS